DEAN'S DOMAIN

THE INSIDE STORY OF DEAN SMITH
AND HIS COLLEGE BASKETBALL EMPIRE

ART CHANSKY

LONGSTREET
Atlanta, Georgia

Published by
LONGSTREET, INC.
A subsidiary of Cox Newspapers
A subsidiary of Cox Enterprises, Inc.
2140 Newmarket Parkway
Suite 122
Marietta, GA 30067

Printed in the United States of America

1st printing 1999

Library of Congress Catalog Card Number: 99-60101

ISBN: 1-56352-540-2

Jacket photograph: Bob Donnan
Jacket and book design by Burtch Bennett Hunter

To Carolina and college basketball fans, near and far,
whose lives Dean Smith has touched

ACKNOWLEDGMENTS

I have what you might call a love-like relationship with Dean Smith. For more than thirty years, I've loved his coaching style and what he stands for as a human being. Now, after he reads this book, I hope he still likes me.

Through four decades at Carolina, Smith became an idiosyncratic icon and a fiercely private person. Any book that examines several sides of this coaching legend must include some stories Smith would not want told, and *Dean's Domain* delves into aspects of Smith's career and life that he's not likely to include in his own forthcoming memoirs. He did not try to stop me from writing *Dean's Domain* (after all, he's a staunch believer in the First Amendment), but it is fair to say that he did not cooperate with special interviews. I once teased him about the private sittings he has granted other authors, and he said, "No one has had more exposure to our program than you have had over the years."

That may be true. First as a student reporter for the *Daily Tar Heel* and later as a local sports columnist and editor, I was fortunate to get as close to Carolina basketball as anyone who has never been a player, coach, or team manager for Smith, or a member of the school's sports information staff. And subsequently, after producing celebratory books on Smith's two NCAA titles and publishing the *Carolina Court* magazine for fourteen years, I indeed have had my share of exposure to Smith and his many players.

Unlike *The Dean's List*, which I wrote in 1996 as a tribute to his greatest teams and games, this book is far more about Smith himself, and his far-reaching influence as a basketball coach and mentor to millions. Beginning with his controversial last six months on the job and then reverting to the start of his career, *Dean's Domain* looks at the power Smith amassed, where it came from, and how he wielded it.

To a large extent I have drawn on my own articles, books, and interview notes. In addition, I offer special thanks to Alfred Hamilton, Ron Morris, and Lee Pace for the stories they have written on Smith. Many former UNC players and team managers and friends of Carolina basketball, too numerous to list, contributed either directly through personal contact or by having been quoted in some of our earlier publications.

Further thanks to the last three sports information directors during Smith's tenure at UNC – Jack Williams, Rick Brewer, and Steve Kirschner – for their help with recollections and/or access to their office files. And I am grateful for the time and insight offered by John Swofford and Dick Baddour and members of their respective UNC athletic department staffs, as well as former and current coaches Larry Brown, Eddie Fogler, Phil Ford, Bill Guthridge, Dave Hanners, Dick Harp, John Lotz, Randy Wiel, and Roy Williams, who through the years have been helpful without ever once violating the confidence that Smith placed in them.

My friend Joel Fishman helped convince Longstreet Press president Chuck Perry and senior editor John Yow that this book on Dean Smith would be better than any other and, thus, worth publishing. Yow's guidance and steady editing hand assured it. Helping me make the Longstreet deadlines, Jan Bolick proved to be an eager research assistant who said she even had some fun along the way. Colleagues at Tar Heel Sports Marketing seemed to understand my weird comings and goings over the eight-month writing process.

I consider myself very lucky to have witnessed, first hand, thirty of Smith's thirty-six seasons as Carolina's head basketball coach, as he rose from a young man making a name for himself to the biggest winner in major-college history, whose name became synonymous with the game. His reign as a successful coach and exemplary person will never be duplicated on any level. I hope you enjoy this inside look at one of the true giants of American sport.

CONTENTS

"C" WORDS

Compassionate. Competitive. Consistent. Controlling. Contradictory. Compelling. Controversial. Classy. Champion College Coach. Dean Smith was all of those in his thirty-six years running the basketball program at the University of North Carolina.

Compassion was integral to Smith's character – both public and private – and his famous "extended family" of former players, coaches, and managers speak of him in the most reverent of terms. He was certainly competitive, whether concocting a comeback from the bench or angling for the best high school recruits. Consistent? Try an unprecedented 879 major-college victories, twenty-seven consecutive years winning at least twenty games, and twenty-three straight bids to the NCAA Tournament. And there was his compulsion to control, heard of by many but experienced mainly by those closest to him – players, coaches, administrators, opponents, referees, and the media who have witnessed first-hand the lengths to which Smith would go to have it his way.

All of those traits were evident in his final coaching days at Carolina. He bade a tearful farewell to his former players and the legions of fans who had followed his program for four decades. He selflessly passed on to successor Bill Guthridge a team talented enough to give Smith his own third national championship, making damn sure the Tar Heels remained a power without him. And, consistent with how he always promised to do it, he stepped aside on the eve of practice, in his own words, "letting Bill take over." Smith also wanted Carolina basketball as he knew it to endure into the next century, which is why he talked to former assistant Roy Williams about succeeding Guthridge. Whether Guthridge coached three, four, or five years, Williams would eventually leave Kansas and return to Chapel Hill. Smith, under contract as a university employee and athletic consultant until the year 2001, was exercising control over the next coach of the Tar Heels, as well. Unless something drastic occurred at Kansas, or within the UNC administration, it would be Williams.

✪

In fact, Smith's pervasive influence played a major role in three hotly debated personnel moves that had already altered the Carolina athletic hierarchy in the minds of many observers. Before giving way to Guthridge, Smith secured Dick Baddour's bid to succeed John Swofford as athletic director. Then, with Smith's recommendation, Baddour hired Carl Torbush to replace Mack Brown as the school's football coach. Though Baddour, Guthridge, and Torbush were all well trained, experienced, and quite capable, the internal promotion of three career assistants within a six-month period dramatically dimmed the star of national prominence that their high-profile predecessors, particularly Smith, had illuminated.

Indeed, Smith at times embodied that kind of contradiction. Paul Hardin, the former UNC chancellor who both supported Smith and clashed with him over the infamous Nike contract, says he "combines modesty and pride in a baffling kind of way." Smith has a favorite paradox – that the only truly free person is the disciplined person – and he has lived that paradox by enjoying immense freedom within a highly structured environment. At times a walking contradiction, Smith could be magnanimous and gregarious one moment, and stubborn and intractable the next. He was a dictator in his private kingdom, but a benevolent one, listening to his assistants and deferring to his senior players.

These divergent characteristics made Dean Edwards Smith a remarkably compelling figure and at the same time make *Dean's Domain*, the author hopes, more than a basketball book with colorful tales of great players and exciting games. This is the story of a man of obvious athletic and intellectual aptitude who rose from modest, Midwestern roots to become the most powerful person at the oldest state university in the nation. Ironically, it was neither position nor influence nor importance he dreamt about as a youngster or sought out later on.

To the contrary, from a burning desire to live his life and lead his basketball program on his own terms grew Smith's view of the world, and it was this immutable agenda that gave him a comfort zone to work from and, at times, hide behind. Smith will deny that he orchestrated his retirement so Guthridge could get the job or that he will have a large say in Guthridge's successor, because he has been careful not to overstep his power base. "You can't control the world," Smith has said wistfully over the years. Only his world.

He also built boundaries between his public and private life, and keeping those boundaries rigid enabled him to remain a hero to Carolina fans for a third of a century. It was also because of those boundaries that most people didn't see much of Smith the son, husband, father, or friend. He made no commercials except for charitable causes, limited his off-court appearances, and was forever deflecting questions about his personal life toward his program and his players.

He relentlessly, and sometimes ruthlessly, defended those players, yet his ultimate goal was to have them set good examples and be solid citizens. In the process he not only mentored hundreds of athletes; he also taught thousands (make that millions) of fans how to be more gracious winners and less-sore losers. Smith preached that sportsmanship and competitiveness were not mutually exclusive, that you could try to crush your opponent, be humble if you succeeded, and remain proud if you failed. And he was the first to remind his own players and those looking on that what they were doing, and what they were watching, was only a game. "If you treat it like life and death, you're going to be dead a lot," he liked to say.

Smith had his own opinion on how the game should be viewed. The official UNC statistics listed team members alphabetically, rather than by scoring average, and minutes played were omitted completely. His TV show highlights rarely included the opposing team making a basket, no matter the outcome of the game, and he disdained close-up, MTV-type clips in favor of wide-angle shots that captured all five of his players in action. For years, Smith successfully kept students and fans from shouting obscenities and waving their arms while opponents attempted free throws. As the only head coach in college basketball who religiously applauded the introduction of the opposing players, he tried to influence the crowd to be supportive and civil. In 1972, Smith successfully talked the students into giving a standing ovation to Maryland's Tom McMillen, who had reneged on his commitment to play for the Tar Heels because of family pressure to stay closer to home. "Remember," Smith told the *Daily Tar Heel* before the game, "Tom really wanted to be one of you."

The classy image he carved out for his basketball team, until the last few years, was that of Carolina Gentlemen – clean cut, blazer-wearing, well-mannered players who always hustled and stayed out of trouble. That image changed in the 1990s, but even that evolution was perfectly in keeping with Smith's professional and personal tenets; the best players had become African Americans who tended to express their individuality on and off the court. And, long before Charlie Scott broke the race barrier at UNC, Smith was color blind in trying to recruit the strongest team possible. When some of his athletes decided to turn pro early, he supported and often encouraged their opportunities to gain financial security for life.

Smith has been called inflexible, but his unparalleled success over four decades of coaching youngsters belies that criticism. Kids of the 1960s and 1970s were far different from those of the 1980s and 1990s – in attitudes and athletic abilities. Had Smith not been willing to learn how adolescent athletes had changed over the years, he would have retired long before 1997. But he still showed no favorites with his players, made no promises to recruits, never belittled an opponent, and always emphasized academics and graduation. In all, 224 of his players earned their degrees out of a possible 232 – perhaps the most astounding number in his own record book.

Smith allowed his seniors to set certain policies and then enforce them. During the 1989 NCAA Tournament, Steve Bucknall, Jeff Lebo, and David May had to decide whether junior J. R. Reid would sit out the second-round game against UCLA for missing curfew the night before. They sent an angry Reid back to Chapel Hill, and Carolina beat the Bruins to stay alive without him. However, Smith had his own rules. To help their adjustment, freshmen could not speak with the media until after the first regular-season game. Their class attendance was closely monitored until they proved they didn't need any help. Players who committed technical fouls always went to the bench for a few minutes, and the next day the whole team ran extra sprints for the transgression.

✪

Much of what Smith accomplished in his thirty-nine years at Carolina, the first three as an assistant to Frank McGuire, was born from his favorite subject on the basketball court – defense. Given the almost impossible job of eclipsing McGuire's legend, Smith's goal at first was merely survival. Even after he survived – and succeeded – those difficult first days remained the underpinning of a remarkable career for an unquestionably proud man. Someone once suggested that former Villanova coach Rollie Massimino would be a good choice to coach the UNC program when he retired, and Smith snapped, "Let him take it over in the condition I got it."

He was clearly a brilliant coach, with intelligence that might have set him apart in any other profession. Among his numerous chances to move to the NBA, the most serious was when one-time Madison Square Garden president Sonny Werblin nearly talked Smith into succeeding Red Holzman as coach of the New York Knicks after the 1982 season. But Smith loved the college game because it emphasized teaching, and practice was his classroom. His many innovations were highly controversial and widely copied, but as much as he enjoyed coming up with them, he always seemed uncomfortable with the notoriety they brought him.

Smith was worldly, well read, and highly spiritual, but he never flaunted it. A staunch liberal democrat, he kept his politics to himself except for an occasional slip of the tongue. His mere presence may have intimidated some people, but inside his own kingdom he was not above playing practical jokes or singing "Happy Birthday" to a fellow employee. Smith worked long hours, watching one more tape, trying to figure out one more move to use. His positive influence instilled faith in others and often turned them around as athletes and human beings. One of his favorite expressions was "learn from defeat, don't dwell on it." Another he borrowed from the Serenity Prayer: "Accept what cannot be changed, change what can, and have the wisdom to know the difference."

A rambling, fractured public speaker, Smith was a master at coach-speak who often left journalists anxious to review their interview notes or tapes to determine exactly what he had said. But he was also a great communicator with his players and assistant coaches. His profound concern for their well being engendered fierce loyalty and created a family atmosphere in which he was the father figure for life. Smith only criticized players in practice or in the privacy of the huddle, and those who suffered his wrath usually wound up feeling that they had let him and the team down. Even those few players who ridiculed him and his program got second and third chances. Smith liked to say that not a single player ever left Carolina mad.

Only accurate criticism bothered him, because it meant he could be doing a better job. He didn't mind the unfounded reproaches about the Tar Heels, and often used them to motivate the team. From his lips came positive reinforcement almost exclusively. After a tough thirteen-point loss to Vanderbilt in 1967, Smith said some things to his players that he later regretted. From that point on, he never discussed a defeat with them before first watching the film or tape of the game and sleeping on it. As he explained, "It's easy to become emotional after the game and sometimes that means you're not rational." He was generally at his unflappable best in the toughest, tightest games, and he always said he felt the most pressure before playing a good team that everyone thought Carolina would beat easily.

After proudly earning his one hundredth, two hundredth, and three hundredth career victories, Smith turned attention away from most subsequent milestones by saying, "It just means I'm old and have been coaching for a long time." He almost refused to acknowledge his seven hundredth and eight hundredth wins and his closing in on the all-time record of Adolph Rupp. Asked if all the talk of the record was a distraction, Smith snipped, "Your question is a distraction." That reaction was in character. Following the 1982 national championship, he completely stonewalled the interview attempts of *Sports Illustrated*'s Frank Deford, who was thus relegated to profiling Smith through the eyes of others and old clip files.

The most important commitments Smith had were to his program and immediate family. After the 1972 Final Four, Smith's fourth in six years, he made a public appearance that conflicted with a date he had made with his teenage children. That rarely happened again. Built into his last UNC contract were a minimum number of Rams Club meetings he had to attend during the summer. He accepted virtually no requests for personal appearances, except an occasional celebrity golf tournament. On the other hand, no commitment to his players was out of the question, and he even made good on a promise prior to the 1982 title game against Georgetown that, if they won, he would run sprints with the team on the first day of practice next season. While most 51-year-old coaches who chained smoked could find a way out of that whimsical wager, there he was on October 15, 1982, huffing and puffing as he lagged behind his hysterical Tar Heels on the Carmichael Auditorium court.

Though he helped spearhead the drive to raise $40 million for UNC's new basketball and swimming complex, Smith resisted having his name attached to the building. At a black-tie dedication dinner on January 17, 1986, he told many of the 2,362 donors in attendance that he begrudgingly agreed because he represented all of his players – past, present, and future. "He agreed because he had no choice; we would have done it anyway," confirmed UNC chancellor Chris Fordham, one of Smith's best friends. Incidentally, Smith had urged many of those former players not to contribute to the building, and he also had tickets waiting for them when they wanted to see a game; he reasoned their accomplishments had built the place and they should not have to pay to get in.

Because of his power and autonomy, Carolina basketball seemed very much like Dean's Nation. His program annually contributed between $4 million and $5 million to the bottom line of UNC's athletic budget, but that number could have been larger had Smith not spent generously on the best hotels and restaurants for his players, as well as on charter planes so they could be back in time for class the next day. Smith did not own the gym where his team played, but he might as well have. Concerts had to be scheduled around his schedule; he once threw the Rolling Stones crew out of his practice for making too much noise while setting up for that night's show. He raised his bushy eyebrows in surprise when he learned that the UNC radio and TV guys had keys to the Smith

Center so they could get into the recording studio on the ground floor.

Visitors who called weeks ahead might get an appointment to see Smith and were greeted warmly in his state-of-the-art office, the inner sanctum, in the UNC basketball suite at the southeast corner of the Deandome. But they also knew it was time to leave when Smith subtly glanced at his watch and explained that a current player wanted to see him or a former Tar Heel would be calling. He liked to say he would interrupt a meeting with the chancellor, or even the president of the United States, if one of his players needed him.

One morning, Smith kept a sportswriter waiting for twenty minutes and then apologetically asked if they could reschedule the meeting because he had to go to lunch with his coaching staff. "I'll be back at 1:30, so any time in the afternoon," Smith said. When the writer suggested the end of the day, Smith said he had to leave at 3:30 to catch a plane. "So," said the writer, both irritated and amused, "any time this afternoon between 1:30 and 3:30." For Dean Smith, it was all about sticking to the agenda he had created for his basketball program and his personal life.

This is the inside story of Dean Smith's sovereignty – the everlasting effect he has had on hundreds of players; the thousands of people he has mentored from near and far; the *hundreds of thousands* of fans and foes alike for whom he was the only Carolina basketball coach they ever knew; indeed, the millions of lives he has touched in some way. This is *Dean's Domain*.

DEAN'S DOMAIN

A GAME OF LOYALTY

Dean Smith arrived early, a rarity for the man who lived by the clock but always seemed to race it. And he wore his game face, also a rarity for the coach who somehow seemed more relaxed the tougher the opposition.

But this was a game of a different kind, one that Smith couldn't control by simply preparing his players in practice and moving them around when the action started. Those in his company on June 12, 1997, would remember a Dean Smith as focused as they had ever seen him – and as sharp-tongued as with even the most incompetent referee.

Smith had taken the short walk down the hall from his suite in the building that bears his name, past his own bust and bigger-than-life photo in the main lobby, headed across the walkway to the Koury Natatorium, and punched the code to unlock the back door to the offices of the Educational Foundation, or Rams Club, on the ground floor of the building.

This was the heart of Dean's domain, a complex built with $40 million of private donations in the 1980s, when Smith and the late Hargrove "Skipper" Bowles went stumping to alumni, boosters, and fans to lead the fund-raising effort themselves. To be sure, Smith moved smoothly through the entire university community, but he was generally more comfortable in and around the "Deandome" than he was at meetings in, say, the chancellor's suite in South Building, whose weather vane atop its tarnished dome once signaled the exact geometric center of the original University of North Carolina campus.

Indeed, this shy man who as a youngster figured he'd teach math and coach in high school some day much preferred his own office – or a closed practice, or his home, or a good golf course, or an expensive Italian restaurant with a private room in the back – to the rarefied atmosphere of the chancellor's office. He had mixed memories of that place, beginning from his earliest days at Carolina when his boss, Frank McGuire, dispatched him to South Building to help sort out an NCAA investigation into McGuire's own program. There, Smith had to dig up evidence that ultimately put McGuire's team on probation and himself into McGuire's job.

But even on his home turf, on this early summer day, Smith was working especially hard on the Nicorette gum he had chewed since giving up chain smoking almost ten years before. He probably would have been happier reaching into his jacket pocket for the pack of unfiltered cigarettes he used to finish off in half a day. He had kicked the habit, cold turkey, the day practice began on October 15, 1988, and although his players remember him being unusually edgy most of the season, he surprised even his wife, a psychiatrist, by not sneaking a single cigarette thereafter. "If I expect my players to be disciplined, then I have to be, too," he said back then.

But, oh, how he must have wanted a smoke today, uncomfortable with what he was there to do, had to do, in the plush paneled boardroom of the Rams Club. At this time of year, Smith usually used the conference room, with its thick carpets and large glass-topped, mahogany table, to listen to presentations from sports agents vying to represent his All-American players in their pro basketball careers. Today's was a very different scenario, and Smith did not relish the role he had to play. But the battle lines had been drawn: a veteran college basketball coach and arguably the most powerful man in the state versus an upstart chancellor who idolized the coach but had his own agenda for the university.

The prize was the school's athletic directorship, vacated when John Swofford departed UNC to become the commissioner of the Atlantic Coast Conference. Back in 1980, Smith had helped the thirty-year-old

Swofford land the promotion to athletic director at UNC, and he counseled Swofford on whether to take the ACC's top job. "Where was (retiring commissioner) Gene Corrigan last Saturday, and the Saturday before that?" Smith said. "He was at any ACC game he wanted to be at, and he didn't care who won. What could be better than that?"

While Carolina's athletic department grew dominant during Swofford's seventeen years at the helm, winning 123 Atlantic Coast Conference championships and twenty-four national titles, he was a hands-off manager who expected problems to be settled by his staff before they ever reached his office. Ironically, it was the autonomy with which Smith had steered his own ship that had spurred such an attitude at UNC. Because the successful basketball coach wanted to preside over his program with little or no interference from the athletic director, most of the other Tar Heel head coaches had tried to do the same.

However, the fiefdom Smith had built over thirty-six years was run by the man still considered to be the most influential in the entire university. Thus, the joke around campus was that the fight over the new AD would prove who really called the shots at Carolina, the chancellor or the head basketball coach.

Dealing from his position as coach of the nation's best collegiate program over the past four decades, Smith favored Dick Baddour, a UNC graduate who had worked for the school for thirty-one years and, for the last eleven, had been the right-hand man to Swofford. While Swofford had been off serving on NCAA committees and building his name nationally, Baddour had directed day-to-day operations. When summoned down the hall to the sumptuous basketball suite in the Smith Center, Baddour had loyally helped Smith and his staff – just as he had other Carolina coaches – find ways within the NCAA rules that continued to give Tar Heel teams an edge over their competition.

Smith liked the short, gray-haired, bespectacled Baddour, whom he believed could maintain Swofford's success, and wanted to repay his loyalty by helping him secure the top job, even if it meant using the full extent of his power. A couple other more self-serving reasons may have also had him pushing the handsome, 53-year-old Baddour. In the first place, Smith abhorred any change that required his precious time, and he had not a single minute to waste getting to know a new athletic director. Also, as he neared retirement, Smith expected to have tremendous influence in naming his successor . . . unless, that is, another athletic director, appointed by a new chancellor, preempted him.

In only two years on the job, chancellor Michael Hooker had already established himself as something of a maverick, a man who saw much fat in the university bureaucracy and immediately began slicing away the layers. In his very first summer in Chapel Hill, Hooker had called Arch Allen back from a beach vacation to fire him as head of the school's development office. Hooker then elevated 38-year-old Matt Kupec, a former Tar Heel football quarterback and Hooker's own fair-haired boy, to be the top fund-raiser at the university.

Kupec, who had returned to UNC in 1992 after ten years as associate vice chancellor at Hofstra University in New York, was putting the finishing touches on the school's widely publicized Bicentennial Campaign, begun by Hooker's predecessor, Paul Hardin. The original goal of $400 million had been surpassed months before the deadline, and Kupec received most of the credit. Because his office had also raised about $100 million every year since, he was considered Carolina's "billion-dollar boy." Not really the prototype of the "slick" fund-raiser, Kupec had a Yankee-cum-good ol' boy mix that allowed him to hit up the high rollers from Wall Street and, with equal success, the hog farmers "down east" in Carolina. That he could talk football with them – particularly the "perfect" touchdown pass he threw to win the 1979 Gator Bowl – didn't hurt. Now, Kupec was at the center of Hooker's long-range plans for UNC in more ways than one.

Hooker, boyishly handsome, often brilliant, and a UNC alumnus, was especially popular with students, mainly because he and his attractive wife Carmen – a former Massachusetts state senator who had raised some eyebrows by going to work in the private health care industry – were so visible at Tar Heel sports events, from football to field hockey. Not only a vocal presence at games, the fiftyish and youthful Hookers almost always presented awards – both academic and athletic – together in public. Many people on campus jokingly referred to her as "Mrs. Chancellor."

Basketball was their unabashed favorite, and Hooker made no effort to hide his affection for Smith. "I have admired Dean Smith since I was a freshman here in 1965," Hooker was to say at Smith's retirement press conference a few months later. "I remember very well in 1965 in

Carmichael (Auditorium) seeing Dean standing with, I believe it was, Rusty Clark and Bill Bunting, and they were having a conversation in the hall, and I just stood and watched for probably ten minutes. Dean has been my hero since then, and I have always held him up to coaches I have worked with through the years as a paragon of integrity, the kind of coach I wanted each of them to be."

His first year back at UNC, Hooker had sat with Carmen in the chancellor's traditional seats on the second row, midcourt at the Smith Center – surrounded by the "buck-some" boosters who had coughed up most of the dough to build the on-campus arena that was the second-largest in the country (after BYU). But when criticism mounted of the passive, "wine-and-cheese" crowds at the Deandome, the Hookers donned light blue T-shirts and moved into the student section behind the basket near the Tar Heel bench. There, they led the rhythmic cheers and sang with the band, and at least once each season Hooker allowed himself to be held up and "passed" from the first row up to the last.

After every home game, Hooker and his wife attended Smith's press conference in the basement of the building and often waited for players outside the locker room to congratulate or console them. To some observers, this was more than just ardent support for the basketball and athletic program; it bordered on hero worship. So there had been no great surprise in May of 1997, when Hooker phoned several prominent members of the UNC board of trustees and Rams Club to tell them he had his top choices for the new athletic director. Insiders had expected that Hooker would be knee deep in that appointment from the moment speculation began about Swofford's departure almost a year before, and they were correct.

There was, however, surprise that the names Hooker first mentioned did not include Baddour, already well known as the basketball coach's favorite candidate. Hooker inquired quietly about Bob Marcum, who had been the athletic director at the University of Massachusetts when Hooker served as president of the UMass system before moving to UNC. Told the board of trustees would never approve a "non-Carolina man" when so many options existed among Tar Heel grads, Hooker then said he wanted Kupec.

Kupec, he reasoned, had already proven himself as a champion fund-raiser, and Hooker cited the need to make sure UNC's annual

$27 million athletic budget kept growing, and could be balanced, each year. Hooker also believed, with Swofford having spent so much time away from the office, that Baddour and the other half-dozen assistant athletic directors were already running the department and could continue doing so no matter who became their new boss. What Hooker did not know, however, was that Baddour was either going to be named athletic director or retire with full benefits from the university and state. As he approached thirty years of service to UNC, and long before Swofford became the favorite as ACC commissioner, Baddour had mentioned his plans to several friends. Clearly, it was not a ploy to help him get the AD job.

Typical of his "just do it" style, Hooker wanted to name the new athletic director as "an emergency hire" – believing there was no need to spend the time and money convening a search committee and interviewing a bunch of candidates who wouldn't have a chance. He had his man and was ready to move on it. But Hooker did not enjoy such complete autonomy; he had to answer to the people who, two years before, had helped him get his job, such as the powerful Charlotte real estate developer Johnny Harris, chairman of the committee to select the new chancellor. When Hooker was told that simply selecting Kupec was impossible because, as a state university, UNC had to post the position for a minimum period and interview whomever a committee deemed viable candidates under the guidelines it would establish, he had no choice but to listen.

Since most channels at Carolina led back to the basketball office, Smith had quickly learned that Hooker wanted someone other than Baddour, and in the ensuing weeks he swung into action, using the power he had carefully cultivated but rarely abused.

Having worked closely with Swofford, Baddour had a head start on the job. Swofford had made no secret of his plans to go after the ACC's top position when Gene Corrigan retired, and, as early as the late fall of 1996, he had told Baddour that he thought his chances of succeeding Corrigan were pretty good. By the first of the year, after the ACC had begun interviewing candidates with neither Swofford's experience nor love of the league, Baddour figured his boss was a goner. So it was then that he first asked Smith to speak on his behalf . . . if Smith felt it appropriate. At the same time, Baddour was careful not to make Smith choose between him and the other widely rumored candidate, Charles Waddell, a one-time UNC three-sport athlete who had embarked upon a different course that he hoped would lead him back to his alma mater.

After playing four seasons as a tight end in the NFL, Waddell returned to UNC to get his MBA and remained visible around the athletic department. From there, he went to work trading government securities for NCNB (later NationsBank) in Charlotte. As a result, renowned bank president and UNC alum Hugh McColl became the first key name on Waddell's resume. The second was Jim Delany, a former Tar Heel basketball player who had risen quickly in college athletics to be commissioner of the Big Ten Conference. In 1990, Delany had plucked Waddell as his assistant and, knowing Waddell's ultimate goal, had given him valuable experience working with the league schools in compliance matters and on marketing and television contracts. Next, the strapping and handsome Southern Pines, North Carolina, native accepted an offer to become vice president for marketing with the new Carolina Panthers and thus was able to add the name of entrepreneurial NFL owner Jerry Richardson to his impressive list of references – all the while eyeing a return to Chapel Hill.

Waddell, ever the visible and active alumnus, had actually jockeyed for the job three years earlier when Swofford had flirted with – and almost won – the athletic directorship at the University of Michigan. Before last-minute negotiations between Swofford and Michigan broke down, the NationsBank jet was warmed up and ready to take off from Douglass Airport in Charlotte. Awaiting the announcement that Swofford had accepted the Michigan post, McColl and Harris were prepared to fly to Chicago to pick up Waddell, who was still at the Big Ten, and "present" him to then-chancellor Hardin as UNC's new athletic director. Deeming it time for Carolina to have the ACC's first black AD, Harris and McColl knew Waddell was ready, willing and able to do the job. They had wanted the deal done virtually overnight, and their influence at UNC could have gotten around any regulations that, ironically, would stop Hooker from trying the same thing three years later.

Even though Waddell had been a two-year reserve on the basketball team (he also ran track at UNC) before playing in the NFL, it was Smith whom he had consulted before each professional move, beginning with an even earlier decision about a coaching career. Pointing out the scarcity of black head coaches in the college and pro ranks, Smith had steered Waddell toward business and eventually athletic administration. Waddell believed that, several times since then, he had made it clear to Smith that his ultimate goal was to run Carolina athletics. Consequently, he was taken aback by the question Smith asked him in February of 1997. Waddell had dropped by the basketball office the afternoon of Carolina's home game with Wake Forest – the Tar Heels' sixth of sixteen straight wins on the way to the Final Four in what would be Smith's last season coaching. Raising the probability that Swofford would be the next ACC Commissioner, Smith asked Waddell if he wanted to "come up here and work for Dick next year."

Waddell watched Carolina crush Wake that night preoccupied by his afternoon conversation with Smith. "I told him I had prepared to be the athletic director, not an assistant," Waddell recalled months later, "that I had gone away to work for three successful, different-type leaders, I had thought, with his (Smith's) blessing. So I knew something was up."

Others began to know it, too. As Smith's choice became clear, the power brokers climbed on board. Of Charlotte bigwigs McColl and Harris, Waddell would later say, "They weren't nearly as enthusiastic about me as they had been before." And when word spread in the summer of 1997 that Hooker was pushing Kupec, Smith unwaveringly reaffirmed his support of Baddour and began taking steps to ensure he would get the job. He wrote a letter to every other coach of a varsity sport at Carolina, asking rhetorically, "If the athletic department is making money – which it is – why do we need a fund-raiser in charge?" In turn, those coaches recommended Baddour.

"I'll go to my grave remembering what that man did for me," Baddour, who quickly heard about Smith's letter, was to say often from that point on.

Over the next few weeks, Smith spoke with key members of the board of trustees, plus prominent people in the UNC Alumni Association and Educational Foundation, emphasizing the success and solvency of the athletic department on the fields and courts. He continued to pose the same question he had asked in his letter to the coaches, while mentioning his concern over the speculation that Hooker might allow Kupec to keep his old position and do both jobs. Smith also took the opportunity to praise Baddour for being a loyal, trustworthy, and highly competent candidate to succeed Swofford. Eventually, even Governor Jim Hunt spoke up for Baddour, who had known the governor for years and whose lawyer brother, Phil Baddour, had worked on Hunt's reelection campaign and twice been elected to the North Carolina General Assembly.

Neither was Smith a stranger to Kupec, who had begun taking psychological ownership of the athletic directorship because of Hooker's backing. Smith had served on the Bicentennial Campaign's steering committee, and Smith was also a regular, if very private, contributor to the campaign. Though legendary for his paternal attitude toward his players and his compassion for causes outside of basketball, Smith could also wield a sharp and surly tongue. He surprised Kupec in an early summer conversation by claiming Kupec had no experience in athletic administration and, thus, little chance to succeed as AD at UNC. Understandably nonplussed by this not very veiled threat from Smith – a man whom he, too, had admired since his student days – Kupec nevertheless continued preparing for his eventual interview with the athletic director's search committee.

Despite years of turning down many requests to serve the university outside of basketball, Smith asked to be on the fourteen-member search committee. Also appointed were head football coach Mack Brown, women's field hockey coach Karen Shelton and Senior Associate Athletic Director Beth Miller, plus representatives from the faculty and staff, board of trustees, alumni association, Rams Club, and one student-athlete.

Brown's place on the committee had much to do with Smith's. While he liked Baddour, Brown had long been critical of what he considered Swofford's passive style of leadership. Publicly, he supported Baddour but privately did not oppose Kupec or Waddell, both of whom Brown believed might be more proactive toward football. So, as long as Smith stayed on the committee, Brown was going to be there, too.

Elson Floyd, executive vice chancellor and Hooker's right-hand man, served as chair, setting an aggressive timetable of six weeks to submit three names Hooker would choose from to recommend to the full board of trustees. Smith and Brown made it to about half of the early meetings, when more than forty applicants were paired down to the short list who would be interviewed by the entire committee.

By this time, the press had gotten wind of the battlelines, and the one-time campus joke had become a statewide question: Would Smith or Hooker get his man?

"I like who the basketball coach likes," one radio talk show host said repeatedly, and it's a fair assumption that many of his listeners felt likewise.

Over Memorial Day weekend, Baddour left town with his wife, Lynda, to plan for his interview. He wanted to come up with a concrete philosophy for the athletic department over the next ten years and filled nearly an entire legal pad doing just that. Though he was a close friend and staunch supporter of Swofford, Baddour knew changes needed to be made, and he planned to emphasize that to the committee. For example, after having reviewed years of complaints about UNC baseball coach Mike Roberts and golf coach Devon Brouse, Hooker had instructed Swofford to terminate them. The chancellor was furious to find out that Swofford had decided to leave those firings to his successor, and Baddour knew what his first two moves would be if he were to get the job. (He was to give both men their "last-season" notice within months.)

Baddour's interview went smoothly, since he had met with long-time associates and supporters who also knew how Smith felt. "I wanted to cover all the issues, to show that I had prepared most of my adult life for this job," Baddour said afterward. "There were a few things I could have said better, but for the most part I was pleased." Still, he could only sit and wait while the other candidates had their turns. "It's a horse race," he said nervously in early June, "and right now I'm not in the lead."

✪

So now came Kupec's turn. Smith originally had a conflict but rearranged his schedule so he could be in the Rams Club conference room with the rest of the committee. As the members took their seats on the light-blue, leather-cushioned chairs for the two o'clock meeting, the arched Carolina-blue ceiling with its few white, puffy clouds belied the tension in the room.

Smith owned a well-protected reputation as Carolina basketball's benevolent dictator, but those who worked with or ran afoul of him had occasionally seen his stormy side. A notorious ref-intimidator during games and hard-balling negotiator with pro agents, he could be stubborn to the point of belligerence. However, even those on the committee, with more than a hundred years of aggregate experience at UNC, had never witnessed the Smith they were about to see. When it came to getting something he wanted, something he believed was best for the university he loved, he could become the mean Dean.

Floyd, a handsome black man who had earned Hooker's trust when many members of Hardin's old staff had been jettisoned, went over the agenda, which included a review of the six-week timetable followed by the interview with Kupec. Smith, his reading glasses perched on the end of the well-known nose that dominated his craggy face, remained silent while continuing to jaw the Nicorette.

The talkative Brown, wearing slacks and a Carolina-blue golf shirt, tried to keep the atmosphere light, interjecting into the discussion of expectations of the new athletic director the fact that one national magazine had already picked his football team to oust Florida State as ACC champion and win the national title by beating Florida in the Orange Bowl.

"I hope they know who's going to replace Leon," Brown cracked of departed tailback and New York Jets rookie Leon Johnson, "because no one has told me."

After about forty-five minutes, the committee took a short break and returned for an executive session, which typically included discussions about or interviews with specific candidates and was always closed to the media. Reporters allowed in for the business portion of the meeting were now asked to leave.

Kupec entered the conference room through the back door, carrying a folder of documents, and went around the table to personally greet each member, a tradition that had struck Smith as funny early in the process. "I've never interviewed for anything in my life," he said. "Where does all this hand-shaking come from?"

Although Kupec hadn't given much thought to being an athletic director until six months before, he had obviously done some thinking since. He passed out to each committee member a thirty-page booklet, neatly bound, that outlined a "twenty-point plan" for the future of the

UNC athletic department. The protocol Floyd had developed was for the candidate to make an opening statement and then have each committee member ask a question. Predictably, these initial questions generally reflected the committee members' own interests. For example, Miller asked each candidate about his view on the importance of gender equity and women's athletics.

The first time Floyd went around the table during Kupec's interview, Smith passed. Smith did, however, jump in when Kupec was asked by someone else about his management style. Referring to his twenty-point plan, Kupec began harmlessly: "I would want the people who work for me . . . ."

"WORK FOR YOU?" Smith interrupted, raising his nasal voice, "I wouldn't work FOR YOU. I might work WITH YOU, but I don't work FOR anyone."

Smith's stance was well known to most people in the athletic department. "I've told all the athletic directors who've been here since I was coaching to stay down the hall, and I'll call them if I need them," he had said over the years.

"Mack and I are the only ones who make money for this department, anyway, and we support all the other sports," Smith continued. "So all we need from an athletic director is more money for football and basketball, then leave us alone and we'll make enough so all of you will be happy."

Floyd went around the table one more time for final questions. When he got to Smith, the coach said, "Well, since you called on me," with a thin smile.

"Do you think experience is important as an athletic director?" Smith asked. Kupec nodded his head and was about to speak, but Smith cut him off again: "Then why do you think you can be a good athletic director without experience?"

"I understand this university," Kupec countered. "I've been an athlete here, I've played the game. I've known a lot of coaches."

As his line of questioning made clear, that wasn't good enough for Smith. Kupec, who had heard from several committee members that Smith had not asked many questions in previous interviews, later confided to friends that he thought the veteran basketball coach had treated him viciously and that he had not handled Smith's inquisition particularly well.

As it happened, the six-foot-three, two-hundred-pound Kupec grew red-faced, his neck bulging over the white collar of his dress shirt. Brown was to say later, "Matt's an athlete, still very competitive. For a minute, I thought he was going to jump over the table and beat the shit out of Dean. The whole thing was pretty embarrassing."

After regaining his composure, Kupec concluded his interview with some strong points about his overall leadership skills and athletic experiences. But the damage had been done. He never got to the twenty-point plan and, after thanking each member of the committee, left the room abruptly. He avoided eye contact with Smith. With some committee members visibly shaken by what had occurred, Floyd adjourned the meeting.

Several members walked out through the back door, hoping to avoid reporters who waited outside of the conference room. And though he was never called on it, Smith's approach left some people upset for days. Trustee Bill Jordan vented to a friend, "You just don't treat any candidate for anything that way." On the other hand, Karen Shelton, in the midst of building her own field hockey dynasty, was unperturbed by Smith's line of questioning. She deemed it "appropriate because Matt was the only candidate interviewed who did not have athletic director's experience."

The day after his interview, Kupec withdrew his name and announced he would remain in his fund-raising position. Floyd said Hooker was not surprised that Kupec had thrown in the towel. "It took an emotional toll on everyone," Floyd said months later.

So that left Baddour and Waddell as two of the candidates the committee eventually presented to Hooker. Aware that Hooker had wanted three names from the committee, Smith asked Kansas Athletic Director and old buddy Bob Frederick to fly in for what was a perfunctory interview. Later, Villanova's Gene DeFilippo (now at Boston College) also met with the committee and actually was the third person recommended to Hooker. But it was clearly a two-horse race – and not a very close one at that.

Hooker would have loved to see Waddell in the job – someone he could hire without the appearance of being beaten by his basketball coach – and he sought, and got, a strong recommendation for Waddell from Big Ten Commissioner Delany. But, in the end, the internal and

external support for Baddour was just too strong. Ten days after Smith
– as he later told a friend – "got Kupec out of it," Baddour was vaca-
tioning with his family at the beach when Hooker called to inform him
that he had been selected as the new AD. Baddour had been staying
close to the beach house, hoping the phone would ring. After it did, he
walked to the top of a sand dune, waved to family members on the
beach below and gave them the "thumbs up" sign.

Baddour might have gotten the job had Smith not intervened, but the
coach's backing pretty much sealed it for him. Hooker, who would
eventually refuse to give Baddour more than a series of one-year contracts, undoubtedly knew that Smith had said on several occasions,
"I've picked the last three athletic directors," implying he was going to
pick this one, too. And, when all was said and done, he did.

Both Kupec and Hooker have declined public comment on the entire
matter.

Certainly, the ordeal was more painful to Kupec, but it may have
offered a more pointed lesson to Hooker. After all, Kupec had been a
Tar Heel athlete and knew of Smith's wide-ranging influence, while
Hooker still had to learn first-hand how powerful Dean Smith was. As
one staff member in the athletic department said succinctly, "Hooker
might be the chancellor, but he found out who's really in charge."

HE DID IT HIS WAY

The power that Dean Edwards Smith had amassed was never more evident than the following October when the winningest coach in the history of major college basketball decided to step down – after thirty-six seasons, 879 victories, thirteen ACC Championships, two NCAA titles and an Olympic gold medal, after having graduated 97 percent of his players, and after having become a living legend close to home, across the country, and abroad.

The son of a Kansas schoolteacher and coach, Smith rose to prominence during the explosion of college basketball popularity. An unknown assistant coach who had succeeded Frank McGuire, another UNC legend whose 1957 Tar Heels had won the national championship by going undefeated, Smith rebuilt a troubled program and dodged his own early demise after five so-so seasons and twice being hanged in effigy by dissatisfied students.

As his stature grew with his own championship run, beginning in 1967, Smith's life was altered forever. A regional phenomenon until that point, he burst into the national spotlight by coaching the 1976 U.S. Olympic team to the gold medal in Montreal – a victory this country badly needed after having lost to the Soviet Union in the controversial 1972 gold medal game in Munich. "It's the only time we took a win-at-all-cost approach," Smith said. "I even ignored some players who broke rules, because we had to win."

But even that golden moment was tinged with an ambivalence that has always seemed to mark Smith's career. He had placed on the Olympic team four members from his own Carolina program and seven in all from the ACC, answering critics that a familiar nucleus would be easier to mold into a cohesive unit in the short preparation time. Privately, he said, "You think I would leave off anyone from our program who deserved it as much as anyone else? How could I face them after that?"

Fortunately, the Americans did bring home the gold medal, and from that point on Smith was a national icon, getting bigger each ensuing year as his Tar Heels appeared more frequently on national television. Before the advent of the shot clock in college basketball, his Four Corners offense triggered a national controversy, as Carolina teams slowed the game down to a crawl to protect, and generally hold, their leads.

After Smith won his long-awaited first NCAA title by beating Georgetown in 1982, on a jumpshot from a skinny freshman named Michael Jordan, Smith earned induction into the Basketball Hall of Fame along with presidential status in his own state and beyond. He was often ushered off the court by police guards or Pinkertons; he rated curbside treatment from airport security that always seemed to know he was coming; he packed banquet rooms and coaching clinics with folks who wanted to hear his often rambling, sometimes fragmented thoughts.

Right through his fifties in the 1980s and his sixties in the 1990s, Smith signed some of the best high school players in the country and produced teams that consistently won. Not even Duke's back-to-back national championships could force Smith into submission. He wound up winning a second national title and taking four more teams to the Final Four in his last seven years on the bench, as the Duke program faded.

Toward the end, in fact, it was clear that the only aspect of Smith's career that had declined was his desire to keep doing all the things his job demanded outside of actual coaching. He had helped create the monstrous and mushrooming growth of college basketball, which had become almost totally dictated by television; upheld his unyielding responsibility to his more than two hundred former players, for whom he would always drop anything; and maintained a keen reluctance to relinquish control over whatever he believed would be good for his program or the game itself.

The desk in his plush, richly paneled office stayed stacked with correspondence and other paperwork. By January each year, Smith had already begun moving the piles to the floor behind his desk to make room for the next stack that was coming from administrative secretary Linda Woods, whom he ran ragged until well into the evenings with chores ranging from assigning complimentary tickets to picking up a late-supper sandwich.

When classes started in late August of 1997, Smith still gave every appearance of coaching another season. He did not participate in the afternoon three-man drills that Bill Guthridge, Phil Ford, and Dave Hanners conducted with the players twice a week, but he did drop by to observe what would be another national championship contender for the Tar Heels.

One late September afternoon, he teasingly asked a magazine reporter and photographer, "Who gave you permission to be down on the floor?" When the reporter answered that Guthridge had let them in, Smith chided, "You're lucky Bill's so nice; I never would have said yes." He then walked by All-American forward Antawn Jamison and playfully slapped the ball out of his hands. The following week, he was testier during an interview in his office for another preseason magazine. He challenged the writer's assumption that Smith was "going small" – referring to a starting lineup that would consist of veteran juniors Jamison, Ademola Okulaja and Vince Carter in the front court. "Sam Perkins wasn't a true center in 1982," Smith said. "I don't know what you're getting at."

Smith's well-documented moodiness could be triggered by speculation over how long he would coach, which had become the hottest sports topic in the state. Yet few expected the bombshell he was about to land. Smith had another great team returning and he had recently been quoted as saying he would "definitely not coach beyond the end of my contract in 2001." That was widely interpreted to mean he would coach four more years, and only in retrospect did it seem he was saying just the opposite. He had, for years, almost promised he would step down suddenly – before the next season, not after the last one – when he could no longer muster the energy to begin practice. And, unquestionably, he would never leave the cupboard bare for his successor. With the distinct possibility that Jamison and perhaps Carter would turn pro early, Carolina would be left with another inexperienced team the following season.

Still, Smith sent shock waves when, on October 9, he declared himself officially burned out from everything but drawing diagrams, running practices and coaching games. He could no longer continue what he still loved without answering the other demands, so he turned the program over to Guthridge, the long-time assistant who had been by his side for thirty years.

At a news conference that attracted media from across the country, Smith sat on the dais with Guthridge, Hooker, and Baddour, highlighting the irony of recent months. No tension was evident from the still-raw battle over the athletic directorship, and Hooker even offered his own special brand of hyperbole: "I don't think any person has done as much for his university in the history of higher education as Dean Smith has done for Carolina." By now, though, surely Hooker's admiration for Smith had been tempered by the reality of the man.

After Carolina had defeated Colorado in the 1997 NCAA Tournament to give Smith the record for all-time, major-college coaching victories, former players and their families lined the hallway beneath Joel Coliseum in Winston-Salem to greet and congratulate the coach. He passed through the gauntlet – nodding at some, smiling at others and reaching out to touch a few – and came to the end of the hallway. As Smith was about to enter the TV interview room, Hooker caught him from behind, yelled "Dean!" and threw a bear hug around Smith that clearly made him uncomfortable. Holding his palms up against Hooker's chest, Smith said, "Thank you, Michael," then turned and walked into the TV room.

It was reminiscent of an incident in practice back in 1970, when Smith's starting point guard Eddie Fogler fired a look-away, bullet pass to a surprised teammate, a rarely used reserve forward, under the basket. The pass hit the teammate squarely in the hands, but he fumbled it out of bounds. Instead of criticizing the player for dropping the ball, Smith turned to Fogler and said without anyone else hearing him, "Know your personnel." When Hooker hugged Smith so conspicuously that day in Winston-Salem, he didn't "know his personnel" as well as he should have. Hooker's education began with the hiring of the athletic director and concluded with the hiring of a new basketball coach.

At his retirement press conference, Smith briefly addressed the silly rumor that Hooker had forced him to resign over the Baddour-Kupec conflict. "I've never had any better relationship with a chancellor, although equally with Chancellor Aycock and Chris Fordham," he said, "We're a happy family." However, it did seem like more was going on than a coach's simple decision on the eve of practice that he no longer could generate the enthusiasm to begin another season. At that very moment, it became clear to anyone who hadn't thought about it before that such timing also put Smith in the position of naming his successor – a position he clearly coveted.

Smith was aware that Hooker had told an alumni group in New York over the last year that, while not looking forward to the day he had to find a new basketball coach, it would be one of his "easiest hires" because UNC was "the pinnacle of college basketball coaching and you would have your pick of all the talented basketball coaches." Making the move a week before practice began precluded Hooker's trying to bring in an outsider or any of the long-rumored next-in-lines from coming – Kansas's Roy Williams, South Carolina's Eddie Fogler or peripatetic pro coach Larry Brown. Besides, even if Smith had chosen to quit after the prior season in April, a phone call to each, telling them he wanted Guthridge to take over, would effectively end their candidacies. None would dare cross this basketball Godfather and even consider interviewing for the job.

Still, it was a great irony that the Guthridge-for-Smith maneuver, unlike the athletic director's position, involved no job posting, no search committee, nor even one formal interview – not even Guthridge's. Earlier in the week, Smith had told Baddour and Hooker that he was quitting and that he wanted Guthridge to have a long-term contract. This one was deemed an "emergency hire," and if university system regulations had to be circumvented, so be it. After all, Baddour was Smith's man. And Hooker had learned, the hard way, who really "ran things" at the University of North Carolina.

✪

As his winning record, and influence, expanded over four decades, Dean Smith rarely used, and almost never abused, the kind of power he wielded in the last few months of his coaching career. Had he tried to do so, ironically, Smith might have never lasted as long. He, more than anyone else, realized that.

As it was, he was in complete control of his destiny during the summer of 1997, when he had begun to suspect that he would not coach another season. The first hint was a conversation he had in August with Baddour, whom he told that his normal and annual revitalization progress was going slower than he ever remembered. Throughout the summer, Smith had also confided to his buddy and business manager Bill Miller that he was considering retirement more and more seriously. Miller, a Charlotte financial planner who had seen something like five hundred straight Carolina games in person, befriended Smith early in his career and, as the coach's income rose dramatically, had made him a rich man through the stock market and other shrewd investments. Recently, Miller, Smith, Fogler, and Williams had bought a large chunk of Kenmure, the mountain golf course outside of Asheville, where the foursome usually spent a weekend together after the basketball season. (A few months after his retirement, Smith and Miller would go in together on a five-bedroom beach house on Figure 8 Island near Wilmington.)

Baddour checked in periodically with Smith over the next few weeks and, as the start of practice approached, had reason to believe he would not have to face, at least for another year, the biggest coaching change in the history of the university. Those hopes came crashing down on Thursday, October 2. On that day Smith informed Baddour and Hooker that he was seriously thinking about stepping aside, but he wanted one more weekend to make sure. Smith was holding his annual "alumni coaching clinic," and over the next three days he had private meetings with Fogler and Williams, as well as phone conversations with some of his oldest and closest friends.

Larry Brown was also in Chapel Hill; he had brought his Philadelphia 76ers team to town for training camp just as he had the Indiana Pacers for four years. Smith did not confide in Brown right away because he did not want to distract his former player and assistant coach, but he quietly used Brown as a barometer over the weekend. Periodically wandering into the arena while the 76ers practiced in the mornings and evenings, Smith always seemed amazed by the 57-year-old Brown's enthusiasm. He doubted he had that kind of fire anymore, and not even his regular chalk talks with the alumni coaches could generate the level of excitement he had always demanded of himself.

Over that weekend, Smith continued to drop in on the 76ers' two-a-days, sitting at the scorer's table along the sideline. There, he would visit with other former players, coaches, and friends whom Brown had allowed in, and he appeared his happiest and most relaxed. At one point, he signed the autograph book of a wide-eyed seven-year-old watching with his mother. "Best wishes, Dean Smith. P.S. Take Care of Mom!" read the inscription. When the practices were over, Smith and Brown often stayed around, doodling more plays on scrap paper and talking basketball. Here Dean Smith was in his element – an empty gym in a teaching environment. Had it been able to remain that way, somehow insulated from the glare of TV lights, media demands, and alumni responsibilities, he might have held off doing what he did that weekend and into Monday.

In breaking the news, Smith even used his famed seniority system with his former assistants. He called only Fogler, Williams and Randy Wiel, head coach at Middle Tennessee, into his office and asked them not to tell their staffs until returning to their respective campuses. One-time Tar Heel player and Williams' assistant Matt Doherty was in Chapel Hill but didn't find out until he was back in Kansas. Looking back, Doherty recalled "something funny" all weekend. The clinic sessions were looser, with more free time, and lots of side conversations went on between Smith, Guthridge and Williams, most likely the second successor to the throne. Smith sat next to Doherty at dinner one night and sighed that he no longer went out recruiting as much as he had in the past, or needed to.

"I didn't realize it then," Doherty said, "but he was saying, 'I'm done. I'm out.'"

None of them was truly surprised. As Smith coached into his sixties, signs of his impending retirement grew stronger every year. He seemed increasingly exhausted after each season, especially of the long hours in the office answering letters and returning phone calls behind the desk perpetually piled with those stacks of paper that he insisted on going through himself, one by one. He had taken a step toward assuaging the media crunch by holding weekly press conferences for forty-five minutes, thus eliminating the endless succession of one-on-one interviews. He might still say yes to the occasional out-of-town writer, but the press conference offered him an easy way to say no – and also gave an indication that Smith's energies were ebbing.

Fogler remembered Smith at ease the afternoon his old coach told him he was quitting. "He said he was retiring and I was happy for him," said Fogler, who had been on Smith's staff for thirteen seasons.

"He never confided in me what his plans were, but for the past three or four years I got the vibes that he was closer to not coaching. The demands were going up and the energy level for the off-court stuff was going down. You could see it coming."

Like many other ex-Tar Heels, Fogler had implored Smith to keep coaching until he broke Adolph Rupp's record for career victories. Once he had, with the 73-56 win over Colorado, Fogler and the other Tar Heel faithful called off the dogs. Their program had become part of college basketball history.

"I said, 'After you break the record,'" Fogler recounted, "'any time you want to retire, it's Hi, Hi Ho Silver, as far as I'm concerned.' If he hadn't broken the record, I would have tried to lay a big guilt trip on him, and there would have been a huge push by his former players to stay until he did it. But I honestly believe that wouldn't have made any difference to him when he was ready to retire. When it came down to it, (1997) was going to be his last year, whether he had the record or not. I don't think the record meant that much to him."

Smith had told Baddour he would call him on Monday with his decision, and the new athletic director remained preoccupied all weekend as he traveled with the football team to a game at TCU. Confiding only in his wife, Lynda, Baddour was hoping for the best but fearing the worst. He intentionally stayed away from the telephone on Monday, figuring he'd miss Smith's call if it came and thereby give the coach another day to think it over.

On Tuesday morning, October 7, Smith called Baddour to say he was coming down to his office to talk to him. "No, Coach," Baddour said, "I'll come up there." The fifty yards or so down the hall from the athletic director's suite to the basketball offices in the Smith

Center seemed like a mile for Baddour, who had spent part of the weekend planning for the news he did not want to get. Baddour remembered Smith looking very calm and relaxed, exactly what he expected of someone who had made an important decision and was comfortable with it. Smith told Baddour that after speaking with former players – Michael Jordan was the first one he told – and coaches and his family, his mind was made up. Baddour's own stomach was sinking while, to the contrary, Smith seemed happy.

"He is by far the most analytical and thoughtful man I've ever known," Baddour said months later. "Before he makes a decision, he looks at things from many more angles than most people and really thinks them through. When he told me, I knew he had considered everything and was comfortable with his decision."

But Baddour was left with a highly sensitive situation, one that had not been faced by his three predecessors over the last thirty years. Now, how to handle Dean Smith's departure had landed in his lap after barely three months on the job.

"From my perspective, it was an awesome responsibility," Baddour recalled. "How do you end a career like he's had? And could it be done with as much class as the man and his program have shown all these years? Then, from a practical side, where does the program go? There was only one clear decision, and that was if Bill would do it. Coach Smith had obviously talked to Bill, and I talked with Bill, and he said he would do it. So then it was a matter of going to the chancellor."

In a typical self-effacing gesture, Smith told Baddour that his retirement announcement could be handled in a press release, that he didn't need a news conference. After he was convinced otherwise, Smith then grew concerned that a media circus would deflect attention away from the undefeated and nationally ranked Carolina football team's Homecoming game against Wake Forest that Saturday.

The news slowly began to leak out on Wednesday evening, when Smith met with his players and the other members of his coaching staff besides Guthridge. His assistants were stunned, but Smith found some levity in the moment. "Coach Guthridge will be the head coach," he began. "Phil (Ford), you'll move up to top assistant. Dave (Hanners), you'll move up and go on the road as a recruiter. And Pat (Sullivan, the former player who had been working in the office), by a 3-2 vote, you'll be joining the staff."

Ironically, several sportswriters were already hanging around the Deandome that afternoon to check out another rumor they had heard. The University of Michigan had called a press conference for the next day, obviously to announce that embattled basketball coach Steve Fisher was resigning or being fired. Calls from several Michigan newspapers were tracing reports that Ford had already agreed to coach the Wolverines. Ford seemed distracted when one reporter asked him about Michigan. "What? I've never talked to anyone from Michigan," he said, hurriedly walking into the UNC locker room. Ford would be the Carolina coach most affected by the retirement of Smith, who had been his mentor and father figure since recruiting Ford out of Rocky Mount High School in 1974.

Though he avoided comparing players, Smith often talked about Ford's play at point guard in glowing terms; he even allowed that the Four Corners, with Ford in the middle, had been so effective that it probably should have been illegal. He unsuccessfully tried to get Ford to go pro after his junior year, when the injury-plagued Tar Heels had driven all the way to the NCAA title game before losing to Marquette. But Ford refused to go and stayed to win National Player of the Year as a senior.

After being named Rookie of the Year in the NBA and making the all-star team, Ford's pro career collapsed in a well-publicized battle with alcohol. Smith urged Ford to enter a rehab clinic in Georgia and tried to get several NBA teams to keep him on their rosters. But less than eight years out of school, Ford had squandered most of his professional fortune and was working a desk job at NCNB (later NationsBank) while attending AA meetings four or five times a week. Typical of the lengths to which he would go, Smith even memorized AA's twelve-step program and attended several meetings with his former star. When Roy Williams left in 1988 to go to Kansas, only someone with Dean Smith's unilateral power could ignore the dozens of applications from experienced coaches and hire a reformed alcoholic without a day of coaching on his resume. But no one questioned the move, and Ford had been welcomed back into the Carolina family with open arms.

Over the next decade, Smith would return to the road recruiting more than he had in many years, taking Ford with him to high school gyms and all-star camps, showing him the ropes and introducing him to the key operatives. He also counseled Ford on his turbulent marriage to his wife, Traci, and helped him out with his fluctuating finances. By now – the time of Smith's retirement – Philip Jackson Ford Jr. had become a respected college basketball coach who, after recruiting the likes of Jerry Stackhouse, Rasheed Wallace and Vince Carter, was being mentioned at Michigan and many other schools with coaching vacancies. No wonder the news dazed him.

"I can't imagine my life without Dean Smith in it," Ford had said in an interview just a week before. "I've known the man since I was seventeen. He's been a major part of every decision I've made since then. He's not only a great coach, but he's just a very good person. I'm lucky."

Word of Smith's retirement spread like a flash fire, first through Chapel Hill and then across the state and nation. When UNC Sports Information Director Steve Kirschner began calling members of the media to tell them of a "major news conference concerning men's basketball" the next day at 2:00 P.M., it could be for only one reason. Any other news about Carolina basketball would have, as Smith suggested, been handled through a press release.

Later Wednesday, as print, radio, and television media were quickly heading to Chapel Hill from as far away as Kansas City, Smith called three other close associates before they heard it on the eleven o'clock news – John Lotz, a former assistant coach and current assistant athletic director at UNC; Betsy Terrell, Smith's first secretary and, with her husband Simon, a long-time best friend; and Brown, who got the message at his Chapel Hill hotel room around midnight. He told them all, "I'm going to let Bill take over."

"I'm sick to my stomach," Brown said. "I can't imagine college basketball without him. He's meant so much to the game. You can talk about Wooden, Leahy, Lombardi, but he's got to be the greatest team-sport coach of all time. I know what this man went through. I'm happy for him, but I feel bad for the game of basketball."

Amidst all the swirling speculation, Smith remembered one other person he should tell before the news leaked out. He called Rick Brewer, the athletic department's communications director and Kirschner's boss, and asked him to in turn call Jack Williams up at

Virginia Tech. Williams had been the long-time sports information director at Carolina who was fired after a messy personal problem – despite Smith's intervention on his behalf. Williams had moved to Virginia Tech with Bill Dooley, the former Tar Heel football coach, but remained an ardent Smith supporter. "He just wanted me to know about it before I saw it on TV," Williams said. "I hadn't worked for the man in almost twenty-five years, but he still thought about me. That's just the way he is."

Tim Peeler of the *Durham Herald-Sun,* holding vigil in the parking lot of the Smith Center, first confirmed the story. He had run into Smith walking into his office late Wednesday and asked him about the rumors and the scheduled press conference. "It's about basketball, so I guess I'll be there," Smith told Peeler, who called his editor and said something big was brewing in Chapel Hill. "There are a lot of things going on right now, but nothing is positive at this point."

After talking to Jamison and several other players, Peeler had it pieced together. Smith had met with his team and, in a rambling, awkward manner, said he was stepping down the next day. "I thought it was a joke," Carter recalled later. "I was waiting for the punchline, but it never came."

Sitting together in the locker room, the Tar Heels had experienced a side of Smith they had only seen when their coach tiptoed around the press or let his mind wander in front of a crowd. With them, he was always clear and succinct and specific about what he wanted done. But on this day, his uneven voice jumped from one subject to another before he finally broke the news. Everyone at the meeting, including Smith, was in or on the verge of tears. Wrestling with his emotions, Smith quickly thanked and shook hands with each player and manager. He left the locker room quickly, and several of the players went upstairs to the darkened basketball office where they were hugged and consoled by the secretaries.

The *Herald-Sun* wasn't going to press until about 1:00 A.M. Thursday morning, and by that time several Internet sites had already "scooped" Peeler. Goheels.com, the website owned by the Tar Heel Sports Radio Network, had a story up by about nine o'clock that evening, tipping off local TV stations for their 11:00 P.M. newscast. ESPN's SportsCenter also had "Smith Stepping Down" that night and, consequently, the world knew.

By the next morning, as numerous TV and satellite trucks began turning the Smith Center parking lot into a scene from *Star Wars*, every newspaper in North Carolina and many across the country had played the story on 1A of its Thursday editions. Reporters poured into town for the confirmation. President Clinton called Smith to offer best wishes.

Kirschner posted several members of his staff at the doors leading into the cavernous Bowles Hall adjacent to the Smith Center, but there was no stopping anyone who wanted to get into what was quickly becoming the biggest media conference in the school's history. Six rows of chairs, each twenty seats across, were set up between the dais and the platforms holding TV cameras from more than two dozen stations and networks. Another twenty photographers and broadcasters knelt down just in front of the dais, waiting and ready to point cameras and microphones at Smith.

Almost every member of the UNC athletic department was in the room – with the notable exception of football coach Mack Brown – along with as many former Carolina players as could get there in time. The current Tar Heel team sat on the leather couches along the right wall, several still red-eyed from the emotional night before. On the outside looking in, hundreds of students, many of whom had spent the night on the front promenade of the Deandome, held up signs against the windows into the Bowles Room eight feet up the brown stucco walls outside of the Koury Natatorium. The biggest poster simply said, "We Love You, Coach," with a big red heart pictured instead of the word *Love*. The sign, as well as the sentiment, was unmistakable to everyone inside.

Finally, a few minutes after two, Smith followed Hooker and Baddour in through a side door near the dais, accompanied by Larry Brown and Georgetown coach John Thompson, one of the many longtime friends who made up the sometimes-maddening mosaic of Smith's personal relationships. Like the volatile Bob Knight, another close coaching compatriot, Thompson was outspoken and controversial. But he had once sent his adopted son to play for UNC and was one of Smith's assistants on the Olympic team. Thompson had flown in from Washington that morning after a call from Linda Woods.

Brown had remained in Chapel Hill after his 76ers broke training camp for their preseason opener against the Knicks at Madison Square

Garden, figuring that being by his old coach's side was enough reason to miss his first game with his new team. Brown, the point guard on Smith's first two teams in 1962 and 1963 and an assistant on his staff from 1965 to 1967, had hugged his mentor and wept in his office just moments before the press conference.

"I have decided to resign as head basketball coach," said Smith, who was upbeat and buoyant until he looked at his players. "It's hard to tell them I won't be their coach this season."

Smith not only addressed the speculation about a rift with Hooker; he also answered rumors about his own health. "I am healthy outside of no exercise, which I will begin on Monday," he said. "It's almost like there is something wrong. I am sixty-six years old. This professor, and I think of myself as faculty, has chosen to retire.

"I've been saying, maybe for the last eight years or so, maybe it's time to go do something else. I enjoy basketball, I enjoy coaching basketball. It's the out-of-season things that I haven't been able to handle very well."

Smith singled out Larry Brown and the passion he still had for the game. "Watching him out on the court, I said, 'I used to be like that,'" Smith said, his voice beginning to waver. "If I can't give this team that kind of enthusiasm, I said I would get out, and that's honestly how I feel."

Typically, he refused to utter the name of a single former player, knowing he could not mention all of them. But he did motion to the current Carolina team, sitting to his left. "What loyalty I've had from all of my players," he continued, his voice finally cracking. "They are really special."

Smith wiped a tear away from his eye and steered most of the press conference toward Guthridge, who was the obvious if not the popular choice to take over. Insisting over the years to stay in the background, Guthridge had been overlooked by the media and fans and, when asked, had said he had no interest in succeeding Smith.

In fact, until Guthridge appeared at the press conference, some people had still expected Ford to be the new head coach. Ford, they reasoned, had been personally groomed for the position; they also figured that his eventual ascension at Carolina was the reason he had turned down the University of Georgia job within the last year. Unwittingly, Ford had also been in the middle of the controversy over the new athletic director. A theory existed that Smith could not push Charles Waddell – a former

UNC three-sport star – for the position because Smith wanted Ford as his successor, and UNC was not ready to have both a black athletic director and a black basketball coach.

The truth was that Smith did not want Ford to succeed him – ironically because of his abiding concern for Ford's ultimate well-being. Smith knew that Ford was not ready to handle the pressures and demands of the Carolina program. Some day, maybe, but not yet. And he would never put Ford in a position to fail and thereby jeopardize his legendary status as one of North Carolina's greatest sports heroes.

So, though he never sought the job, Bill Guthridge agreed to become the new Carolina head coach, signing a long-term contract that could keep him in the position for five years, or until he was sixty-five, and inheriting Smith's Nike deal that would pay him $250,000 the first year and $500,000 each succeeding year he continued to coach.

And as for Dean Smith, he spent an October radically different from any he had seen in more than forty years. On the weekend that Carolina and three hundred other college basketball teams officially opened practice, while signs that said "Thank you, Coach" hung all over Chapel Hill, Smith went to the mountains with Miller to play golf.

CHIP OFF THE OLD BLOCK

Alfred Smith, the basketball coach at Emporia High School, had been called to Principal Rice Brown's office in January of 1934. Brown invited Smith to pull up a chair next to his desk. "We've got a problem with our team," he said.

Smith couldn't imagine. His team was undefeated, and the players were all good boys, none in trouble as far as he knew. He waited for the principal to elaborate.

Brown said the head of the Eastern Kansas Conference had called the day before and complained that Emporia had a black player, Paul Terry, on the team. Terry was the only minority on any team at any high school in the league, and Alfred Smith was damned proud of it.

"So, what's the problem?" he finally said. "Paul's a good student and fine player."

"You have to understand," the principal continued. "They're threatening to drop us from the conference if you keep Terry on the team."

"So they drop us," said Smith, getting irritated. "We'll find other schools to play." "What if I tell you to take Terry off the team?" Brown persisted.

"Then I'll quit and you can let someone else take him off," Coach Smith replied, standing up. "I'm not doing it."

Smith kept his job but was later thrown out of the Kansas coaches' association for using black players.

✪

Young Dean Smith was not even three years old when his father got called on the carpet for having the state's first integrated high school basketball team, but he grew up hearing the story. Not from his dad, but from others in the friendly little town of Emporia. When he was in grade school, traveling to a tournament in nearby Lawrence with the Emporia team, Smith saw for himself an example of his father's iron-willed integrity when it came to racial prejudice.

"We stopped at the Jayhawk Hotel to have a meal," Smith recalled in 1992, "and they wouldn't serve Chick Taylor. So Dad and the rest of the team stomped out and went somewhere else to eat."

Smith learned other, more subtle lessons from his parents while growing up on the Kansas plains. He has long remembered reading the legendary Chip Hilton novels and only years later figured out the method to his parents' madness. Alfred and Vesta Smith wanted their son to like books but, because young Dean preferred playing, knew he would be a reluctant reader. So they gave him sports books that were packed with core values and made heroes of athletes who lived up to the code.

"Those books even had some issues about race in sports, and that was long before Jackie Robinson," Smith said a half-century after he had read his last Chip Hilton story. "My parents had a reason for giving them to me."

They helped shape Smith's character, for one, and not only because Chip Hilton was the ideal athlete. Smith also liked Hilton's coach, "Rock" Rockwell, for the way he treated his players. And he didn't much care for one of Chip's teammates, "Duck" Tucker, a braggart and poor sport who broke the rules and would have never held on to a basketball scholarship to UNC.

Fictional heroes may constitute a small part of the Dean Smith mosaic, but the characters on those pages are eerily representative of both sides of the standards Smith stood for in his forty-plus years of coaching. It's no coincidence that, for most of his career, Smith had basketball players who were assorted versions of Chip Hilton, whether or not they could play well enough to be stars on their own. In 1972, one of his benchwarmers was charged with violating the honor code at UNC. Smith believed he was falsely accused and spoke on his behalf at the student trial. "I wish he were a better basketball player," Smith said, "but, as far as character goes, he's exactly the kind of young man I want my son to grow up to be."

As a son, Smith obviously made his own parents very proud. Born on February 28, 1931, in Emporia, Smith grew up in a world dramatically different from the society through which he would shepherd hundreds of student athletes later in life, making his success as a coach and mentor all the more amazing. Emporia, with only about twelve thousand residents in the 1930s, had two colleges (Kansas State Teachers College and College of Emporia) on opposite ends of town. The Smiths lived in a small, stucco home on Washington Street in a neighborhood filled with many faculty members from Kansas State Teachers.

"Some called Emporia the Athens of Kansas because Greek influence valued culture and education," said Joan Ewing, Smith's older sister by three years. "We had two colleges and seemed to have cultural advantages many small towns did not have." Ewing went on to explain that their family lived by three simple values: education, religion, and thriftiness.

Alfred coached the Emporia basketball team for thirteen years, the football team for twelve and the track team for six. His 1934 basketball squad, with Paul Terry, went on to win the state championship. Vesta taught English at the high school and later served two years as superintendent of Lyon County schools before cutting back to teach college classes in child psychology and development at Emporia, direct the Bible school for First Baptist Church, and eventually study for her masters in education.

Every Sunday, the Smiths took their two children to four hours of church, where Vesta played the organ and Alfred was a deacon. After the morning service, they went home for a meal that had been carefully planned and entirely prepared by the family. Vesta would get upset if a member of the family ate so much as a store-bought cookie. While Vesta put the finishing touches on the usual Sunday lunch of pot roast or chicken, potatoes, vegetables, bread, and Jell-O, Alfred, Dean, and Joan adjourned to the porch for a Ping-Pong round robin to determine who would do the dishes.

Alfred manipulated some of the games, sometimes letting his son catch up and win and other times beating him soundly, to teach Dean values like never quitting and how to accept defeat – traits Carolina basketball teams were to show many years later. But in the meantime, Dean would win the Kansas state thirteen-and-under table tennis championship.

Vesta's elderly and ailing mother, "Grandma Edwards," lived with the Smiths for the last thirteen years of her life, until Joan was thirteen and Dean eleven. Because the family could only afford to take in one extra member, "Grandpa Edwards" had to go to live with Vesta's brother four hours away by car. While other families vacationed in Colorado, the Smiths spent their free time traveling back and forth between relatives' homes. It was Dean's first practical exposure to a lifestyle of sharing and sacrificing. Grandma Edwards slept in the same room as Joan, and Dean bunked out on the sleeping porch until his grandmother died in 1942.

✪

The rules for kids were few and simple in the conservative Kansas environment of the 1940s, with chewing gum and running in the halls the worst transgressions for grade-schoolers. The rules got stricter, albeit no more complicated, as the kids became teenagers. Don't smoke, don't drink, don't stay out late. Teenage sex was an unthinkable. Part of the sacredness of family was an emphasis on virginity until marriage for both boys and girls. Years later, Smith agonized with guilt over a divorce from his first wife and well into his fifties would not smoke or drink in front of his parents.

Until the Smiths bought their first television in 1953, family time centered on the Philco radio in their living room. They listened to Bob Hope on Monday night, Red Skelton and Fibber McGee and Molly on Tuesday, Fred Allen on Wednesday. Jack Benny came on Sunday night before they went back to church for two more hours.

It was over that Philco, after the Sunday meal, that the Philharmonic was playing on December 7, 1941. Dean had gone off to meet his friends, Alfred and Joan were reading the newspaper, and Vesta was napping on the couch, when the symphony was interrupted with news of the attack on Pearl Harbor. Through the next few years, a number of Alfred's former players went off to war, and not all came home. Many of those who did return came by the Smith home to visit with their old coach, a bittersweet time because of the personal losses. Dean recalled those days vividly, another reason that he never treated games as life and death.

"I remember so well the experiences Dad would have with former players," Smith said in 1986. "Almost as soon as one would come home from the war, boom, he'd be over at the house. Yes, I would say it had an impact on me."

Alfred Smith, a veteran of World War I, had volunteered to go back into the army, but at forty-five was too old to enlist. Still, the entire family pitched in during the war, rationing gasoline and learning to use honey and syrup in place of sugar. Alfred spent summers painting and working construction, while Dean, Joan, and Vesta put in hours at the Red Cross Club, rolling bandages, making up CARE packages, and writing letters to the soldiers abroad.

Members of a frugal family anyway, Joan and Dean received an allowance of fifteen cents a week, five cents for church donation, five cents to save, and five cents to spend. Dean often gave his spending money away to friends who had none, and continued practicing that generosity into wealthy adulthood while he professed embarrassment over the amount of money he made. Alfred Smith didn't care much about money, but he used it to challenge Dean with his studies. When Joan went through junior high school making only two B's and the rest A's, Alfred told Dean he would give him one hundred dollars if he could match his sister's record. Dean did, donated most of it to the church, and got hooked. In adulthood, nothing would excite Smith more than competing for money on the golf course.

The great majority of Dean's childhood was spent riding his bike to and from church youth group activities, sandlot pick-up games and, later, organized school athletics. Because his father had a key to the gym, Dean was able to play by himself and then hang around the basketball team before and after practices and games. And while he didn't know he was starting to think like a coach, Smith had fun drawing up plays and making suggestions to his dad. He carried that coach's attitude into junior high school competition.

The various teams he played on gave young Smith close and lasting friendships. One of his school chums in Emporia was Dick Hiskey, who would go on to chair the chemistry department at UNC and serve a term as the school's faculty athletic representative.

However, in one very difficult instance, those friendships also gave Smith an early taste of tragedy. Shad Woodruff, a teammate in junior high school, grew ill one day and was diagnosed with a virulent form of polio. Shad was taken to the hospital, where distraught Dean spent hours standing outside his quarantined room, until Shad eventually succumbed to the disease. While the community mourned and the Smiths fretted over whether their son had been exposed to the crippling disease, because the two boys had drunk from the same soda pop bottle, Dean dealt with his grief privately. Joan remembers him biting his lip and fighting back tears as he spent hours on the porch putting together a scrapbook of articles about his and Shad's junior high teams. He gave it to Woodruff's family.

Eventually, Smith learned to grieve openly, and later in life it was not unusual to see him sitting alone in a pew at the funerals of friends, head bowed, eyes closed and weeping quietly. But Shad's death taught him early to accept death as an act of God, without question or blame, and to cherish positive memories of the deceased. Reading theology became a passion for Smith, and he developed the habit of sending comforting passages from books, articles, and favorite sermons to friends and families of lost loved ones.

✪

In the summer of 1946, after Alfred had retired from coaching, the Smiths moved from Emporia forty-five miles northwest to Topeka. Alfred, who was going to work for the local VA hospital, had actually kept coaching a year longer than planned, so Dean could play for him on the ninth grade football team. That year confirmed to Alfred that father and son would both be better off if he watched from the stands in high school.

An admitted "cocky junior high school athlete," fifteen-year-old Dean Smith was dressed down by his big sister just before the move to Topeka. "Joan gave me a pep talk and helped me understand that I didn't know it all and the world didn't revolve around me," he recalled in 1987. "As a result, I think I went the other way, being overly modest about taking a compliment." Humility arrived at just the right time. "I was about the best athlete I would ever become in the ninth grade," Smith said. "I didn't improve much after that. I was 5-10 and thought I'd grow to about 6-4. But I didn't grow any more at all." Still, he became a starter in three sports as a sophomore at Topeka High School.

Smith really liked the sport of football better, coming up with his own plays and actually trying to set up third down by what he called on first down. Only 150 pounds, he managed to avoid injuries throughout his football career and as a senior called every offense play while leading Topeka to second place in the state playoffs. But whatever his skills, Smith's forte was thinking about the games he played. Father and son spent hours in the family living room drawing diagrams and talking strategy.

Smith's first touchdown pass as a sophomore was caught by Adrian King, a gifted black end who would leave another indelible mark on his teammate's character. A natural athlete at 6-3, King would become the state champion hurdler in the spring, but between the two seasons he had to play on a separate, segregated basketball team at Topeka High. Smith went to the school principal, Buck Weaver, and asked him why blacks and whites couldn't play on the same basketball team, like they did in all the other sports. Smith selfishly wanted to have a better basketball team, but Weaver's unsatisfactory answer stayed with him. The school board worried about trouble at the dances held after home basketball games, and since very few black students watched the main varsity team play, this potential problem would be avoided.

Looking back, Smith always regretted he didn't think of mobilizing the students to protest. But he was just beginning to understand the historical perspective of it all. He was well aware that he played in the same Topeka High gym where Alfred Smith's Emporia Spartans had won the 1934 state title with Terry on their roster. He also knew that down the hall, carved over the library door, was this motto: "By nature all men are alike, but by education become different."

During these years Smith found himself falling under the spell of Kansas basketball, where only twenty-five miles away in Lawrence the successor to the game's inventor, Dr. James Naismith, was coaching the nationally prominent Jayhawks. "Most young men interested in basketball back then would have chosen the University of Kansas," Smith explained years later. "You just grew up that way."

By the time Topeka lost to Wichita East High School, coached by another local legend Ralph Miller, in the 1949 state tournament, Smith was still undecided as to where to go to college. Kansas State coach Tex Winter had offered him a partial scholarship for basketball, but Smith waited for a similar opportunity from Dr. Forrest "Phog" Allen, the coach at KU. It never came, and in the fall of 1949 Dean Edwards Smith enrolled at Kansas on an academic scholarship, planning to major in math and eventually follow his father into coaching. But he had the utmost respect for Dr. Allen and still wanted to show him he could play college basketball.

Allen, or "Doc" to his players, knew of Smith, invited him to try out for the freshman team, and later gave him a job selling programs during varsity football games for extra spending money. Smith also quarterbacked the freshman football team and caught for the frosh baseball squad.

The freshman basketball coach at KU was Dick Harp, who would go on to succeed Allen for eight years, coaching Wilt Chamberlain in the famous triple-overtime loss to UNC in 1957. Almost thirty-five years later, Smith hired Harp as an assistant on his own staff after learning his old coach had been struggling financially. It was a compassionate, but hardly charitable, move. "Dick Harp had the brightest basketball mind of anyone I've ever known," Smith once said. Harp remembered Smith as an inquisitive youngster who soaked up sports knowledge and had amazing retention and comprehension. "I don't think he ever failed to put down anything he thought could be used at a later time, either on paper or committing it to memory," Harp said in 1986. "He asked a lot of questions."

Smith has acknowledged Allen as a major influence on his own career. Always defense-minded, he obviously developed his "run and jump" and "scramble" maneuvers from Allen's old half-court press, when Kansas double-teamed the man with the ball as soon as he crossed midcourt and forced him to pick up his dribble. But he didn't always agree with his college coach about playing only five or six people. "Since I was a sub, I always said I'd remember the guys on the bench," Smith said. And clearly, Smith's own sometimes-obsessive habit of running his players in and out of the game stemmed, at least in part, from his frustrating moments riding the Kansas bench. Just as clearly, the man who would invent the clenched-fist "tired signal" didn't buy Allen's contention that if you couldn't go full steam the entire game you weren't in shape.

Surrounded by bigger and better players, Smith had an unmemorable varsity career. Kansas's outstanding guards, Gil Reich and Dean Kelley, could outshoot him and get the ball to inside scorers Clyde Lovellette and B. H. Born as well as he could. In forty-four games as a college reserve, Smith scored a total of eighty-nine points. He loved to play defense and, especially, take charges.

Smith's shining moment came as a junior in the 1952 NCAA semi-finals win over Santa Clara when he went in, ironically, to run the delay game. Doing what Tar Heel guards would do years later, Smith killed the clock and allowed Kansas to reach the championship game. He played briefly in that game as the Jayhawks, in yet another irony, defeated a St. John's team coached by Frank McGuire, who would eventually move to North Carolina and hire Smith as his assistant.

Never wavering in his desire to be a coach, Smith stayed around Lawrence for a year after he graduated, playing AAU ball and helping Harp with the freshman team. It was before Chamberlain enrolled, but many of the players he coached went on to face UNC for the national championship in 1957.

By the time Smith was out of school, he had met two young women who would have a lasting impact on his life. As a senior, he had dated a girl from Parsons, Kansas, named Joan Guthridge. She had a kid brother who, like Smith, idolized the Jayhawks and wanted to play for them after having grown up listening to their games on the radio. Also like Smith, he would turn out to be a 5-10 guard longer on heart than skills. Bill Guthridge visited Lawrence occasionally while in high school, using the excuse that he wanted to see his sister but really hoping to hang around Hoch Auditorium most of the weekend. One day, walking with Joan, he met Smith and began a relationship that endured over the next four decades and beyond.

Even after Smith stopped dating Joan, he stayed in touch with her brother. The two young men eventually became golfing buddies, and Smith kept track of his friend's career at rival Kansas State. Tex Winter gave Guthridge the same partial scholarship he had offered Smith seven years earlier, and Guthridge played on three straight Big Eight championship teams for the Wildcats.

Smith graduated from Kansas in 1953 with a degree in math and a B-plus average. (He never forgot his only D – in speech – and remarked many years later, "That's probably why I hate to speak in public.") At a party on the night of graduation, he met Ann Cleavinger, a senior, and they were married the following year in her hometown of Manhattan, where Kansas State was located. Their extended honeymoon included a tour of Europe, where Air Force Second Lieutenant Dean E. Smith served as player-coach for the base basketball team while stationed in Furstenfeldbruck, Germany.

A career reserve in college, Smith gave himself plenty of playing time for a team made up of seven air policemen, one of whom stood 6-7. They went 11-0, and one of the victories came over an Air Force team from France coached by Bob Spear. The two young coaches spent several evenings discussing basketball and began a friendship that would last a lifetime. When Spear, after serving as an assistant coach at Navy, was named head coach at the brand-new Air Force Academy in Denver, his first phone call went to Smith, whom he already considered a masterful young teacher of the game. For Smith, Spear's job offer represented a way to leapfrog over the high school level and into college coaching. In late 1955, Spear helped arrange for Smith to serve the rest of his Air Force commitment at the academy, where the two men coached a freshman squad for one year and fielded their first varsity team the following season.

Ann Smith continued to study occupational therapy during her husband's three years as a basketball, baseball, and golf coach at Air Force. But full-time employment had to wait, as Sharon Smith was born in 1955 and eighteen months later came Sandy Smith. A third child, Scott, was born in the summer of 1958, just after his father had taken his next coaching position in Chapel Hill, North Carolina.

In Smith's second season as an assistant at UNC, the Tar Heels and N.C. State played a two-night doubleheader in Raleigh against Kansas and Kansas State. Behind York Larese, Doug Moe, Yogi Poteet and Lee Shaffer, Carolina defeated the Jayhawks and Wildcats. Guthridge, by now a senior for K-State, scored eight points in twenty minutes off the bench against the Heels. The following spring, when visiting Ann's family in Manhattan, Smith played golf with Guthridge, and the two young men first shared their dreams of a lifetime career in coaching. Guthridge went on to join Winter's staff at Kansas State and Smith to succeed McGuire. Then, in June of 1967, after tracking him down while he was coaching a summer league team in Puerto Rico, Smith hired Guthridge to replace Larry Brown at UNC.

✪

Alfred and Vesta Smith lived in Topeka until they were well into their eighties – on the pretty, tree-lined street and in the same house they had built in 1951, when their son was a sophomore at KU and their daughter was on a graduate fellowship at Bowling Green. Joan Smith Ewing had already moved to North Carolina from St. Louis after a divorce in the early 1980s and was making regular trips out to Topeka to look after her parents while working for Democratic Congressmen Ike Andrews and eventually David Price.

Even though her family had always been deeply interested in politics, Joan was often amused by the rumors that her famous brother, by now a well-known liberal, would quit coaching basketball and challenge Republicans John East or Jesse Helms for a U.S. Senate seat. She knew that two of the most time-consuming responsibilities of a senator – attending cocktail parties and giving speeches – were the two activities that Dean Smith disliked most. Besides, there would be hour after hour of sitting in the legislative chambers listening to colleagues argue over questions that often had no clear-cut answers. In basketball, when the game was over, you had either won or lost. Period. And then there would be the next game. She also knew her brother was far too wise to trade an environment that he had created, and clearly controlled, for one of almost constant public scrutiny.

"Dean in politics?" she once said. "I don't think so."

Her parents had been visiting Chapel Hill about once every basketball season for years. Alfred still kept a scoresheet in the stands, marking field goals and free throws for individual players, while Vesta sat silently by his side. They had been in New Orleans for the 1982 national championship, but counted Montreal, where their son had coached the U.S. Olympic team to the gold medal in 1976, their proudest moment. After the Dean E. Smith Student Activities Center opened in January of 1986, the head coach always held back a couple of seats on the front row of the upper-deck loge for when his parents came to town. Early in the second year of the "Deandome," Smith asked a friend with two tickets on the fourth row at the back of the loge if he would switch them for first-row seats. That way, Alfred and Vesta would have fewer stairs to negotiate.

With Vesta's health and memory declining, the Smiths moved to North Carolina in 1988 and settled into Springmoor retirement community in Raleigh. In November of 1991, at age ninety-three, Alfred suffered a heart attack. He rallied during his hospital stay, and on Sunday morning, December 15, he seemed ready to return home. The night before he had talked with old friends in Topeka and written a check for Vesta to get her hair done. That afternoon, he planned to watch on TV as the Tar Heels played Florida State in their first Atlantic Coast Conference game of the season. He did not live to see his son's team upset by the Seminoles. He suffered a second heart attack and died almost immediately. Joan chose not to tell her brother until after the game. Smith was saddened but not surprised when he heard the news.

"I've been saying goodbye to both of them for a long time," he sighed.

Hundreds of cards and letters arrived at the UNC basketball office in the coming weeks, many from former students and athletes of Alfred Smith. One of them was from Paul Terry, the black member of the 1934 Emporia state championship team.

Now ninety-five, and with her husband of sixty-five years gone, Vesta lived only nine more months. Friends who knew her said she died of a broken heart. After her burial next to Alfred at Chapel Hill Memorial Cemetery and a short visit with his five children, Smith went back to his office to get ready for the start of another season, a season Alfred and Vesta would have loved to see. The following April, back in New Orleans, with an integrated team of unselfish and unpretentious players – all of whom would go on to graduate and come back faithfully to see the coach – their son won his second national championship.

CHAPTER FOUR

LYNCH-MOB MENTALITY

Bill Aycock served the University of North Carolina as chancellor from 1957 to 1963, the most colorful and controversial six years in UNC's athletic history. During his tenure, Aycock presided over two painfully public coaching changes that sent the Tar Heel football and basketball programs spiraling out of national prominence.

In 1957, the year of McGuire's Miracle, Carolina's basketball team went 32-0 and captured the NCAA championship with a storybook weekend in Kansas City that at once thrust Atlantic Coast Conference basketball into the nation's consciousness. At the Final Four, the Tar Heels won triple-overtime games against both Michigan State and Kansas within a 24-hour period – a David-and-Goliath tale that more than forty years later remained the most cherished piece of a state's rich athletic tradition. A young, brash TV producer named Castleman D. Chesley had sent the snowy black-and-white picture back to North Carolina, and thousands of fans watched Frank McGuire's team win the title by knocking off Kansas in the Jayhawks' backyard. That his underdog "four Catholics and a Jew" from New York had slain the giant, Wilt Chamberlain, in the process made the story as much folklore as fact.

A charismatic Irishman with a silver tongue, McGuire became a virtual deity upon returning to Chapel Hill from Kansas City – having detoured to make an appearance on *The Ed Sullivan Show* on Sunday night, March 24, 1957. He had already been given a new Cadillac by adoring Carolina alumni, and McGuire soon had open charge accounts at many restaurants and stores around town.

Indeed, the small village on the hill almost wasn't big enough for the bluster of McGuire and the imposing physical stature of big "Sunny Jim" Tatum, Carolina's equally engaging football coach. Tatum had been lured back from Maryland, where he had won his own national championship, fourteen years after coaching Carolina for one season as a 29-year-old in 1942. A good ol' boy to McGuire's city slicker, Tatum put together a program that would ultimately produce UNC's most memorable gridiron victory – a 50-0 smashing of Duke in Durham. They were his boys who dismantled the Blue Devils, but Tatum did not walk the sideline that glorious Saturday of November 26, 1959. The previous summer, he had suddenly and tragically contracted Rocky Mountain Spotted Fever, lapsed into a coma and died within five days. He was forty-six.

Already immersed in responding to an NCAA probe into McGuire's program, in which he enlisted the help of young assistant coach Dean Smith, Aycock then had to bury a football coach one day and hire his successor the next. And this with the 1959 season, expected to be one of Tatum's best, less than two months away. On a Sunday afternoon, Aycock and UNC Athletic Director Chuck Erickson met with each of Tatum's assistant coaches, one by one, and then called in the team captains. They needed unanimous approval to promote Jim Hickey into the head-coaching position.

"On Monday we had a press conference announcing Hickey as the new coach," Aycock recalled in 1986. "There were some rumblings, just as there were with the new basketball coach a few years later. Some people wanted to form a committee and hire another big name. But that wasn't the way I looked at it." Aycock's angelic face and soft-spoken demeanor belied his resolve.

Under pressure from the athletic department to clean up his program, McGuire escalated his own feud with Erickson. The coach and athletic director had clashed for several years over McGuire's freewheeling spending habits and failure to keep receipts and other documentation.

One evening in 1960, Aycock and his wife, Grace, walked over from the chancellor's residence on Raleigh Road to have dinner at the Carolina Inn. Passing the old Pine Room lounge, Aycock noticed a small group of well-heeled athletic boosters, members of the Rams Club, having what looked like a serious conversation. Aycock knew two of the men, Judge Carlisle Higgins and Fred Huffman, and walked in to say hello.

"We're holding a meeting and we're going to fire Chuck Erickson," Huffman brazenly told the chancellor. "We believe he's the cause of McGuire's problems. And we don't want to lose our basketball coach."

Aycock smiled thinly and suggested to the group that they all come by his office the next afternoon to discuss the matter further. The vigilantes arrived at the appointed hour to find chairs neatly arranged for them and reading material stacked up on Aycock's desk. The chancellor proceeded to hand out copies of the university's progress report into the investigation of McGuire's program.

"Please take your time and read through this material," Aycock said, beginning to walk out of his office. "I think you'll find that Coach McGuire's problems are not all because of Chuck Erickson."

The report included certain NCAA allegations, such as illegally paying scouts to help recruit kids from New York City, along with UNC's own charges of poor sportsmanship, unsavory language, and bench behavior that had led to fights during games with N.C. State, Duke, and Wake Forest. When Aycock returned twenty minutes later, the men had been forced into checkmate. None of them could argue that rules and regulations weren't important. They rose en masse, thanked Aycock for his time, and walked out of South Building, never to be heard from again on the matter of firing the athletic director.

But Aycock wasn't just sticking up for Erickson. When McGuire resigned less than a year later and Aycock selected Smith as the new coach, it was Erickson who objected this time.

"It should be my decision," Erickson said.

"The decision has been made," Aycock told him, without raising his voice.

✪

Tatum and McGuire left enormous shadows from which their successors had difficulty escaping. A football team that had been expected to return UNC to the glory days of Charlie "Choo Choo" Justice struggled to only one winning record in the next eight years, the 9-2 season that ended with a 35-0 win over Air Force in the 1963 Gator Bowl. Hickey was well liked but too laid-back, often playing golf on fall mornings before practice. In 1967, young Southeastern Conference trainee Bill Dooley replaced him.

By then, Dean Smith had emerged from the long, painstaking process of rebuilding the Carolina basketball program. He first had to overcome NCAA penalties and Consolidated University sanctions left behind from the McGuire era and then survive constant comparisons with the man who had brought him to Chapel Hill and to whom Smith remained fiercely loyal.

As far back as 1958, the difference in Frank McGuire's style of coaching and what would become Dean Smith's had been evident. McGuire, the master motivator, and Smith, the young tactician, had clashed quite innocently before the Tar Heels played Cincinnati on the third night of the famed Dixie Classic Christmas tournament. The night before at Reynolds Coliseum in Raleigh, Carolina had lost to Michigan State and star forward Johnny Green – the same Spartan team UNC had whipped in triple overtime on the way to the 1957 NCAA title. Top-ranked Cincinnati had been upset by N.C. State, setting up the third-place showdown between the Tar Heels and the Bearcats, who were led by All-American Oscar Robertson. Adding to the tension of an already fight-marred tournament was the breaking of the color line at the annual event by Green and Robertson, the first blacks ever to play in Reynolds Coliseum and the Dixie Classic.

The loss to Michigan State had angered McGuire, who stayed away from the team the entire next day. The Tar Heels were in the locker room, already in uniform, when first-year assistant Smith wrote the match-ups for the Cincinnati game on the chalkboard, with 6-7 defensive stopper Doug Moe assigned to the 6-5 Robertson. McGuire walked in late, just before the team was to take the court for warm-ups. Turning to the blackboard, he said sharply, "Forget about that bullshit. Just go out there and play like you're in the schoolyard . . . like you're in the schoolyard!"

Smith, who had stepped back when McGuire came in, stood silently as the Tar Heels stormed onto the court for what would be a classic confrontation of two of the best teams in the country. Carolina won 72-68 after All-American Lee Shaffer dunked and got fouled in the final minute, sending previously unbeaten Cincinnati home with two losses in three games.

Since McGuire believed in letting his talented schoolyard players freelance on offense, Smith devoted his time to coaching and teaching defense. He brought the presses and double-teams with him that Phog Allen had used at Kansas, forever thinking about how to improve them. Late one night, while they were on a recruiting trip together, McGuire woke up to find Smith sleep-walking in a defensive stance.

Preparation of another kind helped Smith eventually get the head-coaching job at Carolina and stay one step ahead of the lynch mob in his first few turbulent seasons.

✪

"When we got the charges from the NCAA," Aycock recalled in 1985, "most of them had a common element, excessive expenditures and excessive entertainment on the part of Coach McGuire. I asked him about it and he said it wasn't true.

"I said, 'For your own sake and the sake of the university we've got to gather information to refute these charges.' I thought he would help me out. Instead, he said, 'I'll send over Coach Smith.'"

McGuire had met Smith at the 1957 Final Four in Kansas City, when the Tar Heels played Kansas for the national championship. Smith had stayed in the same hotel suite with McGuire, former Carolina coach Ben Carnevale, Air Force head coach Bob Spear – Smith's boss at the time – and University of Denver coach Hoyt Brawner. Aware that McGuire was beginning to look for an assistant to eventually replace the aging and ailing Buck Freeman, Spear acknowledged the brilliance of his young aide and promoted him to McGuire. But Smith thought he had blown his chance for the Carolina job when he answered one of McGuire's questions truthfully.

"Who will you be pulling for tonight?" McGuire asked.

"I have to go with the alma mater," Smith replied, cringing inside.

Later that afternoon, Smith called his father back in Topeka and told him he might have made McGuire mad.

"No, no," Alfred Smith said. "He'll respect you for your honesty."

After the Tar Heels had beaten Kansas in three overtimes, a disappointed Smith returned to the hotel suite and, upon McGuire's request, took several of the North Carolina writers out to eat. Smith later joked that he had selected Eddy's Restaurant because it was the most expensive place in town and had wanted to stick UNC with a big bill. More than a year later, after seeing McGuire again at the 1958 Final Four in Louisville, Smith accepted an offer to join the UNC staff and moved his family to Chapel Hill in August. He could have also taken a job as Harp's assistant at Kansas but believed his career would benefit from seeing how another school did things.

With McGuire controlling recruiting through his famed Underground Railroad to New York and talent scout Harry Gotkin, Smith concentrated on detail work like preparing practice plans for the following season. So it seemed perfectly logical that McGuire would send the thorough, meticulous young man over to help Aycock track down months and months of travel vouchers and expense receipts. But as a result, Smith found himself delicately positioned between the two men for whom he worked, and did not feel good about it.

On one hand, he was digging up dirt on McGuire, who had treated the newcomer to North Carolina like family. Before Smith moved to Chapel Hill, McGuire had put him up, introduced him around town, and spent a couple of days helping him look for a house to buy. They became handball and golfing buddies and grew quite close. On the other hand, McGuire had assigned him to work with the chancellor, and the young coach wanted to do a thorough job. As he pieced together a paper trail of McGuire's miscues, Smith confided only to his wife Ann that McGuire could be in some trouble.

Aycock clearly remembered Smith going about his business, never mentioning McGuire's name. Even after McGuire was ousted and, later, when their friendship turned to bitter rivalry, Smith would speak publicly of his mentor in the most loyal of terms. And if he secretly felt otherwise, he never shared those feelings with Aycock.

"I know he had a right to be appreciative to Frank McGuire for bringing him here," Aycock said, "and he had a right to thank me for hiring him as head coach. There just has never seemed to be a reason why he and I should get into a conversation about Coach McGuire. We haven't shied away from it; it's just never come up."

In fact, Smith was so successfully loyal to both men that each thought he should have the head-coaching job in the summer of 1961. By then, Aycock and McGuire had become open adversaries, particularly after the chancellor, via a letter dated April 28, clearly delivered an ultimatum: clean up the program or your contract will not be renewed after the 1963 season. Believing the rift could be mended, Smith tried to talk McGuire out of quitting and at one point thought he had convinced his boss to stay. But after being courted by a couple of NBA teams, McGuire walked into Aycock's office on August 5, 1961, and within a half-hour had resigned and recommended Smith for the job.

At the same time, McGuire advised Smith not to accept the job, but to go along with him to Philadelphia, where they would coach the NBA Warriors and Wilt Chamberlain. Although tempted, Smith wanted to remain a college coach and had actually spoken again with Harp about returning to Kansas, as well as to Brawner about succeeding him at Denver. So after conferring with his wife, Smith was driven over to the chancellor's office by McGuire, where he accepted the Carolina job and took Aycock on his now-famous words.

"His directions to me were," Smith recalled many times, "make sure our players graduate; ensure they will not embarrass themselves or the university; no problems with gambling and no recruiting violations."

Despite the championship fever McGuire had whipped up, Aycock made no mention of wins and losses. And although Aycock remained as chancellor only for Smith's first two years as head coach, his mandate gave Smith the strength to hang on through some very tough times and mediocre seasons. During the difficult days, and on into his glory years, Smith held Aycock close to his heart.

"After you gave me this opportunity as your basketball coach, you did everything possible to help me succeed," Smith said in a handwritten letter shortly after Aycock went back to teaching at the law school in 1963. "I am very grateful . . . ."

Following the 1980 season, angered and distraught to find out that former chancellors did not automatically receive staff tickets to home basketball games, Smith wrote to Aycock, "Be assured you will have two for next season and I hope you will enjoy the games." And at the end, after 879 victories, thirteen ACC championships, two national titles and an Olympic gold medal, Smith had only one photo of himself in his office – standing with Aycock in the parking lot of the Smith Center in the early 1990s. He had a copy made and sent it to Aycock with yet another inscription of thanks for having had faith in him thirty years earlier.

✪

McGuire's last Carolina team had gone 19-4, placing first in the ACC standings with a 12-2 record, and, if not for the loss of several key players, Smith might have enjoyed the kind of successful transition that Bill Guthridge did thirty-six years later.

The unraveling began in January of 1961 – the final, fractious season of McGuire's tenure – when the NCAA had slapped Carolina with a one-year probation, banning the Tar Heels from post-season play. McGuire and his team believed they could have won the national championship that year and had played out the season with a chip on their shoulders. Their sour attitude contributed to the wild melee at Duke on February 4, when a brawl erupted after Doug Moe spat in the face of Duke sophomore Art Heyman. Dozens of fans joined in and ten Durham policemen had to break it up. Heyman, who had been headed for UNC before his father and McGuire got into an argument, and Carolina's backcourt of Larry Brown and Donnie Walsh were suspended for all remaining ACC games. (Curiously, Moe escaped ejection). Little wonder that Aycock gave Smith a coaching mandate of decorum over wins and losses.

The downward spiral continued when Yogi Poteet and Kenny "Moose" McComb flunked out of school in the spring. And if that wasn't enough, highly recruited forward Billy Galantai, who had already been declared ineligible as a freshman, drew another one-year varsity suspension from the NCAA for having filed a false statement about his amateur eligibility. These were all residuals of the flamboyant McGuire era over which Smith the assistant had little control. But then Smith's best sophomore, Bryan McSweeney, severely sprained an ankle in the third game of the season and never fully recovered. So with four potential starters down and a coaching legend gone, Carolina's stature plummeted on and off the court.

Undaunted, Smith prepared and motivated his team, quickly making it clear that both in practice and in style of play UNC basketball was now in a new pair of hands. Smith had briefly suspended Brown after he was spotted coming out of a Chapel Hill bar during preseason practice, a violation McGuire would have probably let pass. Brown said he was not drinking, only warning other players to get out of the place. But to Dean Smith appearances would mean everything. And as a testimony to the change in on-court philosophy, senior guard Walsh demonstrated Carolina's new emphasis on shot selection. He was the first of many of Smith's players to set a new single-season school record for field goal accuracy, hitting 56 percent of his shots.

Practices, mostly loosey-goosey scrimmages with McGuire, became classrooms under his successor. The drills that Smith had implemented as warm-ups while McGuire sat in the bleachers entertaining cronies and sportswriters were now the staples of a Tar Heel practice. As would become his inviolable custom through the years, Smith used practice to determine who earned playing time in games. McGuire had rarely played more than seven men, and his regulars were set early, changed only by a serious injury or, as the players joked, "a death in the family." McGuire's taunting turned into Smith's teaching.

Offering opinions as he watched his team go up and down the court, McGuire had believed in banding the players together against an enemy – and in practice he was the foil. He had often referred to his 1957 All-American Lennie Rosenbluth, and later Brown, kiddingly as "Jew bastards" and hazed sophomores mercilessly until they had earned his respect. Smith, on the other hand, began by respecting his players and treated them like gentlemen unless they gave him reason to do otherwise.

McGuire had begun each practice by blowing his whistle and calling the team to midcourt, where he told a story about what had happened to him that day or twenty years ago as a New York roughneck. Injecting humor to make a point, McGuire liked to say there was nothing his players could do that he had not done himself. If one of his guys had been hanging out at The Goody Shop or some beer joint on Franklin Street, McGuire made sure the culprit knew he had been spotted. That was penalty enough; McGuire rarely suspended a player.

Smith also called his team to the center jump circle with a shrill whistle, but that's where the similarities ended. Instead of personal war stories, Smith might conduct a brief discussion of world news and, later, "thoughts of the day." Smith occasionally doled out homework, springing pop quizzes on his players the next afternoon. A teacher at heart, he wanted them thinking and alert.

One final, highly visible difference: Smith began closing some practices to the public and the press, leaving what appeared to be a void in the daily awareness of Tar Heel basketball. Going from the magnetic McGuire to the shy Smith seemed to symbolize what many feared to be a subtle de-emphasis of big-time college athletics on the UNC campus. Smith's first season did little to dispel such fears.

Fear of the point-shaving scandals that had rocked college basketball in the late 1950s, coupled with McGuire's recruiting violations, had caused Aycock to limit Smith's first schedule to two non-conference games. And – despite a season-opening blowout of Virginia – as the ACC rivalries heated up, Carolina looked like more and more like a depleted program. Sophomore forward Dieter Krause, declared academically ineligible, missed the second half of the season, and two-sport star Charlie Shaffer joined the team later than expected due to a knee injury incurred during football season. Left with three experienced upperclassmen, Brown, Walsh, and center Jim Hudock, Carolina lost seven of its last nine games to finish with an 8-9 record against the abbreviated schedule imposed by Aycock. For a program that had won the NCAA title only five years before and had been a national power ever since, the thud could be heard across the UNC campus and beyond.

Although the circumstances of Carolina's demise seemed clear, the first rumblings of discord were soon heard among students and fans, and some in Smith's own camp showed less than perfect loyalty. Assistant coach Ken Rosemond, a member of McGuire's fabled 1957 team, had wanted the head job and did not discourage the second-guessing that he should have gotten it. Smith also had a doubter in Erickson, who was still sore that he had had no say in hiring the new coach and thought Smith spent too much money on new carpet for his office and long-distance phone calls.

"Your phone bill is higher than mine and the chancellor's," Erickson told him one day.

"I should hope so," countered Smith. "You and the chancellor are not trying to recruit basketball players."

Given the testy atmosphere that prevailed after his rookie season,

Smith, not yet thirty-two, occasionally had to remind the team that he was the head coach. But he pushed on, never once doubting that he could eventually get the job done. With Poteet having regained his eligibility, McSweeney fully recovered, and a pogo-sticking sophomore named Billy Cunningham set to join the varsity, Smith expected a much-improved team in 1963 and relished the challenge of seeing how the Tar Heels could compete with powerful Duke.

✪

Early that season, Smith led Carolina to what has since been properly placed among his greatest upset victories. The 68-66 stunner over All-American Cotton Nash and the Kentucky Wildcats in December of 1962 began with an ingenious ploy – Smith's attempt to convince his team it really wasn't playing Kentucky. It ended with his taking an emotional walk back to the hotel in Lexington with longtime trainer John Lacey, who served loyally under both McGuire and Smith until his retirement in 1970.

Smith, himself, had serious doubts that the Tar Heels could hang with the Wildcats, coached by one of his idols, Adolph Rupp, because two nights before they had been blown out at Indiana. Then, upon entering the locker room to find Brown, his senior point guard, shivering and broken out in hives, Smith tried something that, in retrospect, might have been a joke. Having to raise his voice over the stomping, screaming crowd upstairs in Memorial Gym, Smith smiled and shouted, "Just make believe you're playing Tennessee." Then he told Poteet not to worry about scoring a single point, only to stick with Nash wherever he went all over the court. And he told Brown to stay out near half court when Carolina had the ball and run the little stall game they had started working on in practice.

Cunningham pulled down seventeen rebounds, Poteet held Nash to twelve points on 3-of-12 shooting, and Brown was so successful spreading out the Kentucky defense that Smith kept the maneuver as a regular part of practice from that point on. Then, one afternoon in Woollen Gym the following January, Brown accidentally invented what was to become the scourge of college basketball, the full-fledged Four Corners.

Standing under the basket talking to his defense, Smith quietly called for a switch from zone to man-to-man against the stall to see if Brown recognized the change. Brown did not, saw what he thought was a breakdown in the zone and drove the lane for a layup. Smith blew his whistle and walked out from under the basket.

"Larry!" he shouted in his 32-year-old nasal voice, "run that again."

This time, Smith motioned for Cunningham to come out of the corner and break toward the goal when Brown made his move. Richard Vinroot left his man underneath and challenged Brown, who fed a perfect bounce pass to Cunningham for another layup. Smith had them run the Four Corners so many times the rest of that practice that Brown said afterward, "I thought it was a conditioning drill because we had done something wrong. Then I got to use it (Four Corners) against Duke in the last game. They were so good, but we hung in there with them until the end of the game."

The 1963 team finished third in the ACC, lost a one-pointer to Wake Forest in the ACC Tournament and had to go home with a 15-6 record. Smith has since maintained that team could have won the conference title with a little more size. The 6-4 Cunningham averaged twenty-three points and sixteen rebounds as a sophomore in 1963, but no other regular stood over 6-3.

Having lost five seniors, including Brown and Poteet, Smith turned the 1964 team over to Cunningham and admittedly did his worst coaching job. He relied too much on Cunningham and set a bad precedent by allowing the Kangaroo Kid to rest at midcourt after starting a fast break with a rebound. That indeed proved ludicrous in retrospect, given the future Carolina teams whose big men would score hundreds of points off the "secondary break." Cunningham had a great year, leading the ACC in scoring and rebounding, but the Tar Heels lost four straight at one point and floundered to a 12-12 record. Smith's problems among UNC alumni and fans quickly intensified.

Opposing crowds were bad enough, taking the long-awaited opportunity to hit Carolina when it was down. Fans from the other Big Four schools (Duke, N.C. State, and Wake Forest) threw debris and hurled obscenities at Smith and the Tar Heels, indelible incidents that cemented the abiding loyalty among so many of his former players; for them the experience was tantamount to having survived war together. But the mockery from opposing crowds could be expected and tolerated. Only a team's own "supporters" can render the ultimate insult that Smith was forced to confront on January 6, 1965.

As the team returned from a 22-point loss at Wake Forest and the bus rolled to a stop next to Woollen, Smith sat silently in the front seat across the aisle from the driver. He says that he at first pretended not to see his likeness hanging from a tree in front of the gym. But junior Jim Smithwick distinctly remembered his coach telling the team to walk off the bus with heads high. The players froze for a moment before Cunningham jumped out, reached up, and pulled the dummy down as the small crowd watching from across the street scattered. One report, denied by the coach, had Smith following Cunningham and chasing after the on-lookers.

Correcting another popular misconception, that was not the night Smith's sister Joan gave him the book *Beyond Ourselves* (with the chapter entitled "The Power of Helplessness" on learning to not worry about what one cannot control). In fact, Joan had read the book many years earlier at the University of Chicago Seminary and had often discussed it with her brother. They had both become admirers of authors Peter and Catherine Marshall.

However, Smith did call on the book's philosophy that night, maintaining, "I'm healthy; I could do a lot of other things." He was unwinding at the home of friends Lou and Florence Vine, who during their twenty years in Chapel Hill had befriended former Carolina coaches Carnevale, Tom Scott and McGuire and had taken McGuire's young assistant under their wing as well.

"I'll never forget the night after that Wake Forest game," Vine said years later. "Dean came over to the house and was so depressed. We sat around, had a few drinks, and Dean finally said, 'Maybe I'm in the wrong business.' Florence and I both told him, 'You've got to stick it out at least another year.'"

Vine insisted that Smith never doubted his own ability to coach, only whether all the criticism was worth it. Fittingly, three days later Smith delivered what he has since called the best pep talk of his career before Carolina upset nationally ranked Duke in Durham. Motivated by that huge win, as well as by a second, less-publicized "hanging" of Smith a week later, the Tar Heels went on to win seven straight games and complete the 1965 regular season with a 15-9 record, second in the ACC. From that point on, Smith's teams would never finish lower than third place.

The coach was hardly out of the woods and would still have to endure an angry letter from students in the *Daily Tar Heel* asking for his ouster, but he had recruited better players to the program and had more on the way. While Cunningham graduated and became the first of Smith's twenty-six NBA first-round draft picks, another superstar was moving up to the varsity. As it happened, Larry Miller proved to be only one of several newcomers who, in 1966, helped Dean Smith finally establish himself as the only basketball coach the University of North Carolina would have – or need – for the next thirty-two years.

RECRUITING STORIES
PART 1

Frank McGuire remained a central figure in Dean Smith's life throughout his first ten years as head coach of the Tar Heels, but not always an object of Smith's affection. During these years the two men developed a rivalry that was at time acrimonious enough to threaten their long friendship.

After the charismatic McGuire resigned amidst swirling controversy in the summer of 1961, Smith had to "re-recruit" rising junior guard Larry Brown and pray that Billy Cunningham, who was in the middle of his freshman year at UNC, would come back. It was Smith's good fortune that McGuire had moved on to pro basketball rather than to one of the several other colleges that had been pursuing him. Had McGuire chosen any of those, Brown and Cunningham might have followed their old coach to his new school. As it was, McGuire's departure did cost Carolina two highly recruited prospects, Judd Rothman and Billy Lawrence, both of whom decided to attend college in New York instead of playing for Smith, who released them from their scholarships.

Smith had coached Brown one season as an assistant and figured his starting point guard would stay. But that summer, Smith wound up in the kitchen of Brown's modest home on Long Island trying to convince him to return to school.

"Coach McGuire was bigger than life, and the relationship I had with Dean as an assistant was much different," Brown said. "All of a sudden Frank is gone and Dean takes over; shit, it was like my whole life changed and I was ready to run.

"I was going to leave school, and my mom said, 'You're staying. This is the man I want you to be with.' Fortunately, my mom liked Dean, because going back to Carolina was the best thing that ever happened to me."

Brooklyn-born Cunningham had landed in Chapel Hill because his father – a tough, Irish, New York City firefighter – had known McGuire's sister for years. After meeting McGuire, the older Cunningham knew where his son was going to college.

"My father said I was going to a Catholic school or to play for Coach McGuire," recalled Billy Cunningham, whose family drove him twelve hours to see Chapel Hill. "I never visited another school, never thought about another one."

Cunningham was home for the summer when Smith replaced McGuire and thought about not going back to complete his freshman year. But, because he had started college in January and had enjoyed his first five months in Chapel Hill, Cunningham returned for the fall semester. He sat out the spring term and began preparing for his first varsity season. An instant star as a sophomore, Cunningham led the ACC in rebounding and was second behind Duke's Art Heyman in scoring. He led the league in both categories as a junior in 1964, but Carolina struggled to a 12-12 record – Smith's last non-winning season.

While some Carolina players began second-guessing their own coach and fans grew apathetic, ironically, another young recruit was electrifying large, supportive crowds at freshman games in Woollen Gym, averaging thirty-six points by scoring from all over the court. Bobby Lewis had not considered Carolina, in fact did not even know Smith had written to him, until he watched the UNC-Notre Dame game on a rainy afternoon in his hometown of Washington, D.C., the previous January. After that game, Lewis had gone through a box of recruiting letters and found one from Smith.

"Good luck with your senior year," Smith wrote in his standard recruiting letter. "When it comes time to look at colleges, I hope you'll consider visiting Chapel Hill." Enthralled with Cunningham after seeing him play on TV, Lewis had made a springtime trip to UNC with his mother and fell in love with the school. He became Smith's first big-name recruiting victory, a victory abetted by Lewis's mother after she had spent considerable time talking with Smith that weekend about the importance of all basketball players earning their degrees.

Lewis and Cunningham would have only one season together on the varsity, so Smith and assistant coach Ken Rosemond stayed in hot pursuit of their next national recruiting target, heralded Pennsylvanian prep star Larry Miller, "the big cat from Catasaqua."

The rugged and handsome Miller had become a schoolboy legend in his home state, where he played for Allentown in the old Eastern League against semipro players twice his age. A one-time 1960s-vintage, hubcap-stealing hood, with an affinity for weightlifting before it was fashionable, Miller averaged thirty points and thirty rebounds a game as a senior and was rated the top high school player in America. He was also considered to be a lock for Duke coach Vic Bubas, who stood at the top of the long list of college coaches trying to get the loquacious, left-handed Miller to join their programs.

One of those coaches didn't even have a college. After three seasons with Wilt Chamberlain and the Philadelphia Warriors, McGuire had chosen not to move with the team to California after the 1964 season. He wanted to get back to the college game and was considering offers from several schools. On a late spring afternoon in 1964, McGuire showed up at Miller's house while Rosemond was also there. "He was recruiting me, even though he didn't know which school he'd be at," Miller said. "He told me it would either be LaSalle or South Carolina, and then he asked to talk to my mother."

Largely due to Rosemond's persistence, Miller agreed to visit Chapel Hill, and while hopping fraternity parties with Lewis and Cunningham he was swept away by the idyllic lifestyle at UNC. During a one-on-one meeting, Smith appealed to Miller's ego and challenged him to start something of his own at Carolina instead of joining Duke's dynasty. Miller finally decided to invite the head coach of the college he would choose to his high school graduation. He waited until virtually the last minute before dialing Smith's number on the eve of the ceremony in June of 1964. Smith's wife, Ann, answered the phone at their Chapel Hill home and got so excited over the news that she drove to Woollen

Gym, where her husband was conducting his summer basketball camp.

When McGuire finally decided on South Carolina and returned to the ACC later that summer, he had missed on Miller. But he immediately began locking horns with Smith over the best high school players in New York City, where thanks to him North Carolina had such a wonderful reputation.

✪

Larry Brown, playing AAU ball for Goodyear at the time, remembered the successful recruiting of Miller as a turning point in the public perception of his mentor. "When he signed Lewis and then Miller, people took notice and said, 'Whoa,'" Brown recalled. "The pieces were starting to fall into place."

After helping Rosemond get the head-coaching job at Georgia after the 1965 season, Smith talked to Lewis and Miller about rumors that they would follow Rosemond. Though they assured him not, Smith's uncomfortable feeling that Rosemond might indeed have "recruited" them made him realize that he needed unyielding loyalty from his new assistant coach. Brown, who had already accomplished his goal of making the 1964 U.S. Olympic team in Tokyo, thought his playing career was over and jumped at the chance to rejoin Smith at Carolina and enter coaching. Their first task was to do some recruiting.

With Cunningham graduating, Smith had little quality support coming up to play with Lewis and Miller, a rising sophomore. But he had his eye on a couple kids who would eventually allow the "L&M Boys" to play their natural positions. Franklin "Rusty" Clark, a 6-10 center from Fayetteville, was a serious student considering Davidson and planning on medical school. Bill Bunting was a 6-8 forward from New Bern with strong family ties to Duke. Once he hired Brown, Smith and his 24-year-old assistant hopscotched across the country in pursuit of the two big men, plus three other high school stars Brown would coach on the heralded freshman team of 1966.

The turning point for Clark came in March of 1965, when he was awarded a Morehead Scholarship to UNC, the most prestigious academic honor in the state. Almost a year earlier, Davidson coach Lefty Driesell had offered a scholarship to Clark, whose older brother, Billy, was in school there.

"It was important to know they didn't have a big man at the time," said Clark, whose parents were both UNC grads and pushing him to go there. "Plus, I never felt exploited or used. (Smith) went overboard to make sure I got a good education. He did that for anybody, and for those who weren't interested he tried to get them interested."

Even though Smith was not a major factor in Clark's college decision, he did everything he could to accommodate his starting center. For example, on the days when Clark had long labs scheduled in the afternoon, Smith held practices in the evening. Still, with a consuming goal to get into medical school, Clark viewed basketball as an avocation and was often frustrated by how much time it took from his studies.

Early in Clark's career, several Tar Heels sneaked some beer into their hotel room one night between a weekend set of games in Charlotte (the legal age was eighteen, but drinking was against team rules). Clark reportedly had one too many. Told to be quiet because the coaches might hear them, Clark began pounding on one of the walls in the room. "I hate you! I hate you!" he yelled, obviously referring to Smith. In fact, he briefly contemplated not playing as a senior in order to concentrate on academics. But by that time he had already helped the Tar Heels reach two Final Fours and set a school record of thirty rebounds in a game against Maryland. "I would have had to leave the state if I didn't play," he said. Clark went on to become a successful physician and one of Smith's most ardent supporters.

In the spring of 1965, while pursuing Bunting and his smooth baseline jumper, Smith went head-to-head with the other three so-called Big Four coaches – N.C. State's Press Maravich and Wake Forest's Bones McKinney, both dynamic and funny men, and Duke's Bubas, who had recruiting down to a science with his famed checklist of phone calls and letters.

Maravich promised Bunting he could play with his son, the soon-to-be-famous "Pistol Pete" Maravich, although that turned out to be folly when the Maraviches bolted for LSU the next summer. McKinney bet Bunting he could be the next Dickie Hemric or Len Chappell, former Deacon All-Americans, and fixed it so Bunting followed and visited with Wake Forest alumnus Arnold Palmer during the 1965 Greater Greensboro Open. But the smart money was on Bubas, who had coached Duke to consecutive Final Fours in 1963 and 1964 and was tough to beat on any kid. Bunting's father had graduated from Duke, and Bubas played the Blue Devils' trump card aggressively.

Compared to that trio of coaches, young Dean Smith was clearly in the shadow. But he sold Bunting the way he had sold Clark and Lewis – and would dozens of players over the years – by talking about the value of education more than the promise of basketball stardom. In the end Bunting chose Carolina, but his decision was influenced less by Smith's pitch than by Bunting's desire to play on the same team with Lewis and Miller and to play forward alongside Clark.

Smith and Brown – who still hadn't even found a place to live in Chapel Hill – were not done yet. Now they went after a point guard to play with Lewis and Miller on the wings, Bunting and Clark underneath. Their main target became Dick Grubar, a 6-4 high school center from Schenectady, New York, who wanted to play guard in college. After a weekend trip to see Carolina and Duke, Grubar was hooked on becoming a Tar Heel. Later, he learned that Duke assistant coach Chuck Daly had called him too slow to play for the Blue Devils, providing extra incentive whenever the rivals met over the next four years.

Also in that ballyhooed freshman class were forward Joe Brown of Valdese, North Carolina, considered the third best player in the state behind Clark and Bunting; Gerald Tuttle, a guard from London, Kentucky, who had waited for a scholarship from Adolph Rupp that never came; and Atlanta's Jim Bostick, the first of only a few players to ever leave Smith's program because there was too much talent. Bostick transferred to Auburn after his sophomore year.

"That was the year Dean made his move, particularly on North Carolina boys," said McKinney, who died in 1996. "Before Dean came along, Wake Forest was the big recruiter in North Carolina. Dean changed that with quiet determination."

✪

One of the first high school stars Smith had recruited at Carolina was more than an outstanding basketball player. Lou Hudson, a brilliant student and player at Greensboro Dudley High School, had wanted to become UNC's first black varsity athlete but failed to make the minimum 900 SAT score then dictated by the Atlantic Coast Conference. When many coaches and administrators were accepting that arbitrary guideline, Smith rejected standardized testing as racially and culturally biased and repeated that argument many times over the next thirty-five years. Hudson, who had finished third in his graduating class of six hundred, instead went to Minnesota, made All-American, and later starred in the NBA.

"My pastor at Binkley Baptist Church, Dr. Robert Seymour, said my first job was to get a black athlete," Smith said. "Of course, I was well aware of that and wanted to, remembering my father's experience back in Kansas. And the Lou Hudsons were there."

Smith already had his own integration story as McGuire's assistant in 1959. Seymour had asked him to join a group of Chapel Hillians hoping to desegregate the restaurant where the basketball team ate its pregame meals. Smith, Seymour, and a black UNC student who was a member of the Binkley congregation walked into The Pines, where they were served without incident.

After Hudson, Smith tried again two years later when he asked a black high school student from Charlotte named Willie Cooper to "walk on" to the freshman team. Cooper did well enough to be invited to join the varsity the next season, but he failed an economics exam as a freshman and decided to concentrate on his studies. About the time Cooper politely declined Smith's invitation to break the color barrier at UNC, fifteen-year-old Charlie Scott had just transferred from his school in Harlem, where he grew up, to Laurinburg Institute in North Carolina, having accepted a partial scholarship to the predominantly black prep school.

Smith found out when Scott later committed to Davidson and, as a rule, did not recruit players who had verbally agreed to attend another college. But he made an exception because he had also learned that Scott was not comfortable with the segregated restaurants and stores in the town of Davidson. After Smith and Brown made a recruiting trip to Laurinburg, Scott visited Chapel Hill on the then-famous Jubilee spring weekend of 1966, when Smokey Robinson & The Miracles and The Temptations performed in Kenan Stadium. Smith made sure Scott was properly "mothered" by Lillian Lee, a close friend of the basketball program and wife of Howard Lee, Chapel Hill's first black mayor.

In further efforts to apprise Scott of the progressive, caring atmosphere on campus, Smith arranged meetings with Dan Pollitt from the law school and Dr. Frank Klingberg and Thal Elliott of the medical school. In response to the suggestion that he was trying to determine whether Scott had the emotional fortitude to become the school's first black scholarship athlete, Smith would later say, "I was only interested in his basketball ability and whether he would do well in the classroom."

Scott loved the weekend, returned to Laurinburg, and told Davidson's Driesell that he was going to Carolina instead. "All hell broke loose after that, with Lefty thinking I'd been stolen from him," said Scott, who confirmed the much-told tale about Driesell jumping out of the bushes the next day to confront Scott as he walked to a movie.

"My loyalty was to Lefty, but my heart was at Carolina," Scott said. "I had to tell him that Carolina was going to be the better school for me in the long run."

Smith and Scott formed a close bond, since both had been put on the firing line in the racist South of the 1960s. Smith saved all of the letters he received criticizing Carolina's march to the new frontier. "One member of the Rams Club wrote and told me he would never give another dollar to the University," Smith said. "I looked it up and he gave ten bucks a year."

As Scott's career unfolded, players within the Carolina program wondered if Smith had not established a double standard to ensure his success. Scott spent a lot of time watching film with the coaches, particularly new assistant John Lotz, who eventually became the best man at his wedding. Also, while Smith liked to keep a fairly tight reign on his players, Scott was allowed to socialize, and eventually live, off campus with friends from nearby predominantly black schools.

When overt racism reared its ugly head, Smith was there to meet it head on. He had to be restrained from going after a fan at South Carolina who called Scott a "big, black baboon." And Smith publicly sided with Scott's claims that prejudice among the lily-white sportswriters had cost him some individual awards, and embarrassment, during his career. In 1969, in fact, Smith supported Scott when he considered sitting out the NCAA East Regional championship game in protest over that season's All-ACC voting. Clearly one of the two or three best players in the league, Scott had been left off five ballots.

It was impossible that five people regarded him as not among the five best players in the league.

Ultimately, signing Scott represented the fulfillment of a major personal and professional goal, and Smith went on to have more recruiting success in the following years. Scott's recruitment cleared the way for fellow New Yorker Bill Chamberlain to join the dream team class of 1972, which included Pennsylvanians Steve Previs and Dennis Wuycik, Craig Corson of New Hampshire, and North Carolinians Kim Huband and Billy Chambers . . . the kind of balance Smith looked for.

✪

Smith's biggest recruiting nemesis continued to be Driesell, who by this time had moved from Davidson to Maryland and was building a powerhouse in College Park. Driesell nearly had George Karl convinced, promising him a starting position "in writing," before Smith landed the pepperpot guard from Pennsylvania – in part by continually calling Karl's girlfriend on the telephone to keep tabs on him.

Then the worm turned – ironically after what had appeared to be one of Smith's biggest recruiting victories. The highly publicized wooing of high school star Tom McMillen during the summer of 1970 wound up a two-horse race between Smith and Driesell. Reporters covered the story more aggressively than ever before, signaling the start of regular recruiting coverage by most newspapers. McMillen, of course, went to Maryland on virtually the last day; the letter of intent he had signed with Carolina was non-binding because he had yet to turn eighteen years old.

McMillen's parents supposedly wanted their son to play closer to their home in Mansfield, Pennsylvania, but the wild stories ranged far from that simple statement of preference – even to the far-flung rumor of a long-ago love affair between McMillen's mother and Virginia coach Bill Gibson, who was also recruiting the 6-11 high school star. Back in Chapel Hill, newspapers reported that Dr. James McMillen would turn Smith in for what he thought might have been illegal recruiting tactics. Paul McMillen, Tom's older brother, had landed a job in a Chapel Hill bank, and stories floated around that Carolina had helped him get it. Nothing came of the rumors, and McMillen appeared set to enroll at UNC in early September.

A few weeks before McMillen jilted the Tar Heels, he had been touring Europe with a U.S. Olympic Development team. Wuycik, a rising junior at Carolina, also played on that team, and McMillen had confided to Wuycik that his parents and another brother, Jay, a former Maryland player, were still pressuring him to change his mind. However, McMillen's last words to Wuycik at Kennedy Airport were, "See you in Chapel Hill." On registration day, McMillen instead showed up in College Park after sending the now-famous telegram to Smith at the Carolina basketball office: Very Very Sorry. Hope You Understand. Going To Maryland For Reasons You Know.

Carolina fans criticized Smith, who was in Germany giving a clinic at the time, for not being home to monitor what had been a testy situation for months. "I don't know what happened," Smith said upon his return. "I spoke with Tom on the phone just a few days before, and everything was fine."

Stealing McMillen seemed fair play to Driesell, since he had lost Scott to Carolina and Smith much the same way. Although the two coaches continued recruiting against each other until Driesell resigned following the controversial death of Len Bias in 1986, none of their subsequent battles measured up against the Scott and McMillen affairs.

The newest challenge was coming from twenty miles down the road, where Norman Sloan had resurrected the N.C. State program by combining talent from his native Indiana and his adopted state. Smith, in fact, had once dreamed of having McMillen and 7-4 Tom Burleson in the same front court and even asked McMillen in the spring of 1970 to call Burleson and say, "Let's go to Carolina together." But Burleson went to State, and with the addition of the following year's class – including David Thompson, Monte Towe, and Tim Stodddard – the Wolfpack lost one game over two seasons, won the 1974 NCAA championship, and defeated archrival Carolina nine straight times.

Thompson had grown up idolizing UNC's Scott and attended Smith's summer camp as a kid. Carolina had close ties to Thompson's high school coach, Ed Peeler, and Smith had every reason to believe the sensational 6-4 forward would someday be a Tar Heel. Plus, black kids from rural North Carolina did not grow up with dreams of playing at N.C. State, whose only minority basketball player, Ed Leftwich, had left school unhappily after his junior year. And Thompson had already told Smith several times that he wanted to come.

Following their 1971 NIT championship, Lotz and tournament MVP Chamberlain visited with Thompson at a restaurant near his home in Shelby, west of Charlotte. They expected to find an excited high school senior ready to follow the success of Scott and Chamberlain in Chapel Hill. Instead they found a sullen and quiet youngster with something obviously weighing on his mind. A few days later, Smith found out that Thompson had signed a letter-of-intent with State coach Norman Sloan, who was already the subject of rumors about an investigation into his recruitment of Thompson.

The week after Lotz and Chamberlain returned, Smith received a telephone call from Sloan, who said he was considering tearing up Thompson's scholarship. Smith told Sloan that was his business but that, certainly, the Tar Heels wanted Thompson if for some reason he wasn't going to State. That's the last Smith heard from Sloan, who obviously decided that having Thompson in his program would be more than adequate compensation for any forthcoming NCAA penalty (a one-year probation, as it turned out). At the ACC spring meetings in Myrtle Beach, South Carolina, the following May, Smith was miffed when Sloan pretended his phone call had never happened.

✪

By any standard, Smith was a highly successful recruiter throughout the 1970s, but, besides Thompson, there was one other player during these years that Carolina wooed hard but failed to win – Bill "Poodles" Willoughby, a silky smooth forward from New Jersey. Smith and his entire staff worked overtime pursuing Poodles against their chief competitor, the big blue machine at the University of Kentucky.

The Carolina coaches strongly suspected Kentucky was cheating with Willoughby, using tactics initiated in the days of Adolph Rupp and apparently continued under his successor, Joe B. Hall. (UK was later investigated and went on NCAA probation.) Smith and his assistants firmly believed that Kentucky was "taking care" of Willoughby's friends and family members, and they would have turned Kentucky in to the NCAA had they come up with any hard evidence. Willoughby eventually signed with the Wildcats in the spring of 1975, but Smith and Carolina had the last laugh. Willoughby failed to show up at Kentucky for his freshman year, opting instead to jump from high school to the NBA, where he played for nine seasons.

The Carolina team Willoughby would have joined was already loaded with talent, including juniors Walter Davis, 6-10 Tom LaGarde, and scrappy guard John Kuester, along with sophomore Phil Ford. The next year, in 1977, the Tar Heels added freshman Mike O'Koren to complete one of Smith's best starting lineups ever. All five later played in the NBA.

Ford, of course, had been the key recruit, because Smith sorely needed a point guard. And after watching him repeatedly in high school, Smith also did not want to play against the six-foot whirling dervish from Rocky Mount, North Carolina. Also recruited by Sloan, Ford had a chance to join seniors Thompson and Towe for one year, then become the leader of the Wolfpack. Though it later washed out that Ford was a Tar Heel all the way, his recruiting story included unique sales pitches from Clemson and Maryland, as well as State.

Driesell offered Ford's high school coach Richard Hicks a part-time job on his staff for eight thousand dollars and insulted the man by further telling him he could supplement his income by running the concession stands at Maryland home games. "I was already an assistant principal getting a coaching stipend, so I wasn't about to do that," said Hicks, who eventually left coaching for full-time high school administration.

Clemson coach Tates Locke had apparently determined the only way he could compete with the Big Four schools was to buy players. He had already landed Skip Wise, a willowy schoolyard legend from Baltimore, whom Ford remembered from a recruiting trip the two had taken together to Washington State.

"I was wearing jeans and a little jacket," Ford recalled of the cross-country flight. "Honeydew – that's what we called Wise – was wearing an all-white suit, a big hat, and high-heeled white shoes. That's when I first realized the difference between the North and South."

After having already flown Ford's father to Clemson (in itself an infraction, though Ford's father didn't realize it), one of the school's booster club members showed up at the Fords' home in the spring of 1974. B. C. Inabinet left a suitcase filled with cash on the dining room table. Philip Jackson Ford Sr. never told his son about the "gift" and, after calling Smith in Chapel Hill to make sure he had not jeopardized young Phil's college career, gave the money back. Recruiting folklore – denied by Smith – has it that Smith told Ford's father to "keep the suitcase and send Phil to Carolina." Locke was fired after the 1975 season, leaving Clemson with a severe NCAA probation. Inabinet died a few years later.

Ford was the best basketball player the state of North Carolina had produced since Thompson. The key recruiters for the two in-state schools locked horns for Ford, exacerbating their rivalry and very nearly resulting in a fistfight between grown men.

Eddie Biedenbach had been one of Sloan's better players when State struggled to win in the late 1960s. A scrappy guard, he had turned into a tenacious recruiter and dogged Ford during a time when recruiters could make unlimited visits to prospects. Eddie Fogler had also been a tough-nosed guard for Smith two years behind Biedenbach. A product of the New York City schoolyards with an acquired touch of Smith's class, Fogler the recruiter could drink all night with O'Koren's Irish cronies in New Jersey and also sweet talk Southern mammas like Mabel Ford.

During the 1974 season, when State was ranked No. 1 and on the way to the national championship, Biedenbach and Fogler were both in Rocky Mount one night to see Ford play, and Biedenbach wrangled an invitation from Ford's father to go back to the house after the game. Of course, Fogler had already been invited, too. Both assistant coaches sat awkwardly in the Ford's living room long after young Phil had gone to bed. Finally, Fogler got up to leave around midnight. Mabel Ford would have none of it, insisting Fogler stay over and have breakfast with the family in the morning. Fogler tried again.

"If you go," she said, pointing into the living room at Biedenbach, "he goes!"

Both coaches wound up staying the night, and Ford eventually picked the Tar Heels. But Biedenbach wouldn't let the matter die, needling Fogler whenever their paths crossed on the recruiting trail. It so angered Fogler that, at one point, he told Smith he might have to punch Biedenbach in the nose the next time it happened.

"I don't condone that," Smith told his assistant, "but if that's the only way you feel you can straighten things out, you have to be yourself."

The confrontation never occurred, and after Thompson graduated State faded toward the middle of the conference. Biedenbach took the head-coaching position at Georgia in 1978, after Carolina had gone 8-4 against the Pack in Ford's four years. Fogler remained in Chapel Hill, helping the Tar Heels to many great recruiting triumphs into the 1980s.

THE LEGEND IS BORN

Dean Smith was mad either at himself or at his assistant coach, Larry Brown.

More than five thousand fans had packed Carmichael Auditorium on Saturday, November 6, 1965, to watch Carolina's own "Sensational Six" – Jim Bostick, Joe Brown, Bill Bunting, Rusty Clark, Dick Grubar and Gerald Tuttle – give notice that the following season the Tar Heels were going to be something special. And sure enough, the highly recruited freshmen of 1965 had beaten the varsity.

Before the game, there had been a distance between the freshman and varsity teams that was unusual for the Carolina program – and that would never exist again. Brown, the 25-year-old former point guard for the Tar Heels, had been integrally involved with recruiting the freshmen. Now, he was their coach. The young, aggressive Brown had felt like he "died and went to heaven" when Smith offered him seven thousand dollars a year to replace Ken Rosemond. "I always wanted to be a coach and after being around Coach McGuire and Coach Smith, I wanted to do what they did."

Brown had jumped into his new job with both feet, taking full advantage of the unlimited visits then permitted with each recruit and setting them all up for Smith to close the deals. Living out of hotel rooms, airports, and rental cars, the usually fit Brown had put on twenty pounds from taking the prospects out for so many good meals and not getting a chance to exercise. Later, as freshman coach, Brown considered the players his guys and wanted to mold them into a unit that would love Carolina as much as he did and eventually help Smith complete his rebuilding of a once-proud basketball program. But this was not the first time his gung-ho nature had gotten him in trouble.

A month earlier, Brown had drawn a reprimand from his boss, who had suggested opening freshman team tryouts to the entire student body. Brown had needed another half-dozen men to fill out the frosh roster and had been surprised to find more than one hundred former high school players waiting for him in Woollen in October of 1965. Since the scholarship kids would play most of the minutes, Brown was looking for determination and dedication from the remainder of the squad. So he decided to make the tryouts an endurance test and put the freshmen through exhausting drills – run, roll over, run, roll over. Brown didn't have the heart to cut anyone and figured those who couldn't take it would quit.

Smith had walked in, watched what looked like Army boot camp for a few minutes, and gone back to his office shaking his head. "I was running 'em so hard he was afraid the scholarship guys were going to quit," Brown recalled, only half-joking. In subsequent meetings, Smith gave Brown a clearer job description: coach the freshmen exactly the way he coached the varsity; use the same practice plans; teach the same offenses and defenses; in short, prepare them to join the system the next year.

Brown prepared them so well, in fact, that they won the first of only two public scrimmages Smith ever held between his freshmen and varsity players. Before the first practice game, Brown had given his squad a rousing pep talk, challenging the frosh to "prove you're as good as they are!" And they had been, at least on this night, winning largely because of the height advantage of the 6-11 Clark and 6-9 Bunting, each of whom scored twenty points.

Smith believed Brown had crossed the line, creating an unhealthy divisiveness in his program. He called Brown into his office the next morning and closed the door. It was the first time he could remember being angry with his young protégé. "Larry, we coach all of the players in the program," he said. "As good as the freshmen are, it's important that they understand they have to wait their turn and pay their dues. I don't want any resentment between the freshmen and upperclassmen next year."

Actually madder at himself, Smith could not fault Brown's intentions. He had created the problem by scheduling a public scrimmage he could not control, or stop, if things got out of hand. But now Smith had another problem. Veterans Bob Lewis and Larry Miller were also mad – and wanted another shot at what they had sarcastically dubbed the "dream team." So four days later, Smith held a public rematch that the varsity won decisively. "Lewis and Miller weren't going to let the matter drop," Smith said. From that point on, the only intra-squad competition played in front of spectators was the annual Blue-White Game, when both teams sat on the same bench as a symbol of togetherness.

Still, the excitement over Brown's freshmen electrified the campus, as students came early to brand new Carmichael Auditorium to watch what were then called the Tar Babies. They won fifteen of sixteen games, losing only at Virginia Tech (they also blew an eighteen-point halftime lead and lost an exhibition to an all-star team of UNC alumni). The success of the frosh took some pressure off another relatively disappointing varsity record of 16-11.

Despite All-ACC players Lewis, who led the league in scoring with a 27-point average, and Miller, fourth in scoring and third in rebounding, Smith knew why his team could not challenge nationally ranked Duke for first place. He needed more height and weight in the middle.

Carolina, finishing third in the ACC with an 8-6 record, had lost two respectable games to Duke in the regular season, by eleven points at home and fourteen in Durham. So Smith had good reasons for not wanting to play the Blue Devils "straight up" when the two teams met again in the ACC Tournament semifinals.

Facing the Duke powerhouse of Steve Vacendak, Jack Marin, Mike Lewis and Bob Verga for a third time, Smith was convinced his team could not win a forty-minute game. So he talked to his assistants Brown and John Lotz about using the same strategy that had succeeded in the Tar Heels' upset of Ohio State earlier in the season.

✪

Imagine the atomic atmosphere at Reynolds Coliseum on Friday night,

March 4, 1966, during the thirteenth and last ACC Tournament to be played on the N.C. State campus. (The post-season event would move to a neutral court beginning the following year.) When three of the Big Four teams and South Carolina advanced to the semifinals double-header, it was no longer a conference tournament. The house that Everett Case built rocked with the intensity of the local rivalries. Duke, headed for its third Final Four appearance in four years, was heavily favored over archrival Carolina to reach the championship game Saturday night. Defending champion N.C. State faced South Carolina, which had hired Frank McGuire as its coach the year before.

With Duke's only possible weakness a lack of quickness up front, Smith planned to open the game in Four Corners and hope Duke would come out of its zone to play man-to-man defense. By spreading the court, slowing down the game, and letting Lewis and Miller take their men one-on-one, Carolina might get an early lead and create some anxiety for the Blue Devils. The fact that only the ACC champion could move on to the NCAA Tournament certainly added to the potential for anxiety, and Duke couldn't risk chasing the smaller and quicker Tar Heels. Instead, when Carolina went into Four Corners on its first possession, Coach Vic Bubas opted for a game of cat and mouse, figuring the crowd at least would be on his side. And he was right.

As Johnny Yokley held the ball in the middle, while seconds and minutes ran off the clock, fans began hurling verbal and physical trash at the UNC bench. Hit in the head with a rolled-up paper bag, Brown turned around and gestured to the crowd.

"I wanted to say to the guy who threw it, 'Hey, he's the head coach; if you're going to throw anything, hit him,'" Brown recalled. "People were yelling, 'C'mon, Smith, play ball,' but he just sat there coaching away."

Smith had not expected such a low-scoring game, thinking Duke would at least apply passive pressure. By halftime, the Tar Heels had attempted only five field goals, but they had successfully kept the ball out of Duke's hands most of the time and trailed only 7-5. Figuring Duke would play the same way in the second half, Smith had a decision to make in the locker room. He went around the stuffy room in the bowels of Reynolds, asking the players if they still believed in what they were doing out there. This would become a regular, if occasional, habit of Smith's when he needed to know if the team agreed with a certain strategy. Smith made eye contact with each player and wanted eye contact in return.

He was especially concerned with Miller, who had lost more games in his sophomore season than during his entire high school career. Earlier in the season, an unhappy Miller had made some critical comments about the team and coaching staff to a *Daily Tar Heel* reporter before sports information director Jack Williams interceded and convinced the young sportswriter to sit on the story. But Miller supported continuing the slowdown style in the second half, although he would take only three shots in the game. He took turns with Yokley standing around in the middle of Four Corners as the Tar Heels inched out to a 17-12 lead.

On the brink of a monumental upset, Carolina got impatient down the stretch and allowed Duke to pull even, 20-20, with less than two minutes to play. Yokley got fouled with 1:40 left and went to the line for a one-and-one. He missed and Duke grabbed the rebound. The Blue Devils by this time had accepted the tempo of the game and were being very careful with the ball. Like a chessmaster, Smith discussed the options with Brown, taking time to teach even during this tight situation.

"Maybe we should foul," Smith said.

"Whaddyamean?" said Brown anxiously.

"Let's foul, and see if they'll miss," Smith said. "Who's their worst foul shooter?"

Brown recalled years later that Smith was testing him to make sure he knew the Duke player with the lowest free-throw percentage. When Brown answered back (Jim) Liccardo, Smith smiled and decided to keep playing tight defense.

"I'm just getting you to think," Smith said out of the side of his mouth.

Duke's Lewis was fouled with four seconds remaining in the game and made one free throw for a 21-20 lead. Carolina threw the ball away trying to get it inbounds, and the horn sounded to end the game. The Blue Devils had escaped and went on to beat State, which had ousted South Carolina, for the ACC title the next night and eventually reached the Final Four.

The coliseum crowd booed Smith roundly as he left the court. Even

Carolina fans, yet to be educated in what their basketball coach might devise, were upset by the strategy. Only five Tar Heels (Lewis, Miller, Yokley, Bob Bennett, and Tom Gauntlett) had played, and the entire team had attempted just fifteen shots in the game. Only a few years later, near the end of close games, Dean's disciples up in the stands would anticipate his next move by raising four fingers. The very next season, however, they never had to hold the ball on anyone.

✪

During Bob Lewis's sophomore year, 1965, Smith had publicly promoted the ability of the lithe, athletic swingman. Even though Lewis went on to average twenty-one points and eight rebounds, Smith came to believe he had encouraged the media to put too much pressure on his young player.

"It was the first time I had ever over-sold a player," Smith said. "I pushed him because I thought it would be good for Bobby, but I was wrong. Although he had averaged over thirty-five points as a freshman, he played against teams he could just jump over. I should have known he would have trouble scoring like that on the varsity."

Consequently, when the 1966-67 season opened, Smith vowed to protect his highly touted sophomores – a task made easier because Carolina already had two established ACC stars. The heralded former freshmen had finally given Smith the height and depth championship basketball teams need, but they didn't have to be headliners right away. For that reason – since it was Lewis's and Miller's team – the Tar Heels clicked smoothly almost from the first day of practice. They won their first nine games by an average of more than twenty-six points and sixteen of their first seventeen, including another win at Kentucky. After five years, Smith had finally put together the kind of club he coveted.

Smith continued preaching and teaching his two basic philosophies, play unselfishly on offense and aggressively on defense. Lewis, who had set the Carolina single-game scoring record, was the poster child for Smith's selfless system in his senior year.

"Before this year I never went into a game when I didn't assume I would score twenty points," Lewis said in 1967, "I expected that of myself. If I only got fourteen, I'd go crazy and start worrying what went wrong. I always want to win and score points. But now I wanted to prove something . . . to show I could do everything else, like set up my teammates and play defense."

The system endured after Lewis turned the starring role over to Miller, and Miller eventually to Charlie Scott; it endured even after Brown left the staff to play in the fledgling American Basketball Association and Bill Guthridge replaced him.

But in the meantime, that freshmen class of 1965 enjoyed quite a run. Joe Brown, Bunting, Clark, Grubar, and Tuttle (Bostick had transferred to Auburn after his sophomore year) won a total of eighty-one games and lost only fifteen, one-third of the defeats coming in three straight Final Fours from 1967 to 1969. They won the ACC regular season outright and the ACC Tournament each of those years, a feat yet to be matched in the conference. They did not lose a single game to N.C. State, Wake Forest, Virginia, or Maryland.

Of course, the big breakthrough came in 1967, when the Tar Heels defeated Duke three times and won their first ACC championship under Smith. The tournament had shifted to the 9,000-seat Greensboro Coliseum, where demand for tickets was so great that the ACC moved the event again the next year to the 11,000-seat Charlotte Coliseum. After the Tar Heels and Blue Devils had advanced to the Saturday night title game, the pressure on Carolina seemed far greater. Only the winner would qualify for the NCAA Tournament, and statewide newspapers that had covered the Duke dynasty were giving the nod to the experienced Vic Bubas over the younger Smith in their third meeting.

"People don't understand what kind of pressure that was," Miller said. "You had to win three games in three days or you weren't called the ACC champion and you weren't going anywhere, no matter what you had done in the regular season.

"I had to tell my parents, 'You can't come down here for the tournament. I couldn't eat, I couldn't sleep, my stomach was in knots."

Smith, of course, had ultimate confidence in Miller and years later poked fun at his alleged suffering. "What a competitor! Larry probably told his parents not to come because he wanted to sell his tickets," the coach kidded. Indeed, Miller justified Smith's faith in him, scoring thirty-two points against Duke on thirteen of fourteen shots from the field in Carolina's 82-73 win.

"I remember the one I missed, too. It was from the corner, and when I let it go I knew it was in," Miller said. "It was just one of those games when I was in a frame of mind. Down the stretch, Dean would be telling me to do this and do that. I said, 'Don't worry, Coach. It's in the bag.'"

Following the game, Smith let himself be carried off the court by his players for the last time in his career. As the Tar Heels lifted their coach into the air, years of frustration fell away. "I just remember how proud Dean was," Larry Brown said. "People didn't understand what he had gone through and what a disadvantage he was under at first."

The Tar Heels rolled past Princeton and Boston College in the NCAA East Regional at Maryland, where Lewis's family threw an all-night party for the team after it had qualified for Smith's first Final Four and Carolina's first in ten years. The team would advance no further this year, but even after one-sided losses to Dayton and Houston, UNC fans were so happy to have at last thrown off Duke's dominance that they walked through the streets of Louisville, chanting, "We're No. 4."

Oddly, most of the players still did not fully credit Smith for their success. Some, who had been referring to him as "Smitty" behind his back, thought he was merely along for the ride with a very talented team. But as the Tar Heels remained rated among the top four teams in both national polls for three consecutive years, Smith slowly but surely became recognized as the brightest young coach in the college game. He officially walked out of McGuire's shadow on February 28, 1968, when South Carolina went to Chapel Hill for Miller's last home appearance. As he came out with his team, McGuire received a standing ovation from the Carolina fans who remembered his remarkable dream season of 1957. But the applause soon turned into a thunderous reception for their own second-ranked Tar Heels, and Smith, as they took the Carmichael Auditorium court.

McGuire and Smith engaged in a heated rivalry over the next five years. Like brothers scrapping in the backyard, the two Carolinas played some classic games, including one that would remain in the hearts of both schools forever.

✪

Smith had developed a stunning, and sometimes stubborn, command of the game, especially evident in tight situations. In the 1968 ACC Tournament semifinals, he had continued to exploit the Tar Heels' height advantage over South Carolina even after the quicker Gamecocks rallied furiously to force overtime. The difference turned out to be sixteen more shots and nine more rebounds for UNC in the 82-79 win.

He also knew when to stop talking strategy. In the tournament finals against N.C. State, the team struggled through a lackluster first half. In the locker room, Smith uttered seven words – "You know what you have to do" – and walked out of the door. They blew State out with fifty-six points in the second half and moved on to establish themselves as undoubtedly the second best team in the nation by sweeping through the East Regional in Raleigh. Carolina drubbed undefeated St. Bonaventure and big Bob Lanier in one game, then edged Lefty Driesell's Davidson Wildcats in the other.

Against the Bonnies, Smith challenged Rusty Clark to play Lanier aggressively from the outset, hoping the Tar Heels would build an early lead and frustrate the seven-foot giant with the size-sixteen shoes. Clark finished with eighteen points and ten rebounds, while most of Lanier's twenty-three and nine came after the 91-72 romp had been decided. The following night, trailing by four points, Smith again said only a few words in the halftime locker room and walked out. The fired-up Clark, on his way to the Regional MVP, sparked a second-half comeback over Davidson, sending UNC to its second straight Final Four in Los Angeles.

That Smith did not have the full cooperation of his players after deciding to hold the ball against UCLA in the national championship game said more about the cockiness of his team than about his coaching prowess. Having just blasted Ohio State in the semifinals, the Tar Heels wanted to prove they could play with towering Lew Alcindor and the top-ranked, once-beaten Bruins. But Smith knew better. With a highly partisan crowd at the LA Sports Arena cheering on what was considered the best college basketball team of all time, Smith had sent the Tar Heels back to the hotel and stayed to watch John Wooden's Bruins destroy Elvin Hayes and Houston in the other semifinal.

Despite his own team's 28-4 record – his best to date – Smith believed the Bruins were so good that his team had no chance to beat them playing a full forty minutes of regular-tempo basketball. Having gone out to the West Coast with two goals – avoid the upset they had suffered the year before against Dayton and then topple UCLA for the national title – his players vehemently disagreed. Young, talented and cocky, the Tar Heels really thought they could do it. And, because they had not been prepared for any special strategy during the prior week, they were stunned to hear about Smith's plan before the championship game on Saturday night, March 23, 1968.

Senior Miller, the two-time ACC Player of the Year, and precocious sophomore Charlie Scott met privately with Smith before the game and argued against playing Four Corners. Both considered such a strategy to be an admission of inferiority, and these players didn't feel inferior.

Ten years, or even five years, later, the Tar Heel players would not have dared challenge their coach. All-American Miller, however, was used to doing things his own way. For example, upon arriving at Carolina, he had objected to mandatory Sunday morning church services for the team because he did not go to church when he lived at home. Smith deemed that logical and acquiesced. And since Miller worked so hard in practice, Smith basically ignored his flamboyant lifestyle, which included an abundance of beer, coeds, and parties. Indeed, Miller never got nailed for sneaking a case of beer on to the team bus for a victorious trip back from Charlottesville, even though Smith, sitting in the front row, must have known half the players were blotto.

As for the supremely confident Scott, he disagreed with the plan against UCLA because the 7-2 Alcindor, with whom he had played back in the Harlem neighborhoods of their hometown New York City, did not intimidate him. But this was not Harlem; it was Los Angeles, with a heavily partisan crowd on hand to watch the Bruins cap off a 29-1 season and win their second straight national championship, the fourth in five years.

Of course, it turned out that Smith knew best. Carolina was not a good-shooting team that year (45.5 percent), and he worried that Alcindor's shot-blocking and the Bruins' zone press would force turnovers and hurried attempts from the field. After Carolina stalled the first half away and left the court trailing by ten points, the 37-year-old Smith deferred to the wishes of Miller and Scott to play UCLA straight up. The Bruins won going away, 78-55, the most lopsided loss to that point in the history of the NCAA finals. Several players grumbled after the game, but the proof had been conclusive. Although it certainly wasn't the outcome he wanted, Smith's strategy of holding the ball had been vindicated. And that was the last time he would go with his players' wishes over his own. In the years ahead, Smith would run Carolina basketball, in his words, as more of a "dictatorship than a democracy."

Like McGuire in 1957, Smith received a brand-new Cadillac from appreciative fans after his team's second-place finish. He accepted the car graciously as a tribute to how hard all of his players had worked over his first seven years as head coach. But, clearly, he had buckled himself into the driver's seat.

✪

As the recruits of 1965 approached the end of their senior season, it became junior Charlie Scott's job to hold their banner high. With Grubar sidelined and the other players exhausted from their pressurized three-year run, Smith allowed an emotional Scott to become a one-man team. His twenty-eight second-half points in the ACC Tournament finals saved the Tar Heels' third consecutive title. Duke had led by ten late in the game when Scott started screaming to his teammates, "Give me the ball!" Carolina won by eleven.

The next week, in the NCAA East Regional at Maryland, Scott rekindled his emotions with the spark of anger. Deeply affected by what he believed to be racial bias in the All-ACC voting (five voters had left the consensus All-American off the first All-ACC team), he nearly boycotted the NCAA East title game against Davidson. Smith gave Scott time away from the team before the game, a chance to sort out his thoughts. Deciding at virtually the last minute to play, Scott dominated with thirty-two points, including the buzzer-beater, to subdue Davidson and Driesell again. Afterward, he spoke softly to the Washington press, charging the ACC with bigotry and hinting the Final Four would be his last college games.

Scott shot poorly in Louisville and, even if he had decided to turn pro, probably lost his chance to be the No. 2 draft pick behind Alcindor. In any case, Purdue and Drake crushed Carolina in the semis and consolation game, respectively, and the class of 1969, despite having lost only fifteen games in three years, went out exactly how it had come in – with two one-sided defeats at the Final Four.

By late in the 1970 season, Smith had not figured out how to replace the class that had won three straight ACC championships. Meanwhile, South Carolina had completed its rebuilding job under McGuire with "bad boy" juniors John Roche, Tom Owens, and John Ribock. Ready to take his second "Carolina" team to the top of the ACC and the national rankings, McGuire also was looking to pay back those who had stomped his earlier clubs. He had been mad at Smith only once before – in 1967, when he thought the Tar Heels had run up the score during a 25-point win in Charlotte. Smith had substituted liberally in the game but said afterward, "I can't tell my players not to try to score."

While rebuilding his new program the same way he had constructed his Tar Heel empire, McGuire had filed that one-sided loss away. And when the Gamecocks began to dominate the ACC, the idea of beating UNC twice in 1970 sounded particularly sweet to the revenge-minded McGuire. Thus, after the two Carolinas had reversed roles, Smith seriously considered holding the ball when the Gamecocks visited Chapel Hill at the end of a season that would stand out like a sore thumb for the rest of his coaching career.

Following their 27-5 record of 1969, the Tar Heels were struggling on the way to an 18-9 finish in Scott's senior year. That turned out to be the last Smith-coached team not to win at least twenty games, and despite Scott's presence there was good reason for the relative mediocrity. Carolina had a number of players sick and hurt, so Smith again told his All-American to shoot any chance he got. Although he had several monster games, Scott hit only 40 percent from the floor and, as Smith later put it, "That was that."

When big, bad South Carolina swaggered in with an undefeated ACC record and No. 1 ranking in the country on February 21 – one week before his thirty-ninth birthday – Smith knew his team lacked the size, skill, and confidence to win playing the Gamecocks' game. He discussed the options with his three seniors – Scott, Eddie Fogler, and Jim Delany. Even though Scott again objected to a hold-the-ball strategy, Smith's decision to "just play" was based on the relative unimportance of the game. The ACC Tournament pairings were already set, so Smith decided to keep his game plan in the can until then. Predictably, South Carolina stayed in its 2-3 zone and won a 79-62 blowout.

Smith's strategy became a moot point when Scott and the Tar Heels lost a shocker to Virginia in the first round of the ACC Tournament, sending the thrice-defending champions stumbling into the NIT, where they suffered an even bigger embarrassment to Manhattan. Scott's All-American career had ended with three straight defeats and six losses in his last ten games wearing a Carolina uniform. And those who still doubted Dean Smith's longevity began to wonder whether he had had his fifteen minutes of basketball fame.

The 1970 season had also marked Smith's first separation from his wife Ann. He had told his players right away – "so you won't hear it from anyone else first" – and added that he and Ann were going to try to work it out with their clergyman. Away from the pressures of a failing marriage and single for the first time in sixteen years, Smith worked hard at maintaining a relationship with his three teenage children and harder at preparing for the 1971 season – his first in nine years without a bona-fide star on the team. Over that summer, Smith thought he had landed super-recruit Tom McMillen. But, ironically, a struggle in McMillen's own family made the non-binding letter of intent he had signed not worth the paper on which it was printed.

✪

Pundits picked the 1971 Tar Heels to finish well down in the ACC standings. Even though they were a so-so 5-2 after seven games, Smith retained faith in his untested team's ability to execute the strategy he had been saving for McGuire and South Carolina. So when the Gamecocks strutted back into Chapel Hill, unbeaten and top-ranked, on January 4, 1971, the Heels took the air out of the ball. This was the game that threw the Smith-McGuire friendship into peril and made South Carolina the new villain of the ACC.

Smith knew that McGuire's pride would not allow his protégé to show him up in front of his old fans. So, even though he had not taught his players much man-to-man defense, McGuire waved them out of the zone when cocky point guard George Karl put the ball on his hip at mid court and refused to play on the Tar Heels' first possession. Two hours later, after watching his team chase Smith's around the court in vain, McGuire had been taught a lesson by his one-time assistant. The Heels had spread the floor, created match-up problems for the Gamecocks, and crushed them in crazed Carmichael.

"Dean's team was fabulous, but the crowd was tough on us," McGuire said following the 79-64 shocker. "Someone stuck gum in Ribock's hair as he was leaving the court. We've never been treated like this anywhere else in the ACC."

Maryland, Virginia, and Duke all copied Smith's strategy, held the ball against South Carolina, and posted slowdown upsets as the Gamecocks became the ACC's poor losers. Against Maryland, McGuire refused to come out of the zone and lost a 31-30 decision.

Tutored mostly by assistant coach Donnie Walsh, who had resigned as a lawyer and joined McGuire's staff, South Carolina started practicing man-to-man defense and beat Smith at his own game in the hard-fought rematch in Columbia in February. By then, it had become clear that the two Carolinas were the class of the ACC. After his team finished first in the regular season (South Carolina was second), Smith easily won ACC Coach of the Year while stifling all doubts about his ability as a tactician as well as a recruiter. Meanwhile, McGuire not only had to rally his team from that mid-season string of losses, he constantly fought off the rumor that he supported the move of South Carolina athletic director and football coach Paul Dietzel to leave the ACC for independent status.

As expected, the Tar Heels and Gamecocks reached the championship game of the ACC Tournament on Saturday night, March 13, in the newly expanded Greensboro Coliseum. Also, as expected, it turned into a taut and tense game, low scoring and mistake-filled by both teams. South Carolina, for example, shot 28 percent, with star senior Roche misfiring on thirteen of his twenty shots. Even with leading scorer Dennis Wuycik fouling out, UNC had several opportunities to extend a small lead in the second half and put the game away, but the Tar Heels missed some easy shots and Karl missed three free throws.

The last few seconds of the game – and of South Carolina's membership in the ACC – turned into some of the most vivid and painful of all time for UNC fans. Leading by one point, the Tar Heels committed two colossal blunders that blew the ACC championship and a chance to move on to the NCAA Tournament. With six seconds remaining, 6-11 center Lee Dedmon allowed 6-3 guard Kevin Joyce to control a jump ball in front of the South Carolina basket. And UNC's Dave Chadwick, playing in place of Wuycik, failed to rotate between the jump circle and the hoop. The Gamecocks' Owens caught Joyce's tip and had a wide-open lay-up for the 52-51 victory. As soon as the game ended, Roche, who personified the intensely bitter rivalry between the schools, walked over, got in Smith's face, and said, "Fuck you. We beat you."

Though he later denied his own uncharacteristic comment, a furious and frustrated Smith was overheard saying on the way off the court, "I'm not taking the blame for this one," clearly referring to the blunders by Dedmon and Chadwick. Smith, his team, and Carolina fans were moribund for days. The devastated players stayed isolated, sullenly preparing for the NIT they had never expected or wanted to play in. For a while, they weren't sure where the depth of their pain came from.

This was the year that Smith became irrefutably bonded to his team, and from there the legend grew. He had taken a group of recruits that had been written off and, without the star system, molded them into a winner that exceeded even their own expectations. The players felt badly for themselves but ached more for their coach, who had demonstrated unyielding faith in them all season. They had caused him to lose to his rival and mentor, McGuire, and watched as a petulant opposing player had abused him.

Slowly, they came out of it. South Carolina's first-round NCAA loss to Penn seemed to buoy the Tar Heels as they headed for New York, gathered themselves and completed a dramatic sweep of the NIT at Madison Square Garden. By beating Massachusetts with Julius Erving, Providence with Ernie DiGregorio and Marvin Barnes, Duke for a third time during the season and Georgia Tech by eighteen points in the title game, they claimed a national title that they discovered still meant something. And, with four starters coming back, Carolina headed into a 1972 season in which Smith cleverly found a way to overcome the loss of McMillen and lead his team back to the Final Four of the NCAA Tournament for the fourth time in six years.

STAR-CROSSED COACH

Contrary to legend, Dean Smith cursed at least once.

Smith supposedly has never uttered a cuss word in public or, perhaps, in private. "My parents taught me that if you swear, it's a sign of a poor vocabulary," Smith once said.

"He never curses," said long-time Dean disciple Phil Ford, "but he talks to you in such a way that, sometimes, you wish he would." So, while locker-room language is as much a part of college and professional sports as, well, the locker room, Smith abstained; he never used blue words to dramatize a situation, dress down his players or officials, or even to express his own frustration.

Except one time.

At the 1975 ACC Tournament, the most hotly contested in history, every game was won by six points or less. There were two overtime games, a one-point decision, and two two-pointers. In the final, UNC beat defending NCAA champion N.C. State by four points.

It had been a long time since Smith and his Tar Heels led the conference, as they had pretty much from 1967 through 1972 when they won four ACC championships and advanced to four Final Fours. In fact, their last golden moment had come in the same Greensboro Coliseum where the 1975 tournament was played. There, Carolina had whipped Maryland for the 1972 ACC title and, following satisfying East Regional wins over newly independent South Carolina and Penn, moved onto the Final Four in Los Angeles. That the Tar Heels had lost to Florida State and missed their long-anticipated crack at Bill Walton and UCLA didn't seem to matter back home. They had solidified their position as the ACC's best basketball program.

But things had changed dramatically in the three years since, thanks to David Thompson and his spectacular N.C. State team. While going 57-1 over two seasons, including the 1974 national title, the Wolfpack extended a winning streak over archrival Carolina that would reach nine straight by 1975. Six of those Tar Heel losses had been by seven points or less, with the last one in overtime after they had seemingly put the game away. Understandable frustration had set in at UNC. Smith and his staff sarcastically referred to Thompson as "Daaavid"— mimicking State Coach Norman Sloan, who tended to wax sappy about his superstar and as well as about how much love the Wolfpack players had for each other. "It fucking makes me want to puke," said one of the UNC coaches, not Smith.

Having lost highly recruited forward Donald Washington to academics and point guard Ray Harrison to emotional problems over the two-year period, Carolina had found the missing pieces to challenge State during the 1974 and 1975 seasons. The Tar Heels' younger players were maturing and new recruits had been added. Smith had beaten Sloan for Phil Ford, the best player in North Carolina, and the Tar Heels had finally broken the streak on February 25, 1975. That game, a 76-74 win at Carmichael Auditorium in which freshman Ford had been sensational, served as a benchmark for how little difference remained between the two teams. Thompson, Monte Towe and Tim Stoddard were still around, but State no longer had 7-4 center Tom Burleson and carried a mortal 20-5 record into the tournament. Carolina was only 18-7 but had won seven of its last nine games.

All things considered, Smith had great hope that his team could win the tournament. But by the time he raged at a referee and uttered the uncharacteristic curse, the Heels had survived one of the most bizarre games in conference history. In the first round, they pulled off a comeback that was perhaps slightly more plausible than their famous win over Duke at Carmichael the year before, when Carolina had rallied from eight points down with seventeen seconds left to tie, and eventually win in overtime. But given the neutral court and all the pressures of the tournament, their 101-100 overtime victory against Wake Forest seemed just as incredible.

Carolina trailed by eight points with fifty-six seconds to play before mounting a furious rally. Wake still had a two-point lead and the ball with ten seconds remaining when Jerry Schellenberg's full-court pass intended for Skip Brown was ruled to have grazed the scoreboard by official Fred Hikel, one of the few people to see it. The refs gave Carolina the ball, and Smith gave his team one last pep talk in the huddle. "Let's take advantage of it," he said. "Phil, go as hard as you can to the basket and, if the shot's there, take it. If not, look for Brad in the corner."

Ford did exactly what he was told and fed an open Brad Hoffman on the right side. Hoffman's twelve-footer sent the game into overtime, where Carolina won by a point. Since almost no one else besides Hikel had seen the ball hit the scoreboard, many fans concluded that Smith and his team had been given a huge gift.

When they faced their second straight overtime game the next night against Clemson, Smith was seething at official Lou Moser, who was known among ACC refs to detest what he considered attempted intimidation from the Carolina bench. "Moser had great animosity for Dean, always called him a 'con man'," recalled a former ACC official. "He, and some of the others, thought Dean was always trying to get an edge. And TV announcers like Al McGuire and Billy Packer hyped that kind of stuff by talking about coaches 'working' officials."

The Tar Heels had played a great first half against nineteenth-ranked Clemson and were still leading by eleven points when Smith called for Four Corners midway through the second half. The aggressive Tigers turned up their defense, and Smith started looking for calls from officials Moser and Hank Nichols. "Hank, that's a foul!" he shrieked once.

Smith respected Nichols as one of the best officials in the game, but had no such feeling for Moser. And although his team wound up shooting thirty-nine free throws compared to nineteen for Clemson, Smith believed there should have been even more fouls called during Clemson's comeback, which tied the game at 64-64. In the overtime, while Ford continued to get banged and jostled in the middle of Four

Corners by rugged Clemson basketball-football player Stan Rome, Smith kept slapping his left forearm with his right hand and yelling, "Lou, call something!"

Finally, Ford hit Mitch Kupchak with a backdoor layup to put the game away. As the final seconds ticked off, Smith held a steely glare on the crewcut Moser, once pointing a finger at him. When the horn sounded, Smith waited to shake hands with Clemson coach Tates Locke until Moser passed by while leaving the court. "You were terrible, Lou," he said.

Ten minutes after the game, Smith had not calmed down, which was unusual for the man who almost always talked to sportswriters with a cool and calculated delivery. Asked on his way to the press conference why he had been so mad at Moser, Smith snapped, "The son of a bitch cheats, and I'm going to get him!"

"How does he cheat?" Smith was asked.

"He cheats," Smith replied.

✪

Considering the foul language coming from other ACC coaches, Smith's transgression was small potatoes. However, it did show the depth of his dislike for Moser, one of several officials he came to mistrust over the years. While other ACC coaches dwelled on particular plays, sending film clips and later videotape of what they thought were blown calls to the commissioner's office, Smith was known to send entire segments of games to demonstrate how he believed basketball should be played.

"Dean was a coach whose team played a certain style," said the former ACC official, "and if his team wasn't allowed to play that style, he was going to get involved from the bench."

Longtime ACC ref Lou Bello, who died in 1990, put it more bluntly: "Dean didn't curse, but he knew that rule book so well he could cram it down your throat."

Forever calling basketball a finesse game, Smith abhorred unnecessary contact in the pivot and hand-checking in the open court. He also got all over referees when he felt they were not hustling or made quantifiable mistakes, such as calling traveling when it did not occur. During

Michael Jordan's freshman year at UNC, he regularly got whistled for walking on his exceedingly quick first step. Smith sent tape after tape to the ACC office, imploring officials to study Jordan's move carefully. The refs finally agreed that, most of the time, Jordan was being penalized unfairly, and they stopped "automatically" calling him for a travel when he started to make a move.

Outside of constantly dogging the officials, Smith's mannerisms and gestures on the bench – the angry clap, the finger point, the two-handed push, the forearm clearing out – still became familiar to ACC fans. Opposing crowds loved to chant "Carolina Refs" when a call went the Tar Heels' way. But Smith rarely agreed he was getting the better end of it.

He grew increasingly critical of how inconsistently ACC games were called after Fred Barakat was named conference supervisor of officials in 1980. Barakat had left his job as head coach of Fairfield University in Connecticut and, while looking for work, called Smith for help. Barakat finally landed the ACC position, thanks more to the recommendations of other ACC coaches Mike Krzyzewski, Jim Valvano, and Bob Staak, all of whom Barakat had known when they coached in the Northeast.

Under Barakat's leadership, the ACC slowly lost its tag as a finesse league. The biggest beneficiary of that change was Duke, which played the most aggressive defense in the ACC. It was probably no coincidence that Duke led the league's resurgent success in the NCAA Tournament, where the tougher teams seemed to survive.

Believing his team to be no more physical than any other, Smith wondered if Barakat purposely assigned stricter officials to the Tar Heels to try to control the Carolina coach. The defiant Dick Paparo, for example, officiated more UNC games in his first twelve seasons in the ACC than veterans John Moreau in twenty-four years and Lenny Wirtz in twenty-eight. It had gotten back to Smith that, at least one time, Barakat had gone in at halftime of a Carolina game and instructed the officials to call a technical foul if he continued to stand up in the second half. Despite no written rules about a supervisor interacting with his officials after a game had started, Smith regarded such conduct as highly unethical.

Ironically, because Barakat became the fall guy and served as a buffer, there was less direct animosity between coaches and officials.

When Smith had gone after Moser in 1975, Norvall Neve served as the ACC's supervisor of officials and did little to diffuse such explosive situations. In fact, Moser wound up in the middle of another Carolina controversy at the end of the 1976 season. By then, most ACC officials had become well known to fans and were heckled by name. That Smith had continually tried to keep Moser from working his games had not been reported in the newspapers, but the story was out there.

Before the 1976 ACC Tournament, the *Durham Morning Herald* published a long feature article about officiating in which referee Jim Hernjak said some complimentary words about Smith and jokingly implied that they even socialized during the off-season. After ACC Commissioner Bob James read the article, he instructed Neve to not assign Hernjak to any UNC games in the tournament at Landover. Hernjak had been selected to work the championship game Saturday night, but when Carolina advanced to the finals against Virginia he was taken off the game.

His replacement? Lou Moser.

The fourth-ranked Tar Heels were heavily favored over the Cavaliers, who had finished sixth in the ACC standings, and they relentlessly and aggressively tried to speed up the tempo of a close game. Virginia ended up going to the foul line thirteen more times than UNC. During the tense final minutes, with the teams virtually deadlocked, every whistle grew in magnitude. Finally, with Virginia holding a one-point lead, Moser called a controversial traveling violation on Carolina guard John Kuester, who was pump-faking a defender. Kuester may have actually dragged his pivot foot, but that Moser made the call was not lost on Carolina fans after their team lost the game, 67-62.

Despite the in-fighting between coaches and officials, and whatever valid points he made, Smith received little sympathy around the league. Carolina had again become the powerhouse of the ACC, and the feeling was that because Smith was such a good coach and had so many talented players, he didn't need any extra help from the officials.

Besides, Smith had made news on a number of different fronts.

✪

After thirteen years as a head coach, the quiet Kansan had turned into one of the more controversial figures in college athletics. Smith hadn't intended it that way, wanting to coach and teach away from the glare of TV and the noisy demands of the other media. But his emerging brilliance had placed him in the spotlight.

Until Ford arrived on the scene, Four Corners had been generally viewed as a late-game strategy to stall for time, not dissimilar to the ball-control spreads many teams had used in the 1940s and 1950s. Carolina had utilized the strategy to run out the clock, much like the way football teams kept the ball on the ground to protect a lead in the closing minutes. But Ford elevated the importance of Four Corners within the Carolina program and altered its perception with the public. Because Ford was so adept at dribbling – he had learned to keep the ball inches off the ground as a kid by practicing on a dirt playground – his Four Corners became one of the most feared weapons in the college game.

Smith, in turn, did not mind deploying the strategy earlier and earlier in the second half. When he stood in front of the bench and held up four fingers, and Ford did the same thing on the court, a buzz of excitement swept through the arena. UNC fans loved it, opponents loathed it. Thus, Smith and his Tar Heels eventually came to elicit more emotion from the Carolina faithful than even Frank McGuire and his arrogant, bad-boy teams. Fans began watching Smith on the bench as much as they did the action on the floor. And as loudly as UNC fans cheered, opposing fans jeered – particularly when their teams were bested by Smith's stratagems.

The turning point had come, almost suddenly, in that 1975 ACC Tournament. After the Tar Heels upended State, 70-66, for the championship, sending them instead of the Wolfpack to the NCAAs, fans and foes alike had begun to realize that Smith would be around for a long time and that his teams were always going to be good. Twice – first after Charlie Scott graduated and then when Robert McAdoo went pro – Smith had been written off. Twice, he had come back strong. From that point on, almost everything he did and said became newsworthy, so unlike his early years at UNC when he still could maintain a relatively private life away from basketball.

When Smith had separated from Ann in 1970, few people had made anything of it. But despite spending many hours with his Baptist pastor, Bob Seymour, Smith continued to agonize over the stigma associated with divorce. He moved out of and back into the house several times – staying at bachelor assistant coach John Lotz's apartment whenever he moved out – but that only served to confuse his teenage children.

"The guilt was incredible," said his sister, Joan. "You stayed married, no matter what, the way we were brought up. That ordeal made him search himself even more."

Smith read books and listened to tapes, trying to accept the notion that a failed marriage did not necessarily mean failure as a husband or a father. He remained friendly with Ann through the years and, even after remarrying in 1976, included her in various family gatherings with the children and eventually the grandchildren.

"We just had two separate lives," recalled Ann, who remained in Chapel Hill and in her job as an occupational therapist at the UNC hospital until retirement. "Dean's life was basketball and mine was working and raising a family. He worked very hard; his life was all basketball. Most trips we took were all around his games and giving clinics."

So intensely private, Smith could not bring himself to talk about the divorce with his own children until several years later. "It was the one time I saw him cry," said daughter Sandy. "He felt so guilty because he thought he had messed up our family."

Smith and Ann attempted reconciliation several times, and she was still listed as his wife in the Carolina media guide as late as 1973. When the final split came early the next year, Smith thought it had become old news by then. But as his professional star rose, his personal life became more public. In his early forties at the time of his divorce, still thin and ruggedly handsome, Smith now confronted rumors about his social life. Elton Casey, one-time sports editor of the *Durham Morning Herald*, thought he continued to see Smith's car in the parking lot of a Durham apartment building, where a certain red-headed nurse from Duke lived.

Casey, who had battled alcoholism and received Smith's personal counsel on his struggle several times, continued to push the issue with the coach. Finally, Smith said firmly yet still imploringly to Casey, "I have needs like any human being, but my private life is no one else's business."

In the face of the encroaching coverage, Smith remained the picture of self-control – except for occasional lapses in judgment. One occurred following a 68-67 home loss to N.C. State and old nemesis Sloan in 1976. The game was on regional television but before implementation of mandatory TV time-outs at the first whistle after the 16-, 12-, 8- and 4-minute marks of each half. Sitting at the scorer's table calling the TV time-outs was Marvin "Skeeter" Francis, an employee of the ACC Commissioner's office who had gone to Wake Forest and been the sports information director there when Bones McKinney coached the Deacons. Francis's job, basically, was to signal for TV time-outs at even intervals during each half.

The Tar Heels had fallen behind State in the second half and were mounting a comeback when Francis called for an official time-out. Smith walked down to the scorer's table, glared at Francis and clapped his hands at him before going back to the huddle. After the game, which had ended when State's Al Green sank a free throw with no time remaining on the clock, Smith faced the media, mentioned Francis's Wake Forest affiliation, and charged him with calling a time-out to interrupt the Tar Heels' momentum.

Several veteran sportswriters, who had covered Carolina for years and knew Smith always had a method to his madness, saw this as an unmistakable loss of composure and criticized him roundly in print. Indeed, Smith had been wrong and felt badly about it right away. He told his assistant coaches he had made a mistake and wrote a letter of apology to Francis. But some critics, relishing this rare gaffe by the usually unflappable Smith, wouldn't let it go and, as time passed, skewed the story to reflect even more poorly on the Carolina coach.

Billy Packer, the TV commentator who had played at Wake Forest when Francis was there, recounted the incident inaccurately in his book, *Hoops! Confessions of a College Basketball Analyst*. He claimed it occurred in 1975, that the opponent had been Wake Forest, and that "Dean essentially accused Skeeter of using television time-outs to help Wake Forest win the game."

Packer also wrote that the procedure of calling time-outs by designated points on the clock was already established, when in fact that policy did not go into effect until the 1980s. "In more than twenty years of watching Dean Smith, it was the only time I've seen him respond emotionally instead of logically," he said.

However, after Smith was named coach of the 1976 U.S. Olympic men's basketball team, Packer was but one member of the media who chastised Smith for the selection of the squad, which included four Tar Heels and seven players in all from the ACC.

✪

At first, Smith did not want to coach the Olympic team in Montreal. His summers were filled with giving clinics, recruiting and, whenever he could sneak it in, golf. Besides, Hank Iba deserved a chance to rebound from 1972 in Munich. There, of course, the United States had lost the gold medal for the first time ever, when the Soviet Union had been given two tries at the winning basket by the international basketball officials. After Sasha Belov scored and the Ruskies claimed the gold, the outraged American team had refused to accept the silver medal.

But the 71-year-old Iba was definitely retiring after serving as the USA coach for three Olympiads. In addition, Iba, whose deliberate offensive style and standard zone defense were considered obsolete in the growing international game, joined fellow Hall of Fame coaches Pete Newell and Red Auerbach, among others, in approaching Smith. Convinced by his father that coaching his country's Olympic team was as much an obligation as a privilege, Smith acquiesced – with two stipulations. He would do it one time and other qualified coaches would get the chance after him; and, as a member of the selection committee for the team, he could pick whomever he wanted from his own program.

Olympic trials were held on the UNC and N.C. State campuses in the spring of 1976. The best-known stars of college basketball came from across the country, but when the team was named it had a decidedly local flavor: Tar Heels Ford, Kupchak, Walter Davis and Tom LaGarde, Duke's Tate Armstrong, Maryland's Steve Sheppard, and N.C. State's Kenny Carr.

Just as Smith always believed in having five starters, three quality substitutes, and a group of reserves who were just happy to be on the team, he wanted compatibility and chemistry and a complete absence of egos on the Olympic squad. Clearly, Smith did not want to deal with twelve players all concerned more about starting and minutes played than winning.

"This was the only time I ever felt my job was to win," said Smith, who named his own right-hand man, Bill Guthridge, and Georgetown's John Thompson as his assistant coaches. "In fact, that's what I was told."

The reaction was swift, near and far. The national media rejected Smith's theory that a familiar nucleus was necessary to offset the relatively short preparation time before the Games opened in July. Local critics, even those coaches whose players had made the team, complained that all the exposure enhanced Smith's recruiting for his own program.

"Having one player on the team is nice," said Duke coach Bill Foster, sarcastically, "having four players is even nicer."

Perhaps more than any other time in his professional career, Smith had been misjudged by his peers. He stacked his lineup with local players not for the future of his program but for the present of the Olympic team. Aware of how much pressure he would be under to reclaim the gold gedal, Smith had not counted on the hailstorm generated by the mere selection of the squad. It made perfect sense to him to take those Tar Heels who were as deserving as any other college players; after all, he knew they would be no trouble.

Actually, two certain starters came from Indiana's undefeated 1976 NCAA champions – guard Quinn Buckner and forward Scott May. Smith projected only one Carolina player to start, envisioning what he considered the perfect backcourt of Buckner and Ford, his All-American point guard. As it happened, Kupchak practiced well and wound up starting inside along with Notre Dame's Adrian Dantley, a personal favorite of Smith's since he recruited him as a high school player. The 6-5 Dantley teased Smith about a conversation they had had during his visit to Chapel Hill, when Smith said he doubted Dantley could play power forward in college.

The Olympic team played hard and partied hard, and Smith basically abandoned any off-court rules as long as he got the results he was looking for during practices and games. He has since admitted that personal transgressions by the players were virtually ignored because "for the first time, I took a win-at-all-costs approach." Smith knew what kind of team he wanted to put on the floor and what style it would employ. "Hustle and play together," he said. "There isn't a man here who can't play offense, but that isn't what's going to win the gold medal for us." With an up-tempo offense and pressing defense, Smith used most of the squad. Duke's Armstrong did not impress Smith at practice and was the only player to languish on the bench, further irritating Foster and causing Armstrong to dedicate his senior season to beating the Tar Heels.

Though the Americans posted mostly one-sided victories, they barely survived a second-round game against Puerto Rico. Behind Marquette star and San Juan native Butch Lee, the Puerto Ricans led late in the second half before losing by a single point. From there, the U.S. advanced to the medal round and defeated Canada in the semifinals and Yugoslavia for a second time in the gold medal game. Watching his team accept their medals, as thousands of Americans waved miniature flags and sang "The Star-Spangled Banner," Smith was overcome with emotion. For the first time in his life, he had felt real pressure to win. And after going through a spring of Olympic trials, an exhibition tour, and the games themselves, he was thoroughly exhausted.

On top of all that, he had recently been married to a Chapel Hill psychiatrist, whom he had met on an airplane the year before and with whom he would later have two daughters, Kristen Caroline and Kelly Marie. Smith and Dr. Linnea Weblemoe had squeezed in a small wedding near her home town in California just before the Olympic trials. And they hadn't bothered with the traditional private romantic honeymoon. Following the ceremony, the Smiths and two other couples had jumped on a plane and headed for Las Vegas for a long weekend. In many ways, it was the perfect marriage because Smith held such deep interest in his players and the psychology of the game.

"His influence on young people shouldn't be taken lightly," Dr. Smith said in 1977. "It's not omnipotence, but he and his players are setting examples to be followed. He handles a loss better than anyone in his family and usually has to be the one to put it in perspective and say we'll go on tomorrow. He doesn't dwell on the games, but he does share some things, mostly the human aspects."

✪

Fortunately, Smith and his assistant coaches had found time to do some recruiting for the upcoming season. The Tar Heels had finished 25-4 and won the ACC regular season in 1976, but they had ended on the sour note of two straight tournament losses. After going down to

Virginia in the ACC finals, they had been rudely ousted by Alabama in their first-round NCAA Tournament game.

The only weakness on that top-ten team had been a lack of depth, underscored dramatically by Ford's knee injury that rendered him ineffective in the NCAA loss. Smith had used basically six players all season, and All-American Kupchak had graduated to the NBA. Among the five freshmen Carolina had signed that spring, the real gem was 6-6 forward Mike O'Koren from Jersey City. Duke, which already had his high school teammate Jim Sparnarkel, thought it would get O'Koren, but the Tar Heels had led all the way thanks to a side of Dean Smith that few recruits ever saw.

O'Koren was an authentic inner-city Irish rowdy, with a wild group of beer-guzzling buddies who would make periodic road trips to Chapel Hill over the next four years. While assistant coach Eddie Fogler, a native New Yorker, had closed down the saloons with O'Koren's rat pack on his trips north, it was Smith who had won over the group. On Smith's recruiting visit, he had loosened his tie and drunk a beer or two with the brood that included O'Koren's mother, Minnie, his older brother Ron, and a rotating gang of friends who seemed to drop by all evening. Smith particularly loved Minnie's baked ziti, eating two helpings in the O'Korens' small tenement apartment. Emotional and animated, O'Koren could make Smith laugh and later in his career once made him cry. After Duke students had ridiculed O'Koren's facial acne with cruel signs and chants, Smith sharply criticized them in the post-game press conference and then drove back to Chapel Hill teary-eyed over his player's shattered feelings.

A great passer with a nose for offensive rebounds, O'Koren easily won the vacant starting position and joined a power-packed lineup of Ford, Kuester, Davis and LaGarde in 1977. The Tar Heels were ranked No. 1 with a 13-1 record when they mysteriously lost three out of four games, the last a twenty-point blowout at Clemson. Suddenly down and doubting themselves, the players dressed at Clemson and waited for Smith to return from his press conference. Expecting harsh words from their coach, they got the opposite. "No practice tomorrow," Smith said. "Then come back Friday ready to go, and I'll tell you how we're going to win a national championship."

Although he never said it publicly, this was one of Smith's favorite teams. It had hustle and heart and had dedicated the season to 1976 captain Kupchak, who had never reached a Final Four. Smith was mad at them only once after a physical loss to N.C. State when, as LaGarde said, they had "kind of chickened out." When LaGarde tore up a knee in February, Smith thought their chances for a national championship went out the window. But with three freshmen centers rotating in LaGarde's spot, Carolina overcame a bizarre series of injuries to win the ACC Tournament and somehow make it all the way to the NCAA title game in Atlanta.

Smith and several team members fought to control their emotions before the ACC championship rematch against Virginia when doctors drained blood from the finger Davis had fractured in the semifinals. Davis's screams and yelps of pain could be heard from the adjacent locker room. At halftime of the brutally aggressive game with the Cavaliers, Smith nearly had the first physical confrontation of his career. Already seeing the season in peril, Smith thought Virginia was intentionally trying to rough up Ford. Walking through the narrow tunnel to the locker rooms in Greensboro, he yelled and poked a finger at UVA forward Marc Iavaroni, as players and coaches from both teams pushed and shoved and swore at each other. Down late in the game, the Tar Heels managed to come back without Davis and despite Ford fouling out. O'Koren and Kuester and a ragtag lineup of Bruce Buckley, Tom Zaliagiris, and Rich Yonakor outscored Virginia over the last six minutes to save the day.

A week later in the NCAA Tournament, still without Davis, Smith uncharacteristically dropped to his hands and knees in front of the bench to coax a win against Purdue. Then, after Davis had returned for the East Regional games against Notre Dame and Kentucky, Ford went down with a wrenched elbow. An interesting footnote to those regional games in College Park, Maryland, came late in the 79-72 win over the Wildcats that sent Carolina on to the Final Four. During a scuffle on the court, Smith ran out to protect his players, and Kentucky center Rick Robey later accused Smith of calling him a "son of a bitch."

By the time Carolina hobbled into Atlanta, Tar Heel fans believed they had the best coach in the country and destiny on their side. A win over Nevada-Las Vegas, when O'Koren hung thirty-one points on the Rebels, sent their heroes into the championship game against

Marquette and retiring coach Al McGuire, soon to be the real darling of destiny.

Over the weekend, rumors were swirling that Smith would leave Carolina to coach at UCLA. The Bruins were two years removed from John Wooden's era, and the Wizard's beleaguered successor Gene Bartow was reportedly moving on to start up the Alabama-Birmingham program. When UCLA athletic director J. D. Morgan had called in 1975 upon Wooden's retirement, Smith had no interest in taking on that challenge. But now, after twenty years in Chapel Hill and his new wife hailing from California, Smith considered the move more seriously. And if things had turned out differently at The Omni on Monday night, March 28, he might actually have gone.

In one of Smith's defining moments as a coach, he went with his system over the momentum of the moment and probably cost Carolina a national championship. Having rallied furiously from a twelve-point deficit, the Tar Heels led Marquette by two points and had the Warriors on the ropes midway through the second half. With Ford injured, Davis playing hurt, and LaGarde on crutches at the end of the bench, Smith chose the strategy that had gotten them all there and consequently killed his own team's momentum. It was as if he, himself, had called the intentional TV time-out he had accused Skeeter Francis of calling the year before.

Smith signaled for Four Corners but, inexplicably, did not put his best team out there to execute it. O'Koren sat at the scorer's table for nearly four minutes, as Carolina held the ball against Marquette's cagey defense. Smith later explained he did not want to burn a time-out to get a player in the game, but his gaffe allowed McGuire's team to catch its breath and roll on to a 67-59 win.

Devastated, the Tar Heels did not blame their coach publicly, although several players and athletic department officials quietly criticized Smith for keeping O'Koren, Ford's chief target in Four Corners, out of the game during the critical stretch. "Why did he let him sit there so long?" lamented one member of the sports information staff.

Strangely, most Carolina fans did not fault their coach – showing, perhaps, the extent to which the legions had fallen into line. But the media continued to pick at Smith about the loss to Marquette. In the months and years to come, the question would dog him so much that he eventually refused to talk about it, leaving that unpalatable chore to his assistants. "We didn't take time-outs in that situation because Coach Smith had confidence in the players on the floor," Fogler said when asked about it. "Judging from the way it turned out, it's something he might do differently next time."

The next time occurred five years later, when with his team trailing by a point in the final minute against Georgetown Smith took a time-out to set up the winning shot. Michael Jordan made it, and only then were the demons of that night in Atlanta exorcised for Smith and those who idolized him.

CHAPTER EIGHT

"DEAN SMITH'S GONNA KICK YOUR ASS!"

Dean Smith gulped a Scotch on the rocks and felt it race down his throat, make a U-turn and climb back up through his nose and head. It had not been a good day at the office for the basketball coach at the University of North Carolina. He was at the home of his friend and confidante, Dr. Earl Somers, a Chapel Hill psychiatrist with whom he often played golf and, almost always, dined after home games. More than as a personal shrink, Smith used Somers as a sounding board – especially to help him anticipate potential problems with his team.

Once, in fact, Smith had Somers as a guest on his weekly TV show to ensure fans that the Tar Heels could bounce back from an emotional loss. However, on this particular Saturday evening, in February of 1975, Smith was trying to deaden the pain of the events that had transpired that afternoon in his own gym, Carmichael Auditorium. A Maryland team that his squad had upset in College Park a month earlier rolled to an unexpectedly easy 22-point win that, in reality, had been over midway through the first half. By then, it was clear that even a team trained by the master of the second-half comeback would or could not muster a rally to threaten the hot-shooting Terrapins.

As he sipped his Scotch in a more pensive manner, Smith remembered thinking that his players, particularly one, had lacked their usual heart, and that bothered him far more than the loss. Teaching, which defined Dean Smith more than coaching, was about encouraging effort as much as execution. And over the years he had become philosophical about defeat, inevitable at least a half-dozen times during the season while playing in the Atlantic Coast Conference.

"Dean," yelled Betty Somers, the striking hostess that evening, from the kitchen, "the phone is for you."

As he walked from the dining room into the kitchen, Smith figured it was one of his assistant coaches, Bill Guthridge or Eddie Fogler, reporting on how the evening visit had gone with high school recruit Dudley Bradley. Although he was from Towson, Maryland, Bradley had not been heavily pursued by Maryland Coach Lefty Driesell, but the way Bradley's home-state school had whipped Carolina that day made Smith wonder if there was now a new dog in the fight. Smith took the receiver and turned away for some privacy.

"Hello," he said.

"Coach Smith, sorry to bother you," said the voice of a local sportswriter whom Smith recognized instantly. "You weren't home, and I just took a guess you were over there."

"Well, it must be important if you tracked me down," Smith replied in his Kansas twang.

"I need to check something out about Walter Davis," the writer continued, referring to one of Smith's star players, a sophomore on the Tar Heels. "We have a report that Walter has been declared ineligible because of a class he failed, or something like that. I heard it from a couple of different sources and before we print anything, I wanted to talk to you."

"I know you have a job to do," Smith began, an almost perfunctory acknowledgment of first-amendment rights from one of North Carolina's staunchest liberal Democrats, "but it would really hurt Walter's feelings to have that come out when he may not be ineligible after all. He does have an incomplete in a class that, technically, is past the deadline. But we're meeting on Monday about it. Walter has worked hard in school, and this would really hurt him and his family if it came out and he didn't have to sit out."

So, the writer inquired, it's not for sure that he's ineligible?

Smith avoided that question, knowing the chances were good he could resolve the issue on Monday. Having already won more than two hundred games and four ACC championships, the 44-year-old Smith's power base was well established in Chapel Hill. He preached academics first, rarely used his influence and almost never abused it. If there was an undercurrent of favoritism for athletes, as existed at almost every major university playing big-time college sports, Smith worked subtly and steadily to make sure it remained well beneath the surface with regard to his basketball program.

"I think we can work it out Monday, and one way or another I'll call you first on it," Smith said to the writer, then adding, "Of course, if Walter's still eligible I don't think there's a story. But if there is one, I promise you'll get it first."

The writer agreed and the two men hung up. Smith went back to his dinner party, ironically in a slightly improved frame of mind. Although a very private matter was now out there, perilously close to the public, he had earned a temporary victory for one of his players; and that reprieve, in accordance with his own priorities, was far more important than the game he had lost that afternoon.

"The inquiring press," Smith said sarcastically, a thin smile appearing, when someone asked who was on the phone.

Not surprisingly, the matter went away Monday. Davis did not miss a game, earned All-America honors and became another of Smith's millionaire professional basketball players. He remained on schedule for graduation until his junior season and ended up taking ten years to finish up his degree work.

✪

"Come to Maryland and get your name in *The Washington Post*," Lefty Driesell used to say, "Go to North Carolina and get your name in the *Chapel Hill Gazette*."

While Driesell cultivated the aggressive, big-city journalism that in the long run helped bring him down, Smith had built relationships with members of a more docile, small-town press, people whom he might one day need to help his players and program. At least that was the case until late in his coaching career, when the "Southern" press grew more aggressive in its coverage, speculative in its reporting, and opinionated in its columns.

Frank McGuire, the irrepressible Irish carpetbagger from New York, captivated the media as well as the fans during his nine years in Chapel Hill, highlighted by his team's fairy-tale 1957 season of 32-0 and the national championship. He made great copy, from his so-called heated rivalry with N.C. State coach Everett Case (they were really close friends) to his colorful stories about the New York City from which he ran his Underground Railroad to Chapel Hill.

On road trips through the ACC, McGuire made a practice of loading the team bus with his cronies and favorite sportswriters, and one particular swing to Virginia and Maryland proved the beginning of the end for his tenure at Carolina. On the way to College Park and Charlottesville, he had treated everyone on the bus to lavish dinners and kept no specific records of who else besides his team participated in the engorgement. Thus, when the NCAA eventually examined expenditures for that road trip, it appeared that McGuire had bought his players more than a good meal. What he had done was not illegal, but no one believed he had spent all that money entertaining a bunch of sports hacks.

But that had been McGuire's way. During his team's storybook weekend in Kansas City – after the 1957 Heels beat Michigan State and Kansas both in triple overtime to win the NCAA title – McGuire had ordered thick steaks for everyone, including several of his favorite sportswriters, at the hotel victory party. He had also wanted the delicacy of Roquefort dressing on all of the salads. That's when the infamous argument erupted between McGuire and then-UNC Athletic Director Chuck Erickson, ending with McGuire reaching into his baggy trousers and pulling out a wad of bills to pay for the "God-damned Roquefort dressing." Sportswriters, some of whom weren't even born then, have recounted that story for years.

By comparison, Dean Smith was Desi Arnaz to McGuire's Lucille Ball. One local newspaper noted, respectfully, "The successor to Frank McGuire, one of the most dynamic men in sports, is not overpowering in personality." But Smith had learned his lessons from McGuire, after all, and ultimately he was considered McGuire's superior at schmoozing the press. At least that was the claim of Smith's enemies; and while there might be some truth to the assertion, Smith also tried to live by a principle instilled since childhood: treat every human being with dignity. He treated even the youngest, most nervous reporters with respect. He once introduced a prominent recruit to the sports editor of the *Daily Tar Heel*, the same student sportswriter whom he had gently admonished a few months before over a story that had claimed Smith did not like South Carolina All-American John Roche as a high school player.

"Say I'm a lousy coach, criticize my strategy," Smith had told the young scribe, almost sadly. "But don't say I can't judge talent. Of course we wanted Roche."

As an assistant to McGuire, Smith had developed friendships with writers and broadcasters who later supported him as a head coach through the lean years of the early '60s. With a photographic memory, and a keen eye for who attended his press conferences, Smith rarely forgot a good word or a bad one. He could remember with uncanny accuracy the names of sportswriters, and their families, after having not seen them for years. And Smith could also kiss up with the best of them. He knew how to acknowledge certain writers, subtly singling them out among the larger group, and praise them for the job they did. Over the years, it helped him develop a relationship with a press corps that criticized him only occasionally.

When the criticism came, Smith never forgot. But unlike many coaches who fumed silently over negative copy and later angrily confronted the writer, Smith often initiated dialogue right away, calling the reporter in question or mentioning it the next time he saw him, in an effort to prove his point. Whether they agreed with him or not, most members of the media respected Smith for his direct approach.

In the 1970s, coaches like N.C. State's Norman Sloan, Duke's Bill Foster, Wake Forest's Carl Tacy, and Virginia's Terry Holland, as well as Driesell, became almost obsessed with Smith's control over the media and the resulting disadvantages for their respective programs. They were convinced that most ACC sportswriters grew up Carolina fans, and that those who did not were quickly wooed into the fold by Smith. Sloan liked to needle certain writers who had graduated from UNC by sarcastically preceding their last name with the words, "Tar Heel," as in, "Well, if it isn't Tar Heel Jones." After the Wolfpack had lost one game to Carolina, a student reporter from the *Daily Tar Heel* asked Sloan, "Did the way we defended you in the second half affect the outcome?" Sloan walked out from around the podium, leaned into the young scribe's face and bellowed, "Who's WE?"

The countless stories about Smith's supposed coaching brilliance rankled Sloan, who slyly demurred that Smith was a great recruiter, implying that he should win because he had the best talent. Sloan pointed out that the only time State had the upper hand on Carolina – its nine-game winning streak over the Tar Heels – he had beaten Smith for two North Carolina high school stars, David Thompson and Tom Burleson.

Unlike Smith, who always closed practices and made his locker room off limits to the press except after games, Duke's Foster had a more casual policy. Writers could watch practice and visit with players while they were dressing. In January 1977, after star guard Tate Armstrong had been lost for the season with a broken wrist, an understandably crazed Foster chased a writer with Tar Heel ties out of a locker room interview with Armstrong, saying, "Can you do this at Carolina?" Foster also tired of the endless piety paid to Smith and UNC in the press. A very funny guy with a keen interest in sports marketing, Foster kept people amused with comments about the world around them. After Carolina's football team fell on hard times under new coach Dick Crum, Foster poked fun at UNC's promotional slogan when he told a group of writers one day, "It looks like Dr. Crum has found a cure for Carolina Fever!"

But Foster wasn't kidding when he said, "I thought Naismith invented basketball, not Deansmith." A proponent of the run-and-shoot style, Foster abhorred so-called Smith innovations such as Four Corners. He even walked out of an NCAA East Regional final when Carolina spread out to hold the ball against Kentucky with fifteen minutes left in the game. In what should have been his most satisfying payback to Smith, Foster could not let himself enjoy the infamous 1979 "7-0" game, when Duke held a stalling Carolina scoreless in the first half and went on to win 47-40. Foster criticized his opponent's choice of strategy on his weekly radio show the next night instead of crowing over how his team had made it backfire.

Tacy and Wake Forest went to the brink of a lawsuit against a Chapel Hill-based ACC insider's newsletter, published by former Tar Heel star Dennis Wuycik, that had claimed the Deacons were holding organized, closed-door workouts with coaches before the official October 15 start of practice. At virtually the last minute, the suit was not filed, but Smith always feared other ACC schools thought Wuycik's newsletter was coming right out of his office. Tacy once tried to literally upstage Smith in recruiting. After Jerry Schellenberg's two free throws clinched Wake's 67-66 upset win at Carmichael Auditorium in 1977, Tacy ran across the court in celebration and shook the hand of visiting prep star Jeff Ruland sitting in the front row. After Smith reported what had happened, ACC Commissioner Bob James penalized Tacy by crediting the impetuous move as one of Wake's official recruiting visits with Ruland, who eventually went to Iona College.

Then there was the famous claim by Holland to a Virginia newspaper that "there's such a gap between the man and the image the man tries to project." Holland conducted perhaps the longest-standing cold war with Carolina over the years, mistaking Smith's fierce competitiveness for ruthlessness. A scuffle between UNC and UVA players and coaches at halftime of the 1977 ACC title game led to Holland's claim – and Smith's response, "He doesn't know me from Adam." Years after the outburst, Holland was better remembered for making the comment than Smith was for being its object. "When Terry said those things, he ended up coming out the loser," Tacy said in 1981. "(Smith's) control of the press, especially in this state, is unbelievable."

Holland and his successor Jeff Jones, a former Cavalier star who had been recruited by Carolina and very nearly went there, long believed Smith used the media to help substantiate his claim that Virginia held and pushed on defense more than the rules allowed. "Some of his comments have bothered me," Jones admitted in January of 1996. "They have not been appropriate and, I don't think, very accurate. Some teams play differently from North Carolina, and I don't think he comes off very well complaining about it."

And, of course, the rivalry between Smith and Driesell was often waged in the media, as writers ran between the Carolina and Maryland locker rooms after games to tell each coach what the other had said about him. When Maryland, without star Charles Pittman, almost upset the eventual national champion Tar Heels in 1982, Driesell thought that Smith was being disingenuous when he said, "Most teams can play one great game without their best player." Their rivalry dated back to when Driesell coached tiny Davidson College, the David to

UNC's Goliath in North Carolina, and the Wildcats lost back-to-back NCAA East Regional title games to the Tar Heels. Before the second game in 1969, Driesell had told *The Washington Post*, "I'd rather die than lose to North Carolina again." (He did lose on Charlie Scott's buzzer-beater).

Almost twenty years later, when Driesell was about to lose his job after the tragic cocaine-related death of Len Bias, Smith publicly stood up for him with the media. Twelve years after that, Smith did very much the same for Jones at Virginia. Of course, there were the cynics who said Smith hated to see Driesell and Jones go because he beat them so regularly on the court and in recruiting and did not want Maryland and Virginia to hire "better" coaches. Smith's career record against Driesell was 31-10, and 14-4 versus Jones.

✪

In the 1980s, with the emergence of Jim Valvano at N.C. State, Bobby Cremins at Georgia Tech, and Mike Krzyzewski at Duke, Smith slowly lost his grip on the media. All three were candid and witty and developed a rapport with members of the press that the more aloof Smith never allowed. And all three handled the rivalry with Carolina differently than their respective predecessors had.

The comedic Valvano, a wise-cracking New Yorker, claimed he wanted a program just like Smith's, saying he planned to "outlive" Smith rather than "outcoach" him. That turned into tragic irony, of course, as Valvano was stricken with cancer at age forty-seven and died in late 1993 after his third year as a TV commentator for ABC and ESPN. The last game he worked was Duke-Carolina in Chapel Hill on March 7. During his ten years at State, Valvano had the best public relationship with Smith of all their fellow coaches. He contended that any great high school basketball player in North Carolina should stay home and play for either him or Smith, and he promised that he himself would be at the airport to stop any such prize recruit from leaving the state. Following Carolina's last game in Carmichael Auditorium, a 90-79 win over State on January 4, 1986, Valvano dragged a smiling Smith back on the court to watch him shoot a layup. "I wanted to score the last basket in Carmichael," said Jimmy V.

Like all rivals of Smith and the Tar Heels, Valvano poked fun at the Carolina program. But he did it privately to friends and writers who he knew would take it all in good fun. During the 1980s, when Carolina had the tag of being a "soft" team, Valvano liked to imitate Smith's big men doing their little pirouette jump hooks around the basket. The post-game pizza and beer parties in his office at Case Athletic Center were a staple for beat writers covering the Wolfpack.

In public, Valvano had nothing but praise for Smith and the Tar Heels. His favorite story, one that he told repeatedly to the press and at speaking engagements, was about getting his hair cut after he had first taken the State job. The barber kept calling Smith the greatest coach of all time and claiming State never had a chance against the Heels.

"What about Norm Sloan? He had a pretty good team in 1973, going 27-0," Valvano proclaimed.

"Yeah," answered the barber, "but can you imagine what Dean Smith would have done with 'em?"

Another story that Valvano told less frequently concerned a blunder he had made in his first year at State as a 35-year-old newcomer to a region dominated by the same man for the last two decades. Bound for a speaking engagement in eastern North Carolina, Valvano had mistakenly taken a flight from Raleigh-Durham Airport to Greenville, South Carolina. When he explained the goof to what he hoped would be a sympathetic porter at the wrong airport, the old black man looked at the coach's striped pants, bright red blazer, and Wolfpack tie that was too short and poorly knotted. Shaking his head, the old man said, "Son, Dean Smith is gonna kick your ass!"

Cremins genuinely liked and admired Smith, dating back to his playing days for McGuire at South Carolina and the night of February 28, 1968, when the Gamecocks had upset the Tar Heels. That's the game Cremins referred to years later when he jokingly asked Smith before the start of an ACC coaches meeting, "Dean, do you remember your first sexual experience?" Smith laughed without answering or knowing exactly where the conversation was going. Cremins went on to tell him, leaving other ACC coaches in hysterics.

UNC had been undefeated in the ACC and already locked up first place in the conference when the Gamecocks came to town the last week of the 1968 regular season. In the final home game for UNC

All-American Larry Miller, the Tar Heels were expected to beat their scrappy visitors, who had been dubbed the "Four Horsemen and a Pony" by South Carolina fans. After Carolina had fallen behind late in the second half, Smith ordered his team to keep fouling Cremins, who was not only the "Pony" but also the Gamecocks' worst free-throw shooter at 59 percent. Cremins went on to make 13 of 16 as South Carolina held on for the 87-86 upset. After the game, sportswriters mobbed Cremins and, upon returning to Columbia, adoring students greeted the team. Late, late that night, Cremins says, he lost his virginity.

Cremins had carried that slapstick kind of humor into the ACC, endearing himself to sportswriters who had already taken to Valvano's sense of humor and Krzyzewski's early accessibility at Duke. Krzyzewski, in fact, during his early years with the Blue Devils had much of the same approach to Smith and Carolina as did Valvano. Understanding that an embittered Foster had been driven out of Durham and the ACC by the omnipotence of the Tar Heel program, Krzyzewski quietly bided his time while rebuilding Duke.

He began to develop one-on-one relationships with local sportswriters, inviting them to his home and calling them up for a tennis game. Keith Drum, sports editor of the *Durham Morning Herald* and a Carolina alum, became one of his closest friends. This kind of camaraderie would be the foundation of Krzyzewski's support when the Blue Devils turned into a national power and darlings of the media.

In their first match-up of 1984, the top-ranked Tar Heels trailed Duke most of the game in Cameron Indoor Stadium. Using all of his guile and coaching intimidation, Smith cajoled his team to a comeback victory, but not before causing a scene at the scorer's table trying to get a sub into the game. Frustrated that the scorekeeper would not blow the horn, Smith tried to hit the button himself and accidentally put twenty more points on the scoreboard for Carolina. No technical foul was assessed. After the game, Krzyzewski blew up in his press conference, claiming a double standard existed in the ACC – Carolina and everyone else. The press seemed sympathetic, and from that point on there began to grow an ironic double standard in the media favoring Duke, right through the Blue Devils' great run of seven Final Fours and two national championships in a nine-year period.

With diplomacy gone, Smith and Krzyzewski conducted much of their rivalry in the press, taking subtle and more blatant shots at each other over everything from players' SAT scores to crowd behavior to beer advertising on college games. Despite the darts being hurled, Krzyzewski for the most part remained every bit as calm and cunning as Smith with the media.

By the end of the 1980s, the crush of cable TV and competing publications had made the media more aggressive than ever. And the quips and quotes writers and broadcasters were getting from Valvano, Cremins, and Krzyzewski were making Smith's oft-fragmented, sometimes evasive answers look tiresome and obsolete by comparison.

Nevertheless, Smith still had his staunch supporters in the press. And when the moronic calls on talk radio and letters to the editor labeled Smith a "choker" and claimed Carolina, which went eight years without reaching the Final Four, would never win another national championship, these loyalists responded where they could. National writers with UNC ties also stood up to defend Smith. Mark Whicker, a former Morehead Scholar, used to smoke cigarettes with Smith outside the locker room when Whicker was a young sportswriter. In fact, Whicker gave Smith a carton (two hundred cigarettes) of unfiltered Kents after the coach won his two hundredth game. Even after moving on to be a renowned columnist in California, Whicker continued to defend Smith in print.

But there was no lighter blue knight than John Kilgo, the Charlotte gadfly who hosted Smith's weekly radio and television shows and published a basketball-oriented, severely slanted tabloid called *Carolina Blue*. Kilgo took on all comers, some within the Carolina camp whom he thought were being too critical, in his opinionated page-two column. An extreme example of the loyalty Smith engendered, Kilgo was often at odds with the rest of the UNC athletic department due to his uneven coverage of basketball. "I don't care what anyone else thinks, especially not the athletic director," Kilgo said in 1993. "There is only one man I want to please." Kilgo shamelessly promoted Smith, referring to him as "The Coach," and put his own spin on everything that happened, good or bad, to Carolina basketball. He arrived at the Thursday night call-in show, *Carolina Blueline*, armed with a folder of editorial clippings he had accumulated for Smith. "This is what one guy wrote about you, Coach," Kilgo would say as he slid the items under Smith's nose during commercial breaks.

Into the 1990s, Smith loosened up with the media and seemed to regain support from writers who by then considered him the elder statesman of college basketball. However redundant or tedious Smith had been, he was still around spouting the same philosophies and almost never getting caught in a contradiction.

Meanwhile, Valvano had fallen out of grace at N.C. State, resigned in 1990 under pressure, and, three years later, lost his battle with cancer. Unfortunately, his legacy of one-liners and recruiting violations overshadowed his accomplishments as a coach who really cared about his kids and his school. Cremins continues to coach at Georgia Tech, but he has never quite rebounded from that strange occurrence in 1993, when he had accepted the job at South Carolina and then, three days later, turned his back on his alma mater to return to Tech. He remains a media favorite but is generally considered a quick-fix recruiter (Kenny Anderson, Stephon Marbury) who struggles as a bench coach. And Krzyzewski also has lost the universal support of sportswriters who had hung on his every word. The mysterious back ailment that had caused him to miss most of the 1995 season resulted in two questionable moves that darkened his once-impeccable image. After that disastrous 13-18 season, he jettisoned interim coach and long-time associate Pete Gaudet and then allowed his sports information office to petition the NCAA to have those games he missed (four wins, fifteen losses) expunged from his overall record.

Smith carried on virtually unchanged through all of this, marching steadily toward the record for major-college coaching victories and rebuilding his base of support among the media. As his Tar Heels won a second national championship in 1993 and visited four Final Fours in the decade before he retired, Smith again became the coach most fans revered and the press trusted for his character, if not his charisma. He grew to like his weekly press gatherings during the season, bantering with writers in an informal setting. Two of his favorites were Eddy "Front Row" Landreth, who while covering the ACC for the *Charlotte Observer* always sat in the first row at press conferences, and thoughtful freelance writer Barry Jacobs, who although having graduated from Duke had won Smith's trust with his integrity and intelligence.

Smith occasionally poked fun at his supposedly media-savvy rivals. Krzyzewski, for example, was the subject of almost annual rumors that he would leave Duke for an NBA job and once called a news conference at Cameron Indoor Stadium to announce he had turned down an offer to coach the Portland Trailblazers. On that very day, in the spring of 1994, Smith pulled into his private parking space behind the Deandome. Asked what his plans were for the afternoon, Smith quipped, "Maybe I'll hold a press conference to say I'm not going anywhere."

As the countdown continued to Adolph Rupp's record, Smith became the biggest ongoing story in college sports. By the time his 1997 team had rallied from a poor start in conference play to win twelve straight, putting Smith within one win of the record, the media attention became so stifling as to actually overshadow the ACC and NCAA Tournaments. Still, he managed it with aplomb, trying as he might to keep his team focused on winning another ACC championship and reaching the Final Four in Indianapolis. When the record came, in an NCAA Tournament second-round win over Colorado, Smith greeted the phalanx of former players who had found their way into Joel Coliseum in Winston-Salem with great warmth and affection.

Clearly, Dean Smith had mellowed. His power of recall remained as strong as ever, and he remembered all that had been written and said about him over the years. However, on the day of his greatest personal accomplishment, when he could have signaled out all the people who had said he'd never get there, he instead waxed philosophical about the UNC administration that "stood behind me when we weren't very good."

Those words stood in marked contrast to the 1982 night in New Orleans, after the Tar Heels had given him his long-awaited first national championship, when Smith opened his post-game press conference with a dart aimed at *Charlotte Observer* sportswriter Frank Barrows. Five years earlier, after Carolina had blown the national championship game to Marquette, Barrows had criticized Smith and predicted he would never win an NCAA title because his philosophy was based so much on winning consistently that his teams lacked the spontaneity to win the big game.

"A very talented sportswriter from Charlotte predicted we'd never be here," Smith said. It was five years later, but Smith still held in his craw one of the relatively few needles he had received from the Fourth Estate that he otherwise owned.

THE BUILDING OF A CHAMPION

Dean Smith received more personal ticket requests for Phil Ford's last home game than he had in his nearly seventeen seasons as Carolina's basketball coach. Big games were always tough, but nothing quite rivaled the afternoon of February 25, 1978, when Ford was to play Blue Heaven for the last time. The senior guard, a three-time All-American and soon to be National Player of the Year, had for four seasons dazzled fans with his unparalleled ability and unfailing enthusiasm for the game. And, though not really the case, it seemed like he had personally resurrected Carolina basketball from State's brief domination.

The Phil Ford era drove ticket demand to a new frenzy. Before his sophomore season, 1976, all of the Carolina-blue, individual wooden armchairs in "three-sided" Carmichael had been replaced by less comfortable aluminum benches, increasing the seating capacity from eighty-eight hundred to ten thousand and angering many Educational Foundation "boosters" who had to squeeze their middle-aged behinds into far narrower spaces. The closer quarters made what had long been considered the "hottest" arena in the ACC even more uncomfortable. Rumors abounded that the janitors were told to turn up the heat for big games, though Smith himself graphically denied the story by often wearing wool, three-piece suits and almost never loosening his tie.

For Ford's finale, the hot box attached to the east side of Woollen Gym would bulge at the steel girders that held the place together. Fans had plenty of time to get to Chapel Hill for the late afternoon game but on this day arrived especially early for the renewal of the arch rivalry – and a game that, in itself, had tremendous importance. Carolina, ranked No. 10 nationally, was playing Duke for the regular-season championship of the ACC and assured at-large bid to the NCAA Tournament. Led by freshmen Gene Banks and Kenny Dennard, sophomore Mike Gminski, and junior Jim Sparnarkel, the Blue Devils had broken their own eight-game losing streak to their hated rivals six weeks earlier in Durham and were looking for their first win in Chapel Hill since 1966. Having emerged as the team to beat in the ACC, Duke came into the game with its first top-twenty ranking in seven years, and scalpers who could get their hands on any of the ten-dollar tickets were asking as much as one hundred dollars each on the open market.

Not only did Smith have to assign every complimentary ticket (he insisted on doing it so he would know where every guest was sitting), he had to somehow get his gimped-up team believing it could win. Ford had missed the previous game at N.C. State with a sprained wrist, O'Koren was trying to play with a severely injured ankle, and reserve center Geff Crompton was serving a one-game suspension for a minor eligibility infraction. While fans filtered into the arena, Smith irritated and motivated his players by telling them they were underdogs and Duke was coming over to prove it. "I don't know if we can win," assistant coach Eddie Fogler said an hour before the game, "but Duke better tie their jockstraps on real tight."

When the Tar Heels took the court for warm-ups, almost every seat was filled, a rarity because of wicked traffic snarls and a perpetual parking problem. One thin driveway ran in front of Carmichael, down which a few hundred lucky cars snaked onto the adjacent intramural fields.

No one got by Sparrow, the old man guarding the driveway, without a pass. One year, Billy Packer arrived to broadcast the game on TV and did not have the credentials to park next to the TV trucks behind the building. Turning the nose of his car into the driveway, he stuck his head out the window and said, "I'm Billy Packer, let me through."

The old man refused to unhook the single cable stretched across the driveway. "Can't get down there without a pass," Sparrow said, barely changing expressions.

"I'm Billy Packer. I'm here to do the game, and if you don't let me in, I'll have your job."

"Can't have it . . . retired six months ago," Sparrow countered, stoic as a statue.

Packer reversed his car and sped off to join the thousands of others looking for a space somewhere along the narrow roads in the middle of campus.

By the 4:00 P.M. tip-off of Ford's final home game, people stood everywhere they were not blocking someone else's view, stacked six deep and ten across the two main portals, all stretching on tiptoes to see the action. The fire marshals had either taken the day off or gotten tickets from Smith. Students who had waited hours to get the precious twenty-five hundred bleacher seats were packed onto the benches, pumped to beat Duke and bid farewell to one of the most popular students ever at Carolina.

Unlike many athletes who hung out mostly with other jocks, Ford liked to run in a number of different circles. A well-known ladies' man, he actually dated two girls simultaneously during much of his college career, one white and one black. So he knew all of their friends, plus most of the extended athletic family at UNC. He also had fans of all ages who idolized his play and personality, many of whom waited for him after every game hoping to catch a glimpse or, better yet, get an autograph.

Ford's swan song only added to his legend, and was probably the one game that did more than any other to turn talk of a new, bigger arena into an actual plan of action. Despite his nagging wrist injury, his seventeen first-half points kept Carolina in the game. Down the stretch, he was at his most magisterial, spinning to the basket and pulling up for jumpers or dishing off acrobatic assists. He finished with thirty-four points as Carolina rallied to win, 87-83, extending Duke's losing streak in Chapel Hill to twelve years. When freshman Al Wood's four free throws in the final minutes settled it, Carmichael erupted like never before. After Ford exchanged an emotional arm wave with students and rushed off the floor through a gauntlet of adoring fans, Blue Heaven remained full and full of sound. The band played, the cheerleaders danced, and the fans sang the Alma Mater and fight song until Ford popped out of the locker room door for a short curtain call.

Over the years, Phil Ford's home finale has become much like Bobby

Thomson's home run in 1951 and Wilt Chamberlain's 100-point game in 1962. Since then, thousands of people have claimed to be there, yet only a fraction of that number was actually in attendance. That so many Tar Heels wished they could have been in Carmichael Auditorium that Saturday afternoon in February, and so few were, gave impetus to the notion of a new Blue Heaven, where more fans could see the games in person and the best players could envision themselves performing.

✪

Following the 1978 season, two important events occurred that would begin taking Carolina to college basketball's next, and top, level. One was a meeting between a thirtyish, a fortyish, and a fiftyish-year-old man in a cramped office of Carmichael Auditorium. The other was the visit to Chapel Hill by a teenage point guard from The Bronx.

Forty-seven-year-old Dean Smith met with UNC Athletic Director Bill Cobey, then in his late thirties, and Ernie Williamson, a former UNC football player who was in his mid-fifties and the executive secretary of the Educational Foundation. They discussed the growing sentiment in favor of building a new basketball arena to replace Carmichael, which had become too small to handle the demand for tickets and whose antiquated locker rooms and basketball offices were becoming a liability in recruiting. Cobey reported on his previous meeting with UNC chancellor Ferebee Taylor, who had told him that the Carolina Challenge fund-raising campaign had almost a year to go and that talk of a new gym for the basketball Tar Heels might slow that drive in the home stretch. Taylor did say that once the Carolina Challenge ended in 1979 formal meetings about an arena could be held. All three men left satisfied that a tangible timetable would be established. Cobey and Taylor would go to the state legislature for funds to build the basketball palace on a site that had already been informally selected off Mason Farm Road on the south end of the UNC campus. But the wise Williamson, who had been at Carolina through the fiasco of constructing Carmichael, knew the politicos in Raleigh were partial to N.C. State and would never agree. If Carolina wanted a first-class arena that would accommodate the continued growth of Smith's program, Williamson knew the Rams Club would have to build it with private donations. And he was pretty sure the boosters would pony up the money for a state-of-the-art coliseum they could some day call their own.

Carmichael Auditorium had been built as a compromise with former coach Frank McGuire, who had petitioned for an eight-sided arena even before his undefeated 1957 team won the national championship. McGuire had often complained to UNC chancellor Bill Aycock and Athletic Director Chuck Erickson that the roof of creaky old Woollen Gym leaked, endangering his players. In 1961, the state legislature failed to approve funding for any new, self-standing buildings on the UNC campus. However, additions to existing structures were permitted, and Aycock proposed an auditorium that would be attached to Woollen. After two more years of legislative wrangling, ground was finally broken in early 1964, and the first game was played there against William & Mary on December 4, 1965.

By the time William D. Carmichael Jr. Auditorium – named for the former vice president and controller of the Consolidated University – opened, McGuire was long gone and Smith had entered his fourth year as head coach of the Tar Heels. In only the third game in what had already been dubbed "Blue Heaven," junior Bobby Lewis scored forty-nine points against Florida State, a school record that still stands. Smith had begun to use the new facility as a recruiting tool to land Lewis and eventually Larry Miller, but he soon found out what a tremendous home-court advantage the three-sided structure gave his team. With noise bouncing off the concrete wall of Woollen behind the student bleachers, Carmichael became such a powerful reverberation chamber that it helped lift the home team and rattled opponents. However, as Smith's program continued its ascension, and with it the fervor surrounding Carolina basketball, Carmichael's limitations became apparent. Tickets to the new edifice became harder to get each ensuing season and eventually almost impossible. Only UNC faculty and staff with enough longevity and high-ranking members of the Rams Club stood a chance. Students had to wait in long lines, sometimes overnight, if they hoped to get one of the relatively few seats issued and paid for by student fees.

Jimmy Black had heard about Carolina basketball and Blue Heaven, but never thought he would experience either firsthand. Heading into the last year of his solid but unheralded high school career, Black intended to play for Jim Valvano at tiny Iona College in New Rochelle, New York. Then, early in the 1978 season, some loose lips began a chain of events that ultimately led to a change in Black's plans. Larry Gillman, the loud-mouthed coach of East Carolina's basketball team at the time, had told the Carolina staff that his New York buddy Valvano was bragging about having the best point guard in New York City locked up for Iona. Black had actually been on the Tar Heels' early recruiting list after a recommendation from Jack Curran, the long-time coach at Archbishop Molloy High School in New York, whose team had played against him. Smith sent Bill Guthridge to see Black play at Cardinal Hayes High School, and in early February, a day after Carolina's loss at Providence College during the week of the great blizzard of 1978, Smith, Guthridge, and Fogler were in Black's home for a recruiting visit. They knew he was committed to Iona and planning to sign a letter of intent there after the season, but they invited him to visit Chapel Hill before he did.

Three weeks later, the day after Ford dazzled Duke, Black courteously asked Valvano if he could make a trip to Carolina before signing with the Gaels. Valvano tried half-heartedly to talk him out of it, knowing full well what the result of such a visit would be. Black, who had relatives in Raleigh, returned to New York from the April weekend in Chapel Hill and told Valvano he would be signing with the Tar Heels instead. Valvano wished him luck and, although he later predicted Black wouldn't play very much at Carolina, the two remained close friends. Ironically, after Valvano took the N.C. State job in 1980, he was to face Black and Carolina six times in two years, losing all six games.

After studying Black a few more times, Smith knew why his future point guard had not been rated among the top fifty high school seniors by the so-called recruiting experts. He was steady, not flashy, and only an average shooter. But Smith liked his fluid ballhandling skills, defensive quickness, and ability to hit free throws in the clutch. Guthridge accurately predicted the eventual success of Carolina's national championship point guard when he wrote in Black's recruiting file: ". . . explosive quickness, defensive potential, good hands, unselfish, savvy . . . the motor we need."

✪

In 1979, true to his word, Chancellor Taylor appointed Hargrove "Skipper" Bowles chairman of a steering committee to head up the fund-raising drive for the new basketball arena. Bowles, who had narrowly missed being elected governor of the state in 1972, was one of UNC's most distinguished alumni and biggest sports fans. He quickly went to work enlisting twenty-four members to join his committee. Plans were made for a fund-raising tour after the 1980 basketball season ended, in conjunction with annual Rams Club meetings in North Carolina and several out-of-state alumni functions. Bowles, along with Williamson, would be at most every stop, drumming up support for the arena project.

Though he found asking people for money personally repugnant, Dean Smith agreed to attend as many meetings as possible. He understood that it was his success that had lit the fire, and that he, more than anyone else, could sell the concept to Carolina alumni and supporters.

During the 1979 season, of course, Smith was busy coaching another Carolina team through one of its biggest challenges. Ford had graduated, leaving junior Dave Colescott, senior walk-on Ged Doughton and freshman Black to try to follow the school's all-time leading scorer and, at the time, assist-maker at point guard. The situation paralleled what Smith had gone through in 1971, after Charlie Scott had graduated and pundits predicted the demise of Carolina basketball. But just as that 1971 team had developed its own personality and went on to win the NIT, Smith's latest team came into its own with some very big wins. One of them occurred early, on December 16, 1978, when Michigan State and their sensational sophomore Earvin "Magic" Johnson visited Carmichael Auditorium. The Tar Heels seized the lead early and controlled the game until late in the second half when Johnson and Greg Kelser rallied the Spartans. After Kelser's last-second shot rolled off the rim, the Heels had a 70-69 win that did wonders for their confidence.

Smith was further buoyed by the presence of high school senior James Worthy in the Carolina locker room after the game. The 6-9 manchild from Gastonia, North Carolina, had abundant skills, explosiveness, and maturity far beyond the normal teenager, and since first visiting Chapel Hill as a seventh-grader at the Carolina Basketball School summer camp, Worthy was ticketed to be a Tar Heel by most scouting services. Trouble was, Worthy was also a big Magic Johnson fan. And after leaving the Carolina locker room, he went down the hall and around the corner to hang out with Magic and his teammates. Worthy had met them all the previous fall during his official recruiting visit to East Lansing.

Convinced Worthy was destined for college stardom, Smith actually worried more about Kentucky than Michigan State. UK assistant coach Leonard Hamilton hailed from Gastonia and knew the Worthy family through James' older brother, Danny, who had worked in Lexington for a couple of years. Smith regarded Worthy as almost obsessively proud and was concerned that all the talk about his going to UNC might actually hurt the Tar Heels' chances. But after returning from a January loss at Clemson that had kept his upstart team from claiming the No. 1 national ranking, Smith got a phone call from Worthy with a verbal commitment.

Carolina had now put some important pieces together toward rebuilding a dominant program. Although Smith would later lose Ralph Sampson to Virginia in another publicized recruiting battle, his 1979 team went on to win the ACC championship over Duke before losing in the second round of the NCAA Tournament to Penn. What's more, only Doughton and Dudley Bradley, another of Smith's self-made players and first-round NBA draft pick, would be graduating. With Worthy and scrappy prep school point guard Jim Braddock coming in, Carolina again looked like the team of the future in the ACC, if not the country.

Unfortunately the Tar Heels suffered a serious blow when freshman Worthy broke his ankle four games into the 1980 ACC regular season. The team managed to regroup during the second half, blowing out Virginia and Duke in the last two home games of O'Koren, Jeff Wolf, Rich Yonakor, John Virgil and Colescott. Even without Worthy, the Heels finished in a tie for second in the conference. But Carolina couldn't kick it to the next level in the post-season, losing a one-sided rematch to Duke a week later in the ACC Tournament semifinals and then dropping a double-overtime game to Texas A&M in the NCAAs. Few UNC fans made the trip to Denton, Texas, angering several Tar Heel players and apparently jeopardizing the new arena. The team had won twenty-three games, but somehow interest seemed on the wane.

Undaunted, Smith hit the road for fund-raising functions and recruiting trips. He, Bowles, and Williamson went off on what they called their "traveling road show," showing boosters and alumni all over the state a scale model of the new arena created by one of the architectural firms vying to design the new home of the Tar Heels. Smith got over his intrinsic shyness and fund-raising phobia by telling one and all the new arena would be a tribute to every Carolina player, past, present, and future. Some substantial pledges came in early, but Smith was more interested in a couple of commitments from New York, where two high school stars were living a hundred miles away from each other – but worlds apart in their upbringing and basketball histories.

Matt Doherty, a 6-7 forward from Hicksville on Long Island, had already committed to the Tar Heels, announcing his choice of schools before his senior season had begun in October of 1979. While other schools continued to recruit the well-known prep player, Carolina basically "baby-sat" him with calls and visits until he could sign a letter of intent. Sam Perkins was a whole different story. Smith had first seen him at the National Sports Festival in Colorado Springs during the summer of 1979, a gangly teenager whose team lost three straight games without much fanfare. Smith wrote down on the back of an envelope, ". . . has quickness, size and ability . . . a must for recruiting."

Among the hundreds of letters he received each year from high school coaches with college prospects, Smith read carefully the one from Julius Grimindl, whose Shaker High School team in upstate New York had a "6-10 player who is interested in North Carolina." Recalling that gangly kid in Colorado, Smith sent Fogler to check him out. Perkins had not been on anyone's recruiting list. In fact, he had only played organized basketball for three years. Before that, he had lived with his grandmother, a devout Jehovah's Witness, in the Bedford-Stuyvesant section of Brooklyn and was not allowed to play ball or even hang out in the playgrounds.

One day, a recreation basketball coach named Herb Crossman had seen a very tall tenth-grader get off the bus in front of Tilden High School. After asking around the 'hood, Crossman found out the kid everyone called "Kareem" because of his height did not even know how to play basketball. "I'll fix that," Crossman said to himself. He first convinced Martha Perkins to let her grandson play for his Brooklyn Hoopsters rec team. A year later, after accepting a job near Albany,

Crossman talked Martha into letting him take the youngster out of the city and into a better environment.

That was the summer of 1978, and less than a year later Perkins was turning heads at Shaker High by dominating games in his very first year of prep basketball. As Smith would discover in a few months, Perkins had speed, quickness, a soft shooting touch, and arms that hung below his waist while standing up straight. Having slipped by everyone but Smith at the National Sports Festival the previous summer, Perkins still attended no all-star camps in 1979. By the time he drove college coaches to the phones with his dominating performance at the Dapper Dan Roundball Classic that August, Perkins had six schools on his list: Carolina, Duke, Notre Dame, San Francisco, Syracuse, and UCLA.

During his senior season, Perkins told UCLA coach Larry Brown that he was going to be a Bruin, sparking national stories about the commitment. But even though his team reached the 1980 Final Four, losing to Louisville in the national championship game, Brown was rumored to be on his way back to the NBA. In April, Perkins signed instead with the Tar Heels, giving them a new center to play with three returning starters, sophomore Worthy, junior Black and senior Wood.

✪

When Carolina won the ACC championship, reached the Final Four and vanquished Virginia in the 1981 national semifinals, even a disappointing loss to Indiana in the championship game couldn't curtail now-skyrocketing interest in the Tar Heels or slow the drive to build a new basketball arena. Athletic director John Swofford, who had succeeded Cobey in the spring of 1980, was to say later, "If you had designed a fund-raising campaign in heaven, you couldn't have come up with better timing, after the team played for the national title one year and won it the next."

By then, it was clear the new "Student Activities Center" would be built in the large ravine beyond South Campus. Half of the projected $30 million price tag had been pledged, allowing UNC to go to Raleigh for approval and to apply for building permits. The project, until that time still tenuous, was now a reality. Hakan-Corley, the local architecture firm that had helped the initial campaign with schematics and the model, was formally chosen as the design company and drew up the plans for an eight-sided domed arena with wide aisles and wider concourses and about twenty-three thousand cushioned seats, not a single sight line more than 150 feet from the playing court.

Those people sending checks, pledging money, or promising gifts were told that the amount of their contributions would determine the location of the season tickets they could eventually buy. That decree helped send the campaign about $5 million over the top in 1984, but also created a controversy about lost home-court advantage that would dog the "Deandome" into the next century. "Maybe it would be better if more of our students were closer to the floor," Smith said in 1996 after ten years of almost constant criticism about what had been tagged the "wine and cheese" crowds at Carolina. "But I can't go back on my word to people. I promised them that if they gave the money, they could pick where they wanted to sit."

In the spring of 1981, UNC officials were ready to break ground. Smith even mentioned to a young recruit from Wilmington that, with a little luck, maybe he could play his senior season in the new building. Sitting on the floor in the den of his house, cradling a basketball as Smith spoke, Michael Jordan just smiled shyly. Some legal and university maneuvering delayed the ground-breaking until spring of 1982, killing Jordan's chances of ever playing anywhere but Carmichael. However, it wasn't long before the Tar Heels' newest superstar had most of his fans fretting that he was too good to stay all four years, anyway.

Clearly, Jordan was not supposed to have been the final piece to Carolina's national championship team. For a while, he wondered whether he should even be going to a Division I school. Jordan's old junior high principal wanted him to consider the Air Force Academy so he would have a decent job waiting after college. For sure, Smith never suspected what was in store. "Eddie (Fogler) was the only member of our staff who thought he might be as good as he turned out in college," Smith said. "Of course, no one could have predicted what he has gone on to do in pro basketball."

A classic late-bloomer, Jordan had been cut from the Laney High School team as a sophomore and nearly gave up the game for good. His mother, Deloris, told him, "You can either go back and prove them wrong or move on to something else." Jordan carried a ball with him everywhere he went that summer and returned to school twice the player. He won a starting position as a junior at Laney. Bill Guthridge had first seen him that season and thought he had outstanding athletic ability and a bright future – good enough to encourage Jordan to enroll at Smith's summer camp in 1980. On the first afternoon, during a pick-up game in Carmichael, Jordan drove part-time assistant coach Roy Williams out of the gym. Throwing open the door to the basketball office, Williams declared, "That's the best 6-4 player I've ever seen!" Fogler and Guthridge went out to sneak a peek for themselves. Guthridge could not believe how much Jordan had improved since the end of the high school season.

Fogler's normal camp routine was to drive around between Carmichael, Woollen, and Chapel Hill High School, checking on the drills and games at each gym. For the rest of that week, he looked up where Jordan was playing, went to that gym and stayed there, mouth agape most of the time. "How we gonna keep this quiet?" he asked himself. It was too late. Dave Odom, the coach at East Carolina University (later at Wake Forest), had watched about ten of Jordan's games and called him one of the best high school players he had ever seen. Odom also worked as the director of Howard Garfinkel's Five-Star Camp in Pittsburgh and told "Garf" he needed to see this kid.

After his second week at the UNC camp, Jordan told the Carolina coaches that he was going to Five-Star. "You don't have to do that," responded Fogler, only half-kidding because he knew what would happen once the rest of college basketball discovered what the Tar Heels already knew. Jordan wound up the only player in Five-Star history to win five individual awards in one week. With Carolina's cover blown, Smith swung into action by scheduling that fall recruiting visit to the Jordan home and spending most of the time talking academics. James and Deloris Jordan were most interested in their son getting a college degree.

That autumn, Jordan took his official recruiting visit to Chapel Hill, also visited N.C. State, and during a trip to the University of South Carolina ate dinner at the Governor's Mansion in Columbia. Dozens of other schools were trying to get Jordan's ear, but it was too late. The kid who had grown up a David Thompson fan rooting against Carolina had decided to become a Tar Heel. Funny, few schools dared to continue recruiting Jordan, who led Laney into the state playoffs as a senior and then, in the spring, turned down an invitation to play in the

Albert Schweitzer Games in Germany so he could graduate with honors. He had no idea how different his life would be one year later.

✪

Smith looked awful the morning after the 1981 national championship loss to Indiana in Philadelphia. Having had a late dinner, and presumably and understandably several scotches, he joined the team in the lobby of the St. David's Inn for the return trip to Chapel Hill. The Tar Heels, No. 2 in the country, were equally long-faced boarding the bus to the airport. Forty-eight hours earlier, Carolina fans had woken up from celebrating one of their most dynamic victories. Behind Wood's astonishing thirty-nine points, their team had rudely ousted Virginia and Sampson from the Final Four. It had been a bitter defeat for the Cavaliers, who had twice rallied to beat the Heels during the regular season.

His Democratic leaning aside, Smith felt terrible the Monday of the championship game after finding out that President Ronald Reagan had been shot during an apparent assassination attempt in Washington. Never having considered basketball anything more than sport, Smith was ambivalent about the title game being played that night. When personal matters arose, he was much less a coach and far more a father to his players. He would let them go home to a sick parent and miss practice. Smith gave them books to read to help with their studies. In this case, he wanted them to understand the importance of their president being shot and, whether or not the game was played, planned to have the team say a prayer for Reagan.

About three o'clock that afternoon, with Reagan out of danger, NBC and the NCAA decided to go on with the championship game. After building an early lead against Bob Knight's Hoosiers, the Tar Heels began to fade as halftime approached. And when Worthy, who had recovered courageously from his broken ankle, went to the bench early in the second half with his fourth foul, it was all but over. Only after the 63-50 loss did Worthy and his teammates begin to realize how hard they had worked, how close they had come. They pledged at a breakfast meeting the next morning to get back to the Final Four and win it all in 1982. Everyone would return the following season except for Wood and guard Mike Pepper, a part-time starter.

Michael Jordan never figured he would be the guy to replace Wood in the lineup. Upon arriving at Carolina, he was just hoping to fit in somewhere. Smith reinforced Jordan's status as just another freshman when he refused to let him pose with the four incumbent starters for the cover of *Sports Illustrated*, which had picked Carolina No. 1. "You haven't proven anything yet like the others," Smith told him.

Also early in that first year, Smith called Jordan into his office one day before practice began. "What would you like to be called?" Smith asked him. Having heard that Jordan had picked up the nickname "Magic," Smith observed that that one had already been taken by Earvin Johnson. "Wouldn't you prefer to make a new name for yourself?" he asked.

The lesson stayed with Jordan. Although it was too late for the 1982 UNC media guide, which listed him as "Mike," Jordan decided to be called simply Michael. The new name also stayed with him.

Jordan missed two weeks of preseason practice with a sprained ankle, but Smith still listed him on the blackboard with the starters before the opener against Kansas in Charlotte. Much to his own surprise, Jordan began to blossom. He scored in double figures his first six college games and twenty-nine of Carolina's thirty-four on the season, attempting the most field goals on the team and hitting 53 percent from the floor. He answered a mild shooting slump at mid-season by staying after practice and taking eighty-two extra shots every day for a week. Guthridge suggested it to Jordan, telling him that Walter Davis had shaken a similar slump in 1977 by taking seventy-seven extra shots after practice. By the end of the season, Jordan had improved so dramatically in every aspect of his game that Smith considered him his best offensive rebounder and the number-one option when a zone defense denied Worthy and Perkins the ball. Without him, the Tar Heels would never have survived the ACC Tournament in Greensboro.

With Virginia packing under the basket in the nationally televised final, Jordan nailed four jumpers that kept Carolina alive in a game that seemed to be slipping away. The Cavaliers, who had won the last meeting by sixteen points in Charlottesville, hit six of their first eight field goal attempts of the second half to lead by three and stake their claim to the ACC title. Worthy and Perkins could not get free inside the zone, so Smith called on his freshman to take the biggest shots of his basketball career. Jordan hit a jumper from the deep corner to cut Virginia's lead to a point, 39-38. After the Cavaliers' first miss of the second half, Jordan hit again from right of the key to give Carolina the lead, 40-39.

When Virginia turned the ball over, Smith saw his chance to gain control of the game. He usually consulted with his assistant coaches before spreading the court, but this time he jumped off the bench and held up four fingers, ordering the famous stall for which he would be roundly criticized in the days, weeks, and months ahead. After the Heels held the ball for three minutes and inched Virginia away from the basket, Jordan popped free for a jumper at the top of the key. The Cavs scored, Smith called the same play, and Jordan hit almost the identical shot. It maintained Carolina's three-point lead and, eventually, delivered the ACC title by the controversial 47-45 score. Despite the furor that followed, Smith knew exactly what he was doing. Freshman Jordan had scored the last four field goals of the game for his top-ranked team, allowing the Tar Heels to counter Virginia's refusal to come out of the zone. By taking the gamble to stall that ultimately resulted in a shot clock for college basketball, Smith preserved his program's best chance for a national championship.

The East Region was to be played in Charlotte and Raleigh, and as of 1982 no team forced to play outside its natural region had gone on to win the NCAA Tournament. With enormous pressure building on the Tar Heels, perhaps they couldn't have survived the 52-50 scare to James Madison if the game were not in Charlotte. Then, with the players sleeping in their own beds and going to classes like regular students, they commuted to Raleigh, put all five starters in double figures for both regional victories over Alabama and Villanova and won the hard-fought trip back to the Final Four. The ticket to New Orleans ultimately vindicated Smith's strategy; Virginia meanwhile got knocked out of the Southeast Regional by an Alabama-Birmingham team playing on its home court.

Carolina came close to not reaching the championship game against Georgetown. After holding a double-digit lead on Houston in Saturday's semifinal, the Heels had to stave off a Cougar rally sparked by Clyde Drexler. Finally, Worthy's driving dunk late in the second half cemented a return to the Monday night title game.

Of all that has been written and recited about that epic against

John Thompson's Hoyas – Worthy's determination and dominating performance, Jordan's winning shot – the key was Smith's ability to lift the pressure of finally "winning the big one" for him from his players' shoulders.

"I could feel it all the way down the bench," Fogler recalled. "But I honestly don't think he did. He was as loose before and during the game as I ever remembered him. To the rest of us, if we had lost, suicide would have been an option."

As those tense final seconds wound down, players, assistant coaches, the trainer, and managers marveled at the head coach's composure in what should have been a personally maddening moment. It was much to the contrary. When his team looked bewildered after having lost the lead, Smith called time-out with thirty-two seconds remaining and, according to those who were inside that huddle and many others before and since, was never better at any point in his career. He knew what Georgetown would do, he knew who would be open for the shot, and he gave him the confidence to take it.

"Knock it in, Michael," Smith said as the huddle broke.

Jordan later admitted closing his eyes as the biggest basket of Dean Smith's career left his hands, perhaps symbolizing the blind confidence his coach had put in him before the season and the dream he had the night before of taking the winning shot. As it spun perfectly toward the rim, the hearts of Tar Heels everywhere from New Orleans to New Zealand pounded. Would it be, could it be, the night the national title finally came their way?

When the ball fell through the net, and Georgetown then threw it away at the other end, Smith compassionately hugged his old pal Thompson and then searched out each of his players to say thank you, hugged well-wishers in an atypical display of emotion, and then went searching for his family.

The long and painstaking building of a champion had been completed.

On April 17, 1982, with Smith donning a hard hat and holding a shovel during ground-breaking ceremonies in Chapel Hill, the building of a champion began.

Raleigh News and Observer

Frank McGuire (center), with assistant coach Dean Smith (right), in 1959.

Hugh Morton

Dean's father, Alfred Smith.

BOWERS B.
BROWN L.
BROWN B.
BURNS C.
CALLAHAN P.
CUNNINGHAM B.
COOKE M.
KATZ A.
GALANTAI B.
KRAUSE D.
SWEENEY B.
POTEET Y.
RESPRESS R.
RONNER T.
SHAFFER C.
TAYLOR B.
VINROOT R.

The Dean's list: Smith's first roster, 1962.

Rich Clarkson

(left to right) John Lotz, Smith, Larry Brown, and Bob Lewis
at Smith's first appearance in the Final Four, 1967.

Charlie Cooper / Durham Morning Herald

Smith with 1968's returning starters: Larry Miller, Bill Bunting, Rusty Clark, and Dick Grubar.

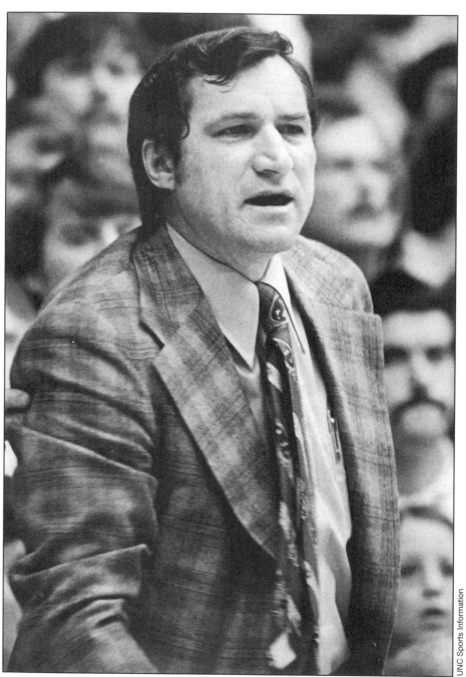

Smith adopts the blow-dry look, early 1970s.

(left to right) Bill Guthridge, Smith, John Thompson, and Tom LaGarde at the 1976 Olympics in Montreal.

Rich Clarkson

Golf cronies: (left to right) Dr. Chris Fordham, Dr. Earl Somers, Bill Guthridge,
Doug Moe, Simon Terrell, Larry Brown, and Smith.

Smith interviewed by Billy Packer.

Smith, irate at Stanford coach Dick DiBiaso in the 1977 Rainbow Classic.

UNC Sports Information

Hugh Morton

Smith congratulated by Frank McGuire after UNC's NCAA championship in 1982 – exactly twenty-five years after "McGuire's Miracle."

Bob Donnan

James Worthy and Michael Jordan at 1982 victory celebration back at Chapel Hill.

Bob Donnan

Jordan outrebounds Virginia's Ralph Sampson, as Sam Perkins (41) maneuvers underneath.

Bob Donnan

Jordan nearing the end of his college career — with Guthridge, Smith, and Eddie Fogler.

Robert Crawford

Jordan announces that he'll turn pro, May 1984.

Smith teaching: (left to right) Bill Guthridge, Dave Hanners, Dick Harp, Eddie Fogler, Phil Ford, John Kuester, Roy Williams, and Randy Wiel.

Bob Donnan

Smith coaching: practice starting in 1982.

Hugh Morton

Smith with Dick Vitale.

Hugh Morton

Robert Crawford

Smith clinching his thirteenth and final ACC championship, as Ademola Okulaja (13) shouts encouragement.

Smith ties Adolph Rupp's record, versus Fairfield, March 13, 1997.

Jim Hawkins

Smith instructs Phil Ford. Will he eventually head the program?

Smith doing CBS commentary, with Greg Gumbel and Clark Kellogg.

With Jordan in attendance, Smith receives the prestigious "University Award."

RECRUITING STORIES PART 2

On Sunday, March 20, 1983, while driving to Raleigh-Durham Airport for a flight to New York City, Dean Smith discussed strategy with two of his assistant coaches. The day before, the Tar Heels had clobbered James Madison in the Greensboro Coliseum to open defense of their 1982 NCAA Tournament championship, but no one was celebrating. This particular skull session did not include Xs and Os, although it had a lot to do with ACC rival Virginia. Smith, Bill Guthridge, and Eddie Fogler were on their way to a recruiting visit at the home of Kenny Smith, who had been pursued by Virginia for months before Carolina ever got involved with the high school All-American guard from Queens. How to make up the lost ground? How to offset the influence of Virginia assistant coach Jim Larranaga, an alumnus of Kenny Smith's high school, Archbishop Molloy, and close friend of Molloy coach Jack Curran? And who else, after the late start, could help convince Smith that Carolina was the best choice for him?

"Maybe Ernie Lorch," Fogler suggested. Old-timer Lorch coached Smith's AAU Riverside Church team that was annually among the best in the New York summer leagues. The Carolina coaches had known the cagey Lorch for years but were not sure whether he could boost Carolina's cause or not.

"Why don't you asked Kenny when we get there?" Smith told Fogler.

Kenny Smith had already visited Chapel Hill, but with Virginia still the clear leader the Tar Heels were scrambling. Since Jim Braddock was graduating and Buzz Peterson had torn up his knee early in the season, Carolina's point guard plans were up in the air. Two hours later, they were in the middle-class home of William and Ann Smith when Fogler asked his preplanned question. "What about Ernie Lorch, should we contact him?" Fogler asked Kenny Smith.

"No, I don't think so," Smith said, smiling.

"By the way, where did Coach Lorch go to school?" Fogler continued, ad-libbing.

"I don't know where he went as an undergraduate," Smith answered, smiling again, "but he went to Virginia law school."

Fogler fell out of his chair onto the living room carpet and feigned a heart attack, as the group broke up in laughter. Carolina's strategy had backfired, but from that point on the ice was broken and the UNC coaches left New York feeling better about their chances.

Still, they were worried about the upcoming McDonald's Game the following April in Atlanta, where Ralph Sampson was to receive his second straight Wooden Award as the nation's top collegiate player. By then the college basketball season would be over, with either Carolina or Virginia undoubtedly having made big headlines in the NCAA Tournament. The two teams had tied for first place in the ACC regular season and seemed to be on another collision course in post-season play. The Tar Heels were favored to reach their third straight Final Four, while the Cavaliers, with Sampson playing his last year, were the odds-on pick to win the national championship.

Turns out neither happened. Carolina got knocked out of the East Regional by Georgia, and in an even more unlikely occurrence Virginia lost for the second time in two weeks to Cinderella N.C. State in the West Regional. By the time the McDonald's Game rolled around, Dean Smith had convinced Kenny Smith to wear light blue. Virginia, now facing the post-Sampson era with a depleted team, was bitterly disappointed and angered by what they regarded as Kenny Smith's defection. Nicknamed "Jet" for his blazing speed, Smith had essentially been stolen by the Tar Heels in the last few months of recruiting.

Larranaga took it personally, unwittingly insulting the young man by telling a New York newspaper that he had made a mistake by choosing Carolina. Head coach Terry Holland, far more diplomatic, simply said, "I'm not sure they know exactly what they have." Virginia knew and would have a constant reminder over the next four years, when Kenny Smith and Carolina faced the Cavaliers nine times, winning eight.

Dean Smith dominated the 1980s in recruiting and on the court, heightening the irony that while winning more games than any other college basketball coach (UNC finished ranked in the top ten for nine straight years) his teams would not get back to another Final Four until 1991.

The Tar Heels appeared weekly on national television and continued to supply a steady stream of players into the NBA. Twice, in 1984 and 1987, Carolina went through the ACC regular season with unblemished 14-0 records, remarkable for a school that seemed to be everyone's archenemy. However, after Worthy, Jordan, and Perkins departed, the power players were replaced by superstar-less lineups of leading scorers and solid supporters. They came from different states and divergent backgrounds, and the first of what would become a constant complement of foreigners joined the Tar Heels.

✪

Before Roy Williams had left Owen High School in Swannanoa, North Carolina, to join Smith's staff in 1977, he had coached a pudgy eleven-year-old named Brad Daugherty at his summer camp. On a subsequent visit home to see his mother, Williams learned that Daugherty had given up basketball for baseball and fishing. Williams went back to the mountains in the summer of 1980 and couldn't believe what he saw. The former fatty had grown to 6-8 and taken up basketball again. While he still needed to lose weight, Daugherty was dominating local pick-up games, some with small-college players. Because he had started school early, Daugherty was still only fourteen and entering the eleventh grade.

After learning that the young giant wanted to play college basketball, Williams laid down three options for him. Being blessed with size and talent, Daugherty could work as hard as he could and play at any level; work a little and play for a small college; or not work at all and maybe still get an offer somewhere. Williams then went back to tell his boss what he had seen. Smith sent Fogler up for a second opinion and after getting the same report scheduled an official visit the next fall without ever having seen Daugherty play basketball. After watching Daugherty shoot around the gym, Smith was amazed at the skill and dexterity of someone his size. Believing that Smith's teaching skills could improve his game more than any other coach, Daugherty turned down scholarship offers from Clemson and Maryland to sign with the Tar Heels. He watched them win the national championship on television the following March, and eight months later he was forced into their starting lineup as a 6-10, sixteen-year-old freshman because Worthy had turned pro following his junior year.

❂

On Daugherty's official visit to Chapel Hill, he had sat on the front row with future Tar Heel teammate Steve Hale during Carolina's dramatic comeback win over Virginia in Carmichael Auditorium. From Jenks, Oklahoma, and a virtual unknown, Hale was a gifted student and hard-nosed competitor – Smith's kind of basketball player. The son of a coach at Oral Roberts in Tulsa, Hale also relished the challenge of trying to play at Carolina when few people except Smith thought the herky-jerky lefty had a chance. "I had no idea how good I was," recalled Hale, who joined the freshman class with Daugherty and the highly recruited Curtis Hunter of Durham. "I came in with no goals because I didn't know whether they would be too high or too low."

When Hale played and shot poorly as a freshman in 1983, Smith called him into the office, shut the door, and challenged him to apply the same hard work to basketball as he did to his pre-med studies. Hale spent hours in the gym and by his junior year had turned into Carolina's best all-around player, setting the single-season school record for free-throw accuracy. He twice had nine assists in a game and once had thirteen, at the time second only to Phil Ford's fourteen.

❂

Warren Martin, who had entered UNC a year before Daugherty, Hunter, and Hale, was so awkward as a 6-10 ninth-grader that kids in school humiliated him with cruel jokes. "They laughed at him so much it hurt," recalled his high school coach, Howard West, at Tunstall, Virginia. When West first met him, Martin was a clumsy fifteen-year-old who didn't even know the rules of basketball at the time. Told that he would have to work harder than other kids, and that it would be easier to quit, Martin took the tougher road. Practicing privately with West year-round, Martin made the varsity as a junior and averaged eleven points and eight rebounds.

At Dean Smith's annual high school coaching clinic in October of 1980, West mentioned he had a seven-foot rising senior that Carolina might want to look at. Guthridge and Fogler went to see Martin the next month and knew their report would interest Smith. While many other coaches had already passed on the gawky Martin, the UNC assistants liked his effort and attitude and, especially, his soft hands. "If big guys can catch and shoot, we can teach them everything else," Smith has said through the years. Early in Martin's senior year, when he averaged twenty points a game, most of the college coaches who came calling were from East Carolina, Richmond, James Madison and Jacksonville. When the UNC staff started showing up, Virginia, Virginia Tech, and Villanova weren't far behind.

"I think Coach Smith can teach me more about basketball. He can pick up where Coach West left off," Martin said upon announcing his decision. His schoolmates continued to snicker. After Martin had played on a national championship team in 1982 and four years later scored the first Carolina basket in the brand-new Deandome, even Coach West shook his head. "That he's even playing in the ACC is just amazing, when you consider how far he's come," he said. "It's just mind-boggling."

❂

In the early 1970s, a brash, two-sport star at Durham Hillside High School had made constant headlines in basketball and tennis. John Lucas had not only been a celebrated athlete, he was the son of respected educators in the community, John Lucas Sr., the principal at Hillside, and Blondola Lucas, a middle school guidance counselor.

Though Lucas had been attracting college basketball recruiters since his junior year in high school, two things about him troubled Dean

Smith. First, he had an unconventional, mostly left-handed, game with a one-arm push shot instead of a jumper. After watching him play and sending his assistants back several times, Smith was not convinced Lucas could make the jump to ACC basketball. And second, if Smith did take the chance, he wondered how much pressure would come from the influential black community in Durham for Lucas to play at Carolina. If he took Lucas and then did not play him, it might hurt UNC's chances with other black athletes in the future.

Of course, Smith had underrated the competitive Lucas, who went to Maryland and started all four years for Lefty Driesell. Never wanting to doubt Lucas in public, or his own ability to evaluate players, Smith only later confided that had he known Lucas was going to be that good, he surely would have gone after him more aggressively.

Nearly fifteen years passed before Smith was faced with a similar dilemma, this one involving a player from Chapel Hill High School. Ranzino Smith, whose father had named him after former N.C. State star Sammy Ranzino, had been something of a local hero since averaging thirty points a game in junior high school. When he moved up to tenth and eleventh grade, Smith did not slow down. Though only six feet tall and a chunky 190 pounds, Ranzino continued to put up big numbers and hang around the UNC campus whenever he could. His dream was to play for the Tar Heels.

Dean Smith knew about his young namesake. In fact, during one session of his summer camp in 1983, the Carolina coach called Ranzino out from the crowd during a free-throw-shooting clinic. Asked to demonstrate the proper form, Ranzino made ten straight foul shots while the coach he idolized spoke. Later that summer, Dean Smith held a meeting in his office with Ranzino and his parents. Dozens of recruiters had watched the young Smith lead Chapel Hill into the state championship game for two straight years, and their schools were set to offer him scholarships. Chapel Hill coach Ken Miller had told them all, "Carolina's his first choice." Dean Smith also offered Ranzino a scholarship that day – with one caveat. He wanted the Smith family to understand how hard he thought it would be for a six-foot shooting guard to play a lot of minutes in the ACC.

"He's a great young man from an outstanding family," Smith said, "and I wanted him to understand that if playing time was the most important thing for Ranzino and his family then he should probably go somewhere else."

In fact, Smith said he would keep the scholarship offer open while Ranzino visited some other campuses. But Ranzino and his parents said they didn't want to waste any other school's time and money. They were going to take their chances with the Tar Heels. Smith played in all but four games as a freshman and went on to have some key performances for Carolina. Subbing for the injured Hale in the 1985 NCAA Tournament, his two free throws sealed the Sweet Sixteen win over Auburn. As a senior, he scored twenty-seven points in Carolina's stunning 123-97 upset of Loyola Marymount in the 1988 West Regional.

✪

The best high school shooter ever recruited by Carolina came from Carlisle, Pennsylvania, and rivaled Jim Thorpe as that town's greatest sports hero. "Every single time he shoots, no matter from where, I think it's going in," Fogler said of Jeff Lebo in the winter of 1985. Since first being discovered as a ninth-grader, Lebo had received hundreds of recruiting letters. But the first one had come from Dean Smith, and Lebo spent the next three years not only preparing to go to Carolina but getting ready to play there. Lebo was always small, and even after he had grown to six feet some people questioned if he could compete in the ACC.

"Dean Smith was like a God where I came from," Lebo recalled in 1995. "The first time he came to one of my games, the whole gym hushed. It was like Jesus Christ walked in. I was embarrassed for him, and I never wanted to let him down from that point on." Though he didn't commit to UNC until he had made all of his recruiting visits, Lebo said there was never a doubt. He spent his entire senior year in high school making sure that, when he got to Carolina, he didn't embarrass himself.

"I remember, after I signed, working out late at night and saying to myself, 'I wonder if Kenny Smith is doing this. I don't think Steve Hale is doing this. I know those guys aren't out there running at this time.' When I worked out in the gym, I always stayed an extra fifteen minutes. It helped me overcome the fear that I couldn't play at that level."

Smith certainly thought Lebo could play for the Tar Heels, but he doubted that he would improve a great deal during his college career. The son of a coach, Lebo knew how to play basketball as well as any Carolina recruit, and he earned a starting position as a freshman. But Smith figured that as other players around the conference and country caught up, those with more speed and size might pass him by. Lebo had a solid college career but proved his coach prophetic by averaging more points and shooting for a better percentage as a sophomore than in his last two seasons. However, also as Smith predicted, Lebo continued to excel in the fundamentals. As a junior, the only year he made All-ACC, Lebo set the UNC record for assists in one game (seventeen) and the single-season record for free-throw percentage until Shammond Williams broke it in 1998.

✪

When Danny Ferry, another high school All-American who had grown up dreaming of playing for Carolina, went to Duke after Smith could not promise him a starting position, Lebo was left with two less-heralded freshmen classmates who had similarly interesting careers. In making the earliest verbal commitment ever to UNC, Kevin Madden was keeping a promise he had made to his ailing mother after his sophomore year in high school. Before she died, Helen Madden had asked her son to play for the Tar Heels. Kevin had grown up watching them on TV with his mom, who was also his best friend. Steve Bucknall had never heard of Carolina or Dean Smith when he arrived from London to attend Governor Dummer Academy in Massachusetts. And Bill Guthridge was scouting another high school player in the winter of 1985 when he noticed how hard Bucknall played, especially going for rebounds. Carolina forgot about the other guy and wound up offering Bucknall a scholarship.

Unlike Lebo, Madden and Bucknall came on strongest at the end of their careers. They both made second-team All-ACC in 1989, when they combined with Lebo and J. R. Reid to lead the Tar Heels to their first ACC Championship in seven years. Once only a bit player, Bucknall scored thirty points in a late-season win over Clemson and then made the critical three-point play that decided the tournament title game against Ferry and Duke.

✪

Those close to the Carolina basketball program insisted that Dean Smith had "backed off" recruiting Ferry in order to successfully land Reid the following year. Though Ferry went on to win ACC Player of the Year twice, Smith had apparently questioned his quickness and could not promise him a great deal of playing time as a freshman. Duke coach Mike Krzyzewski took advantage of Smith's ambivalence, telling Ferry, "We want you more than they do. There's a position for you here."

With Joe Wolf and Dave Popson having two seasons left with the Tar Heels, Smith faced a recurring dilemma, one that often cost Carolina in the short run while upholding Smith's long-time principle of not "recruiting over" players already in school. Unless a freshman was considerably better than a returning player, he had to wait his turn. Brad Daugherty would graduate after the 1986 season, leaving a frontcourt position open the following season. Furthermore, besides chasing Reid for the better part of five years, Smith also had his eye on a 6-10 center from suburban Los Angeles named Scott Williams. He figured to get one, if not both, and chose not to match Krzyzewski's recruiting intensity over Ferry.

A highly publicized player since before his sophomore year at Kempsville High School in Virginia Beach, Reid's first varsity game had been watched by coaches from five major colleges. The Tar Heels had known about him since he had attended Smith's summer camp after his seventh-, eighth-, and ninth-grade years. Besides, Herman and Jean Reid were both graduates of St. Augustine's College in Raleigh and long-time Carolina fans.

Despite Iowa and UCLA remaining on Reid's recruiting list, the three finalists were clearly Carolina, Virginia, and Maryland. The Cavaliers and Terrapins also believed they had unique advantages to match the Tar Heels' winning tradition and the communications curriculum Reid sought. As the home-state school, Virginia boasted the successful career of another native, Ralph Sampson, who had gone to a Final Four and won three national player of the year awards. Still smarting from the loss of Kenny Smith, one Cavalier assistant coach (not Larranaga) promised that Reid was "one player Carolina would not outrecruit us for, I guarantee it." Maryland's Driesell hailed from Norfolk and was so well connected in the Tidewater Area that he believed he had the inside track. As it turned out, Driesell resigned at Maryland before Reid's freshman year.

Reid decided he would not pick a school until the following spring and did not even take all of his official visits in the fall. He did go to Chapel Hill November 9 for the Carolina-Clemson football game and sat on the bench at the basketball Blue-White game. Rumors persisted throughout his senior season that it was down to UNC and Virginia. The surprise announcement came, off the cuff, after Kempsville's first-round state playoff game the following March. Indeed, it had boiled down to Carolina's winning tradition, its communications department, and Williams's commitment to the Tar Heels the previous November. "I'll be able to play power forward, which is where I want to play," Reid said.

Smith and his program were now at the apex, the undisputed Rolls Royce of college basketball, with rival coaches and recruiting gurus alike saying the Tar Heels simply selected those high school players they wanted. Of course, this was before Duke began its run of Final Fours and Ferry turned out to be a better college player than Reid.

Starring as a freshman for the team that went unbeaten in the ACC and 32-4 overall, Reid's reputation might have been responsible for UNC's stunning loss to Syracuse in the NCAA East Regional championship game at the Meadowlands. In the regional semifinal, Reid had scored thirty-one points on 15-of-18 shooting against Notre Dame, and the New York press went wild. The *New York Post* carried a huge sports-front photo of Reid and a long feature story. Syracuse, maligned for its NCAA losses under coach Jim Boeheim, used the article as motivation. Boeheim's assistants made sure all the players saw the *Post* feature, and some brought it with them to the Meadowlands. Syracuse jumped out 8-0 and never trailed in the game, winning 79-75 after Kenny Smith's three-pointer for a tie missed from the corner and Syracuse hit a free throw with one second left.

Dean Smith had had a little too much faith in one of his prime recruits that day. After Lebo had spent the prior twenty-four hours in bed with the flu but insisted he could play, Smith acquiesced and left Lebo in the game for twenty-eight minutes. The team's leading three-point shooter went 0-5 from the arc and was generally out of it. Smith forever regretted that he had not sat Lebo and given more time to Ranzino Smith, who had shot 4-5 and scored eleven points in seventeen minutes. But the real key was how Syracuse center Ronnie Seikaly had his way with Reid inside, scoring twenty-six points and grabbing eleven rebounds while his usually inconsistent teammate Derrick Coleman took down fourteen rebounds. Reid played well, with fifteen points and six rebounds, but had listened to Seikaly and Coleman yap at him the entire game about being the "super freshman."

✪

Rick Fox, a handsome Bahamian, had taken up basketball late and defied all odds by playing two years at an Indiana high school and then winning a scholarship to Carolina. When he arrived in the United States from Nassau, almost the only thing he knew about American college basketball was what he had seen on a large-screen TV in the lobby of a resort hotel. He and some teenage friends had crossed the bridge to Paradise Island on the night of March 29, 1982. Bouncing from one hotel to the next, Fox stopped to watch the basketball game showing on the big tube. He saw No. 52 (James Worthy) make a breakaway dunk on Georgetown. He watched No. 23 (Michael Jordan) sink a jumper from the corner with only seconds remaining. He was mesmerized by the victory celebration.

A few months later, the fifteen-year-old Fox played his first refereed game when an Indiana church ministry arrived in Nassau to conduct several basketball clinics. He got hooked on the sport and convinced his parents to let him attend the church's camp that summer back in Indiana. After returning home, Fox then begged his parents to let him transfer schools and play high school ball in America. In the summer of 1985, after his parents had conceded and Fox had played his sophomore year at Warsaw (Indiana) High School, his coaches took him to the Five-Star prep camp in Pittsburgh. Dean Smith sat down in a folding chair at courtside, ready to scout Reid and Lloyd Daniels, the two most heralded high school players in the camp all-star game. About five minutes into the game, Smith began squinting at the typewritten lineup sheet. He had forgotten his reading glasses and had to ask the coach sitting next to him the name of the kid out there hounding Daniels into turnovers.

"That's our player, Rick Fox, from Warsaw," said Pete Smith, one of Fox's coaches.

Less than a year earlier, Fox had humored Pete Smith and Warsaw head coach Al Rhodes by stating his goal to play for North Carolina. They had waited for Fox to walk away before rolling their eyes at each other. Now, the head coach at North Carolina was asking them about the naïve youngster who had made them laugh. And sure enough, impressed by Fox's hustle and savvy, Smith began recruiting him. By the time Fox's junior year was over, Indiana, Purdue, and Georgia Tech were among the schools offering him scholarships. Rhodes had worked overtime with Fox, but remained flabbergasted by the youngster's improvement and natural ability.

"He had the tremendous ability to learn in two or three weeks what might have taken other players several months," Rhodes said, struggling for an explanation. "Across the U.S. and the world, there are lots of concert pianists who have never played the piano. Rick Fox was a basketball player who just had to start playing basketball."

✪

The route Hubert Davis took to major college basketball was paved by a long-term family relationship. Davis's uncle Walter had been a Tar Heel hero of the 1970s and one of Dean Smith's personal favorites. Before enrolling at Carolina, Charlotte native Walter Davis had attended a year of prep school in Delaware. Homesick for the South, Walter often spent weekends visiting his older brother Hubert in suburban Virginia. Bill Guthridge came to recruit Walter and also got to know Hubert, his wife Bobbie, and their three-year-old son, Hubert Jr. In a thank-you note to the Davises, Guthridge added a playful-but-prophetic footnote: "At this time we want to officially begin the recruitment of Hubert Jr."

During Walter's four years in Chapel Hill, Hubert and Hubert Jr. were frequent visitors to Carmichael Auditorium and the Tar Heel locker room. Inevitably, Hubert dreamed of following his uncle's path. Because Smith and Guthridge had known the extended Davis family so well, they were especially saddened by the death of Bobbie from cancer in 1986. Smith held a place in his program for Hubert Jr., who had grown into a fine athlete in his own right but was not considered a major Division I college basketball player. After visiting with Hubert and his father, Smith delivered much the same speech he had given to Ranzino Smith five years before. He knew Davis wasn't interested in any other school, but when he offered the scholarship offer in the spring of 1988, he worried that Davis might be sitting on the bench for all four years.

"We're happy to have him, but I told Hubert it's going to be difficult to play at this level, and he understands that," said Smith, whose infamous statement has since become a point of humor around the Carolina basketball office. After one day of practice in October of 1988, a wide-eyed Guthridge said simply, "Hubert is a lot better than we thought."

The following January, Davis got a chance to show everyone how much better. Helping fill in for the injured Lebo, freshman Hubert played eighteen minutes at Duke and scored eight crucial points in Carolina's twenty-point win over the favored Blue Devils. Three years later, he had thirty-five points on the same Cameron Indoor Stadium court to complete his improbable journey toward All-American and the NBA, proving, once again, how inexact the science of high school recruiting can be.

✪

Dean Smith's record for evaluating talent was unsurpassed in the college game, yet he misread quite a few players besides Davis. In the spring of 1977, he gave a scholarship to a skinny youngster named Mike Pepper, whom he figured would be a decent practice player and just happy to wear a Carolina uniform; Pepper wound up starting for the 1981 team that won the ACC championship and played for the NCAA title. In 1988, Smith blew a chance to take Bobby Hurley and, in the spring of 1995, told Antawn Jamison that he could use a year of prep school before enrolling at UNC. And, of course, there were some who went the other way, guys who contributed less than expected – like Popson, Hunter, Geff Crompton, and Ed Stahl. Donald Washington and Clifford Rozier, who played twenty years apart, didn't last long enough to show off their considerable talents.

Through four decades, Smith tried to recruit quietly, minimizing publicity until players made it on the college level. He wanted to lower expectations, knowing anything could happen when high school athletes moved up to major college competition and into campus classrooms, all the while juggling the pitfalls of personal life.

"James Worthy was the only high school recruit I was sure would be an outstanding college player," Smith said, "and his career was jeopardized by an injury. You never know what can take place. That's why I liked to call them all prospects."

Indeed, into the 1990s, Carolina continued to sign its share of those top prospects as Smith passed his sixtieth birthday and became a grandfather for the fifth time. His Tar Heels captured another national championship and earned four more trips to the Final Four in his last seven seasons on the bench, a record unmatched by any other college basketball coach except John Wooden. But it was that recruiting success that caused the first serious problems in his program. With many high school players seeking sudden stardom in college and an early exit to pro basketball, some were less patient with his seniority system. When two of those players bolted before their junior years, it left the Tar Heels shorthanded for one of the few times in three decades and signaled the beginning of the end for Dean Smith.

CHAPTER ELEVEN

TOUGH LOSSES

For one of the few times in his coaching career, Dean Smith was visibly shaken. With six minutes to play in the 1984 NCAA East Regional semifinal against Indiana, Carolina trailed the underdog and unheralded Hoosiers by twelve points, and Smith was far from his cool, composed self in the face of this crisis.

Opposing emotions split the capacity crowd at the Omni in Atlanta on Thursday night, March 22. One half of the arena, divided between fans from Indiana and the other schools in the regional tournament, cheered wildly for the upset in the making. For the other half, clad in Carolina blue, absolute panic had set in. The anxiety had made its way down to the Tar Heel bench, where Smith almost always stayed isolated from the crowd and focused on the game. But what was happening right in front of him had turned even the Dean of discipline so ashen that his own players were alarmed.

A decided favorite and ranked No. 1 in the country for much of the season, Carolina could not gain control of this game. Early on, the Tar Heel traps and defensive pressure had bothered Indiana's unsure ball handlers. But since midway through the first half, Bob Knight's team had regained its poise and was actually using the Carolina strategy to its advantage. Schooled by Knight for an entire week prior to the game, the Hoosiers quickly but precisely passed, and reversed, the ball before Carolina could successfully trap any of them. Every defensive double-team left an offensive player open, and Indiana found him over and over again during each agonizing possession. With the thirty-second clock not yet instituted in college basketball, Indiana held the ball for as long as needed until the right shot materialized, waiting for freshman Steve Alford or center Uwe Blab or senior forward Mike Giomi to get open and in position to shoot in rhythm. With growing confidence each trip down the court, Knight's team was hitting 65 percent of its shots.

The ultimate percentage player, Smith stuck to what had worked all season and over the past few years. Believing that superior talent and depth would win most of the time, Smith favored speeding up the game by pressuring on defense and trying to get an inferior opponent to crack. The Carolina traps were actually getting Indiana open shots, but instead of backing off and accepting a slower game, Smith told his team at each time-out to trap harder, rotate quicker.

He had also begun a policy of sitting a key player down with two personal fouls in the first half. All-American Michael Jordan had played only eight minutes before picking up his second foul, and Indiana led at halftime, 32-28. Billy Packer, broadcasting the game for CBS, continually questioned Smith's leaving of Jordan on the bench for so long. Now, Jordan was trying to make up for lost time. Dogged by Indiana's Dan Dakich all over the court, Jordan showed the immaturity of a twenty-year-old college junior. While Michael's poor performance became Dakich's claim to fame, this was a case of Jordan stopping himself rather than any one defender shutting him down.

"In his best day, Dan Dakich couldn't stop Michael Jordan," recalled Matt Doherty, a senior who played his last game for Carolina that night. "He could bump him and foul him, but it was Michael who stopped Michael. After sitting for so long in the first half, he was trying to take over the game. He was pressing so much that he was using up all his energy."

Jordan played the entire second half before fouling out with two minutes left in the game. He scored only thirteen points and had one rebound, but Carolina still managed a remarkable comeback that cut the lead to two points in the closing moments. A key play occurred when Steve Hale knocked the ball away from Alford in the backcourt and, in the scramble, fouled Alford just as the ten-second count was expiring. Smith stayed on his feet, twice walking down the bench to see who on his deep and talented team might be able to help turn the tide of what would be a monumental defeat. He put in freshman forward Joe Wolf to replace sophomore center Brad Daugherty, who was playing with two dislocated fingers. And he continued to sub in Hale for Kenny Smith, who wore a half-cast on his broken wrist from earlier in the season.

Before his freshman point guard's injury against LSU on January 29, Smith had believed his was the best team in the country – better, even, than the 1982 national championship Tar Heels. Although James Worthy had been gone for two years, they still had senior Sam Perkins, junior Jordan and sophomore Daugherty – all future NBA stars. Doherty was the same role player he had been in '82, only two years older and wiser as a senior. Off the bench came scrappy sophomore Hale, who had filled in brilliantly while Kenny Smith missed eight games, juniors Warren Martin and Buzz Peterson and freshmen Wolf and Dave Popson. They had opened the season with twenty-one straight wins and finished as the first undefeated team in the ACC in ten years.

Smith had tried to put Kenny Smith back into the lineup the last week of the regular season, disrupting a team that had barely missed a beat with Hale at the point. Smith admitted it was a gamble, but having his freshman point guard's speed was worth it. As it happened, with player Smith wearing the awkward apparatus on his left hand, Coach Smith got the opposite results he was hoping for. The Tar Heels survived double-overtime to beat Duke in the regular-season finale and finish 14-0 in conference play, but a week later they lost to the Blue Devils in the semifinals of the ACC Tournament when Smith thought they hadn't tried as hard as possible. And they had had an unusually tough time with Temple in their first NCAA game in Charlotte five days before the regional semifinals.

Now behind to an Indiana team that could not normally stay within ten points of the Tar Heels, Smith knew they were all in trouble. He was as animated as he had ever been in a game over the final, frustrating minutes, sweating from the brow while shouting instructions and using body English on almost every play as Indiana clung to the lead.

In literally the last few seconds, Smith seemed unaware that Carolina could not win. His team trailed by four points, but still he watched hopefully as the last shot flew futilely toward the basket. When the horn sounded, Smith grimaced in pain as reality set in. He shook Knight's hand but did not linger with his old friend, then ran off the court and down the hall to the locker room.

He could not hold back his own tears as he talked briefly to the players before heading for the post-game press conference. He told them they were a great basketball team and reminded them that the best team doesn't always win. He thanked them for their effort throughout the season, refusing to mention anything about the game that had just ended.

Back in 1968, he had decided to never talk to the team about a loss immediately afterward, but he would blame this one on himself for months to come. Had he sublimated the players' extraordinary individual talent too much? Having long disdained the showing up of an opponent as poor sportsmanship, Smith had been miffed at Jordan in January for "cuff dunking" the ball on a breakaway in the final seconds of a twelve-point win at Maryland. Smith had insisted the spectacular play be left out of his TV show highlights the following Sunday.

Now a season that had begun with such promise was over. After shaking each player's hand, Smith walked out to face the press. Jordan and Perkins sat stunned in the solemn locker room. Doherty cried so hard in front of TV cameras that he had hecklers on his answering machine when he returned home. The three had played their last game in a Tar Heel uniform.

"The reason it is disappointing," Smith said to the media, red-eyed and holding a handkerchief, "is because this is the third time I thought we had the best team in the country. I thought we were the best team in 1977 before we had all of the injuries, and again in 1982, when we did win (the NCAA title)."

Having lost to Georgia in the East Regional final the year before, two tremendously talented Tar Heel teams had now failed to get back to the Final Four in Jordan's last two seasons. Predictably, Smith drew heavy criticism from home and around college basketball. Making matters worse, the player Carolina looked to as its next superstar chose to go elsewhere. Danny Manning, the 6-9 forward from Greensboro who had grown up a Tar Heel fan, followed his father to Kansas, where Larry Brown had hired him as an assistant coach. Smith claimed he was not upset by what his assistant coaches and fans considered a breach of loyalty by Brown, whom Smith had helped get the Kansas job. But Eddie Fogler, who had recruited Manning, remained mad at Brown for several years, believing Smith would never have allowed Carolina to recruit Manning if he had lived in Kansas.

But, for Carolina, the worst was yet to come. In the most ironic stretch of Smith's coaching career, his teams won more games than any other in the nation, continued to dominate the ACC, ran their string of consecutive trips to the NCAA Sweet Sixteen to nine, and yet went eight straight years without reaching the Final Four. As extra salt in the wound, the newest national power, Duke, made four trips to the Final Four. Untimely injuries and illnesses, a run of bad luck, and players turning pro early all conspired to leave Dean Smith, in his fifties and in his prime, at the crossroads of his professional life.

✪

Unlike most dejected Carolina fans, Smith was happy with Jordan's decision to turn pro after his junior year. He was happy for Jordan, whom he considered ready for the next level and who became an instant millionaire. And he was happy for his 1985 team, whose high expectations had just plummeted. Smith knew what Jordan's senior year would have been like: a preseason ranking in the top five for the team, and for the returning National Player of the Year zones, double- and triple-teaming, and trick defenses. Smith sincerely believed the departure was best for Jordan and, in the long run, best for a team that would now have to rely on others to make up for the loss.

He had long ago learned that, regardless of coaching, winning depended on who had the best players and how well those players performed. Thus, Smith maintained an even tougher standard for his own superstars. Perkins, for example, notorious for not liking practice, had spent more than one afternoon in Carmichael Auditorium, running the arena steps wearing a weighted vest. That's why Smith liked his 1985 team so much – not a superstar in the bunch. Certainly, Brad Daugherty and Kenny Smith were on the way, but neither was focusing yet on a pro basketball career. Martin, a seven-foot junior, was a project playing his fourth year in the program. And sophomore forwards Wolf and Popson were ready to live up to their recruiting raves.

But, unquestionably, Smith's favorite competitor on the team was Hale, whose heart and hustle far surpassed his talent. Through hard work, Hale had made himself into an outstanding all-around player. After filling in for Kenny Smith the year before at point guard, he was taking over the position that Jordan would have played as a senior. Carolina had already compiled a surprising 22-7 record, when Hale personally preserved one of Smith's most unfathomable streaks, coaching teams to either first place or second place in the ACC for nineteen straight years. During that span, each of the other eight schools in the league (except South Carolina, which withdrew after the 1971 season) had finished last at least once.

The Tar Heels traveled to Duke on the final day of the 1985 regular season needing a win to clinch at least second place, which in itself, according to Smith and Daugherty, was amazing. Using Jordan's early exit to lower expectations, Smith had continually motivated his players by reminding them – so claimed Daugherty – that they had been picked to finish last in the ACC. Actually the team had been picked to finish fourth, but the exaggeration was typical of Smith, who for years had been ridiculed by the press, as well as by rival fans and coaches, for finding a reason to proclaim his team an underdog. His favorite ploy was using "common scores" of games played against the same opponents. For example, Carolina had needed overtime to beat Maryland by one, while Duke had beaten the Terps by twenty.

Smith needed no such stretch this time. Duke had blown out the Tar Heels a month earlier, winning for the first time in Chapel Hill since 1966. Hoping for the best but predicting the worst, Smith faced the rematch before a wild Cameron Indoor Stadium crowd bidding farewell to senior Dan Meagher, a regular target of the UNC coach's cryptic comments about dirty play. On the other hand, by now one the many hallmarks of Smith's career had become winning on the road. Upon his retirement, Carolina had won more than 60 percent of its ACC away games over the prior thirty years. Key to that was Smith's insistence that his teams play with poise early in the game and build confidence by frustrating the home fans.

Though he rarely got caught comparing wins, Smith occasionally admitted that "beating Duke at Duke" ranked among his most favorite moments. He often talked to his players about shutting up the home crowd and walking off the court in a silenced gym. In thirty-six years, his Tar Heels won 145 ACC road games. So it was no real shock that Carolina led by seven at the half and went on to beat Duke by ten. Daugherty had twenty-three points and twelve rebounds, but Hale was Mr. Clutch over the last four minutes to secure the victory. His driving, three-point play with the Duke crowd roaring and on its feet put the game away; the Heels wound up with a tie for first in the ACC and high hopes for the post-season.

The team reached the ACC championship game against Georgia Tech and was favored to win the title even though the 1985 tournament was played at the Omni in Atlanta. Admittedly, the rationale of the odds-makers was quirky: Tech had already taken both regular-season games from UNC and a dependable old adage maintained that it was hard to beat a good team three times in the same year. Carolina outshot and out-rebounded the Jackets but committed twenty-one turnovers to Tech's eight and lost again, 57-54. Smith warmly congratulated a bawling Bobby Cremins, whose team had been so bad just four years earlier that former player Lee Goza once forgot which end of the court he was shooting at and had scored a basket for the Tar Heels. Smith could afford to be cordial, since the Heels' success in the ACC regular season assured them of an at-large bid to the NCAA Tournament.

Hale, by now the team's inspirational leader, suffered a separated shoulder that cost Carolina a chance to reach the 1985 Final Four. Late in the first-round game at South Bend, Indiana, Middle Tennessee State's Kerry Hammonds clobbered Hale from behind on a breakaway layup – a flagrant foul that, according to Smith, should have resulted in Hammonds's ejection. The Tar Heels won that game, plus two more to reach the Elite Eight, but they couldn't contain Villanova's guards, John Jensen and Gary McLain, in the regional final. They squandered an eight-point lead at the end of the first half and lost to the Cinderella team that went on to stun Georgetown for the national championship a week later.

The combination of Kenny Smith's broken wrist on a similar break-away the year before, and now Hale's mid-flight injury, put Smith on the warpath with the NCAA officiating committee. He campaigned for assessing a flagrant technical foul to a player who, while chasing a play, initiated contact with an airborne opponent, and that rule eventually got passed.

The following season, Carolina won its first twenty-one games for the second time in three years and stood 25-1 when Hale suffered another serious injury that again killed his team's hope in the NCAA Tournament. This time, late in the Heels' first loss at the brand-new Dean Smith Center, Hale took a knee to the chest against Maryland and missed the last three games of the regular season with a collapsed lung. He returned for the tournaments but was never the same player.

A team that had been ranked No. 1 in both polls for most of the season stumbled to five losses in its last eight games, including another to Maryland in the first round of the ACC Tournament. That loss sent once-cocky Carolina reeling out to the NCAA West Regional, where in Ogden, Utah, Smith struggled to re-instill confidence in his depleted team. The Heels managed harrowing wins over Utah and Alabama-Birmingham, but in the West Regional Sweet Sixteen game, a heavily bandaged Hale shot only 2-10 against Louisville, and UNC lost to the eventual national champion for the second straight year. Hale's otherwise brilliant career had ended with him tangled in white tape. He and Daugherty, the Class of 1986, were the first Carolina players in twenty years to not participate in a Final Four, a fact that made Smith both proud and despondent.

Smith endured another key loss after the 1986 season, when his chief recruiter Fogler took the head-coaching position at Wichita State. An outstanding judge of talent, Fogler had been in the middle of Carolina's biggest recruiting coups over the past twelve years. Roy Williams, not allowed to go out recruiting as the part-time assistant, was quickly promoted and subsequently got some unfair criticism over the next two years for losing recruits to other schools. Williams was still learning the ropes, but the big deterrent for high school players looking at UNC was the incoming class that included forwards J. R. Reid and Scott Williams, considered Carolina's front court of the future. Indeed, with a blend of upper and lower classmen, Smith's 1987 team went through the ACC unbeaten for the second time in four years, a remarkable feat, and entered the NCAA Tournament the No. 1 seed in the East and a favorite to win the national championship in New Orleans.

Two extremely difficult defeats rendered a 32-4 season a relative failure in the eyes of Carolina critics and fans alike. First came a one-point loss in the ACC Tournament championship game to N.C. State, a team that had lost twice during the regular season to Smith's juggernaut by a combined thirty-five points. The Tar Heels had barely survived a double-overtime game against Virginia in the semifinals, and Smith thought his team would be fired up for the final.

That assumption underscored a common knock on Smith, who considered self-motivation as important as any words he could utter in the locker room. While a couple of players chose to stay back and talk about their respective girlfriends as the rest of the team went out to shoot informally, N.C. State coach Jim Valvano stayed in the face of every Wolfpack player. State played a brilliant, totally inspired game, beating Carolina's traps and shooting well enough to get the lead and hang on for a 68-67 win. Irritated by his team's lackadaisical play early, Smith stayed hot right to the end. Atypically, he clenched his teeth and placed his hand over the lens of a TV camera that had followed him off the court.

The second loss ended the season and remained one of the most devastating debacles of Smith's entire career. This was the 79-75 heartbreaker to Syracuse in the East Regional championship game at the Meadowlands that left Smith second-guessing himself for playing Jeff Lebo, who had spent the prior twenty-four hours in bed with the flu and whose ineffectiveness on both ends of the court made a huge difference. Smith was even more crushed by this game than he had been after the 1984 Indiana loss; his senior class of Kenny Smith, Wolf, Popson and Curtis Hunter had won 115 games and twice gone undefeated in the ACC regular season, but did not win even one ACC Tournament or reach the Final Four. Overcome with emotion, he could not finish his press conference after the game and left the podium in tears.

Ranked No. 1 for most of the season, the Tar Heels returned home to watch the Final Four on television and try to take cover from the hailstorm of criticism, most of which was directed at Smith. Assistant Bill Guthridge remained particularly bitter for several weeks, stewing in his office over what he considered savagely unfair treatment of his boss. "We sure have a lousy program," Guthridge said sarcastically; "32-4 is really a terrible season."

Guthridge was mostly angry at what college basketball had become, a TV-dominated sport in which the first three months of the season meant very little compared to how teams fared in the NCAA Tournament. Carolina had enjoyed a phenomenal year, winning those thirty-two games with no superstar and playing without a true small forward. But all that meant little to most people, who had expected the Tar Heels to be back in New Orleans and became derisive when they didn't make it there.

✪

The 1988 season was going to be tough enough, anyway. Three starters, two of them All-ACC players, were gone. Lebo would have to play out of position at point guard until freshman King Rice was ready. And Smith had to deal with two true freshmen, one red-shirt frosh, and sophomore Kevin Madden, back from a year's suspension to work on his studies. He did have a potentially outstanding front court in sophomore postmen Reid and Williams, whom he had recruited with the 1981-82 tandem of Worthy and Perkins in mind. But a phone call Smith received early on the morning of October 16, 1987, the day after practice had started, made all that seem very unimportant indeed.

Out in Hacienda Heights, California, a bedroom community forty-five miles east of Los Angeles, Scott Williams's parents were dead after an unthinkable tragedy. Al and Rita Williams were delightful people, funny and ebullient, who considered themselves extremely lucky that their gangly, 6-10 son had improved so dramatically as a basketball player that he could earn a scholarship to play for the Tar Heels. Al Williams had coordinated the recruiting of his son, which heated up after Scott had held his own against the more-heralded Reid at summer all-star camps in 1985. Carolina had "discovered" Williams, too, and sent Fogler out west twice that summer and fall. Anxious to hear from Smith, Rita Williams blurted out when the head coach finally telephoned, "My husband has been waiting for you to call!"

Against the less-aggressive overtures of UCLA, the Tar Heels had become the school of choice for the Williams family. That was clear to everyone in November when Rita paid her own way to accompany Scott on his official visit to Chapel Hill, wearing a light blue warm-up suit to the UNC-Florida State football game and the Blue-White basketball scrimmage. Thus, despite the three thousand miles in between, the Williamses had become a popular part of the Carolina basketball family. And after Scott had arrived in Chapel Hill in the fall of 1986, Tar Heel insiders were surprised to learn that Al and Rita Williams had separated and were planning to divorce. Smith had asked his friend Earl Somers, a local psychiatrist, for advice on how to handle his sensitive freshman center.

Smith called Somers again that October Friday morning, after learning that, the night before, Al Williams had gone to the apartment building of his estranged wife, shot her, and then killed himself. The horrid homicide-suicide had torn apart the city of Hacienda Heights and reverberated clear across the country. Somers said he would be there when Smith told Williams about his parents. Upon receiving the message that Smith wanted to see him right away, Williams caught a ride to the basketball office with his roommate and teammate Jeff Denny.

Keeping his conversation with Williams private over the years, Smith has said only, "It was the most difficult thing I have had to do in my life."

After hearing that his parents were dead and that Guthridge and Lillian Lee, a friend and surrogate parent to many black athletes at Carolina, would accompany him to California that afternoon, Williams wanted to walk back to his dorm room at Granville Towers more than a mile away. Somers suggested to Smith that they unobtrusively follow Williams in a car because, as Smith said later, "we weren't sure what Scott would do." That evening, Williams, Guthridge and Lee flew to Los Angeles to complete the funeral arrangements.

At the second practice of the season, Smith spoke with his players, most of whom had already heard. Despite Carolina's usually grueling early regimen, the team did not work out for very long and were given the weekend off. The next morning, Smith and his wife departed for California, leaving the basketball program to assistant coaches Roy Williams and Dick Harp. While waiting for a connecting flight in Atlanta, Smith began suffering severe nosebleeds. Linnea called her husband's doctor, who advised him to come home. They decided to continue on to Los Angeles, and upon returning to Chapel Hill, Smith was confined to bed for four days until the nosebleeds subsided.

It marked only the second time in twenty-nine years that Smith had missed practice, the other time also having been for a funeral – that of veteran sportswriter and long-time friend Bob Quincy. Guthridge waited until the following Monday to bring Williams back to North Carolina, and it was left to Williams to decide when, and if, he would rejoin the team for practice. Again with Somers' advice, Smith counseled his players to support Williams by being there when he needed them and leaving him alone when he wanted solitude. Lil Lee hovered a little more closely over Williams, who responded by regularly spending evenings with her family and consuming mounds of her home-cooked spaghetti.

Williams decided to play and, despite frequent lapses of concentration in practice, won the starting center position and had a productive sophomore campaign in what turned out to be an unusual season for Smith and the Tar Heels. They posted their second straight first-place finish in the ACC (Smith won Coach of the Year) but lost three times to archrival Duke. The third defeat came in the finals of the ACC Tournament, despite the fact that Smith encouraged his players to approach the event as they had in the days when only the champion received an NCAA bid.

After the NCAA field opened to allow more than one team from each conference, Smith had clearly begun placing more importance on the regular season. Considered the best league in college basketball, the ACC's top two or three teams in the standings always rated at-large invitations to the big dance. Consequently, Smith had considered the ACC Tournament "for fun" and did not want his players to use up a lot of the emotion they would need when NCAA play opened the next week. However, against conference rivals who still regarded beating Carolina and winning the tournament paramount, playing "for fun" hadn't cut it throughout the mid-1980s.

Stung by criticism from media and fans about his team's uninspired play in recent ACC Tournaments, Smith felt the urgency of winning the event for the first time in six years. But even after the Tar Heels had advanced to the championship game against Duke on Sunday, March 13, 1988, in the Greensboro Coliseum, it became clear that the players were not taking the tournament that seriously.

After beating Maryland in Saturday's semifinals, the team (without the coach, who seldom took meals with his players) went out to dinner at

Slug's At The Pines in Chapel Hill, where Reid took the opportunity to play a practical joke on teammate Steve Bucknall. While Bucknall was in the bathroom, Reid held his fork in the flame of the table candle. Bucknall burned his mouth and, as the rest of the team cackled, threatened to kick Reid's ass. "Buck was mad and wanted to fight, but everyone else was cracking up on the way outside," recalled teammate Marty Hensley.

Witnessed by several diners, the incident eventually made the news. And after Bucknall, a starter, managed only four points and Reid seven against Duke, many Carolina fans blamed them for the 65-61 loss. Holding a five-point lead, the Tar Heels had made one field goal for the last twelve minutes of the game, shooting 28 percent in the second half. Smith got some heat around the water cooler, too, for not being in touch with his team the way Duke coach Mike Krzyzewski supposedly was. He refused comment on the altercation, punishing the two players privately and calling it an internal affair. "It's team dynamics," he said. "We're a family and it stays there."

Whether or not the family had been as focused as its coach on regaining the ACC championship, it still got booted from its own home with the loss to Duke. The winner of the tournament final had already been ticketed by the NCAA selection committee for first- and second-round games in the East Regional at the Dean Smith Center. Thousands of UNC fans had bought tickets, believing somehow the committee would let their team stay home. Instead, Duke played in the Deandome, winning two games and beginning its march to the Final Four in Kansas City. And while Carolina went West to post a stunning victory over run-and-gun Loyola Marymount, it did not get out of the regional for the sixth straight year, losing to Arizona in the Elite Eight at the Kingdome in Seattle. That made three losses in the regional final in the last four years and four in the past six.

If his team did not make it, Smith always attended the annual coaching convention at the Final Four, took in the games on Saturday and generally went home on Sunday morning. This time, he remained in Kansas City to happily watch his alma mater, Kansas, his protégé, Larry Brown, and the player he almost had, Danny Manning, upset Oklahoma to win the NCAA title. Within the next month, Brown had fled back to the NBA, and Smith was again trying to help Kansas pick a new coach. Smith campaigned for his own assistant, Roy Williams, who eventually got the job after a half-dozen head coaches retreated from rumors that the Jayhawks were going on NCAA probation for recruiting violations in the Brown era.

Now fifty-seven, and thinking about how many more years he would do this, Smith had some decisions of his own to make. When he replaced Williams with Phil Ford, who had no coaching experience, Smith knew he would have to put his own career in reverse if he ever wanted to bring North Carolina another national championship.

PROFESSIONAL HELP

Brad Daugherty, all seven feet, 275 pounds and twenty-one years of him, walked through the lobby of the New York Hilton on the morning of June 17, 1986. He spotted an empty seat at a table filled with very tall youngsters and one thirtyish balding man.

"Hey, dudes," Daugherty said as he sat down. "What's up, David?"

David Falk, the balding dude, nodded and smiled uncomfortably. Minutes later, he got up and looked around nervously as he said good-bye to the basketball players at the table and walked away. The dudes continued chowing down on a lumberjack's breakfast, compliments of the NBA.

It bothered Falk that he had virtually snubbed Daugherty, but he was scared to talk to the big, baby-faced center from the mountains of North Carolina. Falk and his boss, Donald Dell, had been with Daugherty and his parents within the last month in Dean Smith's office in Chapel Hill. ProServ, which Dell owned and where Falk worked, had been invited with other sports agencies to pitch Daugherty, an All-American at Carolina and sure first-round draft pick that night in the Felt Forum of Madison Square Garden. After the ProServ pitch ended, Smith had told Falk not to have any more contact with Daugherty until the player was ready to select an agent. "No bumps," Smith said sharply to Falk, referring to the recruiting term that meant a not-so-accidental meeting. "I mean that."

Falk did not know it yet, but he and ProServ were on their way out with the Carolina basketball program. That was hard to imagine, since for the previous two years ProServ had helped Michael Jordan become the hottest young pro sports star in America. Before Jordan had ever played a game in Chicago, Falk convinced Nike to name a shoe after the third pick in the 1984 NBA draft, and millions of pairs of red-and-white "Air Jordans" were sold in the first year alone. ProServ had also arranged deals with Coke, McDonalds, and Chevrolet for the former Tar Heel and newest wonder of the Windy City. But, while Smith had known Dell and ProServ cofounder Frank Craighill for years, he wasn't so sure about the younger member of the firm. Falk had sat quietly during ProServ's presentation to the families of Jordan and Sam Perkins in 1984 and James Worthy in 1982, and Smith somehow couldn't believe that this "gopher," as Smith referred to him, had become a well-known sports agent in his own right and capable of guarding his players' futures.

With Jordan now a megastar, Smith grew particularly leery of Falk. He read how Kareem Abdul-Jabbar had lost virtually everything and was suing his agent for mishandling his pro basketball fortune. So Smith was keeping close watch over Jordan when several real estate investments that Falk had made for his Tar Heel alumnus went sour. While questioning Falk about what happened, Smith believed he had caught the agent in a lie, although Falk claimed it was a misunderstanding. Nevertheless, once Dean Smith suspected that his bedrock principle of honesty had been violated, it made no difference how much money someone was making for one of his players.

Much of Smith's suspicious nature was earned. Early in his head-coaching career at Carolina, when criticism was ringing down from alumni and students, he understandably had trouble trusting anyone. His ex-boss Frank McGuire embraced an "us against the world" attitude, and indeed Smith's Christian faith in his fellow man was put to a test. He had the memory of three elephants, and anyone who had wronged him faced a long, hard climb back into his good graces. A student named Alfred Hamilton had foolishly added his name to seven other signatures on a 1965 letter to the *Daily Tar Heel*, suggesting that Smith be fired and replaced by assistant coach Larry Brown. Hamilton became a journalist and later a loyal Smith worshipper, but he occasionally heard about "the letter" from Smith over the next thirty years.

Falk exemplified Smith's tendency to judge people on the periphery of his program according to his first impression. Student reporters who might have had sophomoric traits were still asked about them years later. "Oh, you were on time," Smith might say to someone whom he knew was often late as a kid – even if that kid was now fifty years old and, himself, had been kept waiting by Smith. So Falk had a tough road earning Smith's respect, especially after he started getting rich off Jordan and filling almost all of Michael's private time with endorsement commitments. "Falk takes the credit, but anyone could have done that for Michael," Smith claimed in the mid-1980s. "Michael has no time to himself anymore, they've got him so tightly scheduled."

Early on, Falk had nothing but praise for Smith. "Other players aren't as fortunate as Michael," Falk said in 1987. "They were their whole college teams, and when they got to the pros they found it difficult to blend in. As great as Michael and James Worthy and Sam Perkins were, they weren't bigger than the Carolina program." Later, responding to Smith's rap against him, Falk sang a different tune. "Dean says he gave us Michael, and he's right," Falk said in an interview two years before Smith retired. "He recommended Donald and Frank to Michael. He denies that he's since told others not to come with us, but I know (he has)."

Out of deference to Dell and Craighill, a 1961 UNC graduate, Smith continued to allow ProServ to make presentations to his future pros. But he set the agenda and, although claiming the player and his parents made the final decision, insisted that all agents play by his rules. For Daugherty, it meant no contact while the player was making up his mind about who would represent him. But Daugherty had decided and wanted to tell Falk he was going with ProServ. When the players, parents, and media boarded the chartered bus to ride the twenty blocks to the NBA Draft, Daugherty jumped into an empty seat right in front of Falk. "I'm going with you," Daugherty said, turning back to Falk. "That's great, but please tell Coach Smith to call Donald," Falk said to Daugherty, he insists, three separate times.

When Daugherty told Smith of his decision – and that he had already informed Falk – Smith hit the roof. He called Dell and accused Falk of tampering and breaking his self-imposed "no-bump" rules. He also met again with Daugherty, who was selected No. 1 in the draft by Philadelphia and eventually hired ProServ's competitor, Advantage International, to represent him. Smith had earned an ironclad reputation for protecting his players, and few agents dared to "bump" a Carolina pro prospect. Once, Smith got word that a good-looking woman who worked for an agent was in Chapel Hill trying to find Perkins, and he dispatched team managers to warn his player.

Despite having turned Jordan into the most marketable pro athlete of all time, Falk did not sign another Carolina basketball player. Furthermore, he expected to never sign another Tar Heel as long as Bill Guthridge, or any other of Dean's disciples, held the head-coaching job at UNC. After reaching superstar status, himself, as an agent, Falk no longer minced words.

"Dean won't change," said Falk, who broke away from ProServ in 1993 to open his own agency, FAME (Falk Athletic Management Enterprises). Elaborating on his charge that Smith actively steered his players elsewhere, Falk declared, "Stackhouse would have come with us. . . ." In fact, Falk was particularly annoyed when word got back to him that Smith, in a conversation with Jerry Stackhouse, had referred to Falk as a "crook."

Falk has gotten wildly wealthy negotiating enormous contracts for athletes (he sold FAME in 1998 for a $100 million), but for every player who has sworn by him there is one who felt forgotten in the twilight of his career. One such incident would be enough to alienate Smith, considered among his former players to be a caretaker for life – not just during their playing days. Falk, like all agents, did not operate that way; he looked for new stars every season.

"He cut me out my last year in Dallas," said ex-Tar Heel Tom LaGarde, a first-round draft choice in 1977 who played four seasons at center for the NBA Mavericks. "Falk started pushing them to draft some big guy from Wyoming, and if he hadn't done that I could have stuck another year for a couple of hundred thousand dollars. I'm not surprised Dean feels that way about him. I think Falk's full of shit, myself." When the Mavericks released LaGarde, he turned to Smith and his European contacts to help him land a six-figure deal in Italy for three years. LaGarde has had very little to do with Falk ever since.

Curiously, while Smith did not push another player to ProServ or FAME, he has apparently never advised Jordan to fire Falk. Nevertheless, after putting Jordan's famous face on everything from the silver screen (Falk was executive producer of *Space Jam*) to perfume ads, Falk remained miffed about his broken Carolina connection.

"I can't live my life to please Dean Smith," said Falk, who claims he paid more in income taxes the first year he was on his own than he made in salary and bonuses for the seventeen years combined he worked for ProServ. "I think he's a great coach with a great program that really teaches kids how to play. But in the long run, he cost some of those kids money by telling them not to go with us.

"We had Wuycik, Karl, Jones, LaGarde, Ford, Bradley, O'Koren, Worthy, and Michael, and Sam for six days before he changed his mind. LaGarde was the No. 9 pick, and he made three times the money that Walter Davis did at No. 5. LaGarde wound up making more than the No. 1 pick that year (Kent Benson, Indiana, 1977)."

Ironically, in one way Smith even helped Falk's relationship with Jordan. Falk knew how close Smith and Jordan were (and could only imagine what was being said between the two), so he was careful not to give Smith any ammunition. When Jordan balked at paying ProServ 4 percent commission on his second NBA contract in 1988, Falk not only demurred but also told Jordan he would reduce the agency's take on endorsement deals from 20 to 15 percent. Years later, after *Space Jam* was in the can, Falk waived what would have been a seven-figure production fee and took only a percentage of what the movie and its merchandising made in profits. That still amounted to millions, but the move further solidified the relationship between Jordan and Falk. In the end, the agent treated the athlete more than fairly.

How much influence had Dean Smith had over the relationship? On some level, Falk knew that Smith was watching and would be quizzing Jordan the next time they played golf together. Such was the power Smith still held over the head of the most powerful agent in the world, someone he had essentially blown off more than ten years before.

✪

Twenty-six of Dean Smith's players were selected in the first round of the NBA draft over thirty-seven years, from Billy Cunningham in 1965 through Vince Carter and Antawn Jamison in 1998. That number could increase, if Ed Cota were to go in the first round or any of the young talent Smith left behind were to mature into solid pro prospects. Among the obvious first-rounders, can't-miss pros were Cunningham, Charlie Scott, Bobby Jones, Phil Ford, Worthy, Jordan and Perkins, Daugherty, and Rasheed Wallace. Many others, of less renown, at the very least earned good livings as pros.

For every Bob McAdoo, the NBA Rookie of the Year and MVP, was a Dudley Bradley, who never scored in double figures. For every Mitch Kupchak, who continually overcame injuries to win an NBA title, was a LaGarde, who never fully recovered from a blown knee his senior season to reach his pro potential. For every Walter Davis, another NBA Rookie of the Year and two-time all-star, was a Mike O'Koren, USA Today's best all-around pro player who did not make an all-star team. For every Kenny Smith, who set NBA records for three-pointers, was a Joe Wolf, a career journeyman whose biggest claim to fame was lasting twelve years with seven different NBA teams. For every Hubert Davis, a great shooter who made it, was an Al Wood, a better shooter who didn't. And for every Rick Fox, who turned out to be a better pro than college player, was an Eric Montross or Jerry Stackhouse, who turned out worse.

The common denominator? They all played for Dean Smith and were considered anywhere from sure shots to good gambles by the various NBA teams that drafted them. Smith cajoled some pro coaches and general managers into picking his players, such as J. R. Reid in 1989 and Pete Chilcutt in 1991. Others needed no convincing. "You don't have to teach Carolina players much," Pat Riley was already saying in 1986. "They come to us with the fundamentals, running, passing, moving without the ball . . . and they understand the pressure at the top, that they are expected to produce night after night."

No coach has put anywhere near as many players into pro basketball. Smith's legions have filled more roster spots, played more minutes, scored more points, and, largely due to Jordan, made more money than the respective alumni of any other college program. Eleven different Tar Heels were members of twenty-five NBA championship teams between 1976 and 1998. In all, seventy-one of Smith's Tar Heels were drafted somewhere by someone in the NBA, and dozens more played in the CBA and overseas. Smith's consuming goal was that any of his graduates who wanted to continue playing basketball would find a job in short pants. He was successful almost all of the time, particularly with players trying to squeeze out one or two years of active duty.

Smith got Geff Crompton, who barely played two full seasons in college, onto the roster of the Denver Nuggets, who in 1978 were coached by Larry Brown. Darrell Elston, a one-year regular in college, played two seasons in the old ABA. John Kuester, overshadowed by four fellow starters who would be first-round draft choices, signed as a free agent, lasted three years as a player and is still a pro assistant coach. Scott Williams's name wasn't called on draft day, but Jordan convinced the Bulls to sign him as a free agent for the 1991 season, the first of the first three-straight titles in Chicago. Williams left Chicago for Philadelphia in 1993 with three championship rings.

George Lynch, whose heart far exceeded his talent, road the coattails of Carolina's 1993 national championship to a big pro contract with the Lakers, and that sustained him when he got traded to Vancouver three years later. And Kevin Salvadori, hardly considered a legitimate college player at one point, has hung on the better part of four years as a back-up center in the NBA. Like Chilcutt three years before him, Salvadori was a long shot as a high school recruit before red-shirting as a freshman. They both developed rapidly and made big money playing pro ball when hundreds of other players with similar, if not greater, ability never got a chance.

✪

Ten years separated the first two Carolina basketball players who turned pro with college eligibility remaining. Although All-American Scott almost went pro following his junior year and Smith had suggested to Bill Chamberlain that he leave school after Chamberlain led the Tar Heels to the 1971 NIT championship, Robert McAdoo was the first to go early.

McAdoo, who played only one season in Chapel Hill, was an unusual case. He might never have been in the UNC program had not Tom McMillen changed his mind and enrolled at Maryland in the fall of 1970 after having committed to play for the Tar Heels the previous summer. But Smith found himself in need of a big man for the 1972 season, when McMillen would have joined the varsity. He had followed the progress of Greensboro's McAdoo, an immensely talented player who had led Vincennes (Indiana) to the 1970 junior college national championship. Because he hailed from North Carolina, McAdoo was the perfect "exception" for Smith to make to his policy of not taking "prominent" transfers. There had been junior college transfers before and would be after (Jeb Barlow in 1981), including another the very same year, McAdoo's Greensboro buddy Roger Jamison, who also stayed only one season. But McAdoo was the first player to step in and start who had not come up through the ranks of the program.

Although he was needed because McMillen's defection had left a huge void in the middle of an otherwise outstanding team, McAdoo's one winter in Carolina blue changed the very special chemistry the 1971 team had enjoyed on its way to the ACC regular-season championship and NIT title. An agonizing loss to South Carolina in the ACC Tournament finals had drawn the team even closer, and the Tar Heels had impressively swept through the NIT behind MVP and New York native Chamberlain. That overachieving team became part of Smith's legend as a coach, but in actuality it had high school All-Americans galore in Chamberlain, Dennis Wuycik, Steve Previs, and George Karl.

With all four returning and McAdoo replacing the departed Lee Dedmon at center, the 1972 Tar Heels were a near-unanimous pick to win the ACC and challenge the UCLA dynasty. However, McAdoo joined a tightly knit group that had been through Carolina's version of freshman boot camp. This group included Chamberlain, who, though now a senior coming off a spectacular NIT performance, faced new competition for minutes from McAdoo and heralded sophomore Bobby Jones. With what he remembered as a "big-headed" attitude, Chamberlain drew an early suspension from Smith for failing to run a wind sprint in practice. It set the tone for a turbulent season.

Meanwhile, the 6-9 McAdoo had earned a starting berth with his long arms and long-range shooting ability. Though his teammates were glad to have such a talent, the veterans were somewhat uncomfortable with – perhaps resentful of – McAdoo's instant emergence. *Sports Illustrated* even referred to him in a feature story as "a tall, dark stranger in the middle." As the season progressed with the highly ranked Tar Heels marching methodically toward first place, the ACC Tournament championship and another Final Four, their closeness of the year before had dissipated.

Carolina could not be challenged on the court as the strongest team in the league, but internally there slowly grew a case of what Smith called "senioritis." Among the symptoms was increasing speculation about the pro careers of seniors Wuycik and Chamberlain and junior McAdoo, considered the best prospect of all three. After making All-ACC and All-America – followed by winning the MVP in the ACC Tournament – in his one year at Carolina, McAdoo knew he had a chance to turn pro. Smith did not encourage him either way, only saying, "Make sure you get what you're worth." The old Buffalo Braves took McAdoo with the second overall pick in the 1972 draft; he won Rookie of the Year his first season in the NBA, MVP his third. McAdoo went on to play fourteen years and then became a pro assistant coach.

Although he would still have to face McMillen in a Maryland uniform for two more years, Smith did not mind taking his chances the season following McAdoo's departure. Having lost four starters, and with a sophomore named David Thompson joining the N.C. State varsity, he was ready for the pressure to be off the Tar Heels.

✪

It would be ten years before Smith again lost a player early to the pros. Exactly in between, after the 1977 season, he tried to interest Phil Ford in leaving school for the big bucks. The prototypical college player, Ford loved life in Chapel Hill and did not seriously consider passing up his senior year. Smith did not push the point.

After Carolina won Smith's first national championship in 1982, he did not have to push the point with James Worthy. Everything fell into place perfectly for the 6-8 phenom from Gastonia, North Carolina, who had won Final Four MVP honors with a bravura, 28-point performance against Georgetown at the Superdome in New Orleans. Worthy was ready, his pro career had already been jeopardized once by a brutal injury during his freshman year, and the powerful Los Angeles Lakers had deftly acquired the No. 1 pick in the 1982 NBA draft from

Cleveland for two players named Dan Ford and Chad Kinch. After Virginia's Ralph Sampson announced he was staying in college for his senior year, Lakers' General Manager Jerry West told Smith he wanted Worthy over Georgia's Dominique Wilkins.

Smith saw the golden opportunity clearly and would not let Worthy pass it up – especially after the potentially career-ending injury Worthy had already suffered. Smith also saw the irony between Worthy's last games of his sophomore and junior seasons. In 1981, Carolina led Indiana in the NCAA Tournament final in Philadelphia when official Booker Turner hit Worthy with his third and fourth fouls. "Two terrible calls," Smith said many times following that night's loss to Indiana. A year later, Worthy played his greatest college game, hitting thirteen of seventeen shots against Georgetown, including four consecutive monster dunks in the second half.

Smith's instincts proved eerily correct. After signing a million-dollar deal with the Lakers, Worthy fractured his left shin and knee in his rookie year. Had that injury occurred while he was still in college, Worthy's durability surely would have been questioned and his draft status adversely affected. He recovered to become a seven-time NBA all-star and have his jersey retired by the Lakers.

The decision was less clear-cut two years later with Michael Jordan, who in Smith's mind was never a Worthy. "I was more sure about James becoming a good college player than almost anyone else we've ever had at Carolina," said Smith, who was in the middle of a mild family squabble over Jordan's future. After he made National Player of the Year as a junior, Michael and his mother, Deloris, favored his staying at UNC for one more season. Smith knew Jordan would be in the top three in the 1984 draft and thought it was time to go; James Jordan, Michael's father, agreed. Not until the morning of May 11 did the family settle on a decision. Flanked by Smith and his parents at a press conference in Carmichael Auditorium, the 21-year-old, still-unpolished Jordan said unconvincingly it was time to move on. Only weeks earlier, he had maintained, "Sam (Perkins) had his senior game and gave his senior speech at the banquet. I'm going to have my senior game and give my senior speech."

Again, Smith was right, but it wouldn't be until Jordan turned into a rookie sensation that certain Carolina fans gave in. The night of

Jordan's announcement, assistant coach Eddie Fogler was married at the Hotel Europa in Chapel Hill. Dozens of Carolina basketball people – coaches and former players as well as long-time fans – attended the wedding. Among the guests was Jimmie Dempsey, who had known Smith since the Frank McGuire days. As friends, they played golf together and drank more than one Scotch over dinner. When the NCAA still allowed it, Dempsey picked up recruits and their families in his private plane and flew them to Chapel Hill. He and his wife, Tassie, fed the basketball players fried chicken in the Rams Club parking lot before every home football game and were considered "godparents" to the Tar Heels. Dempsey knew Jordan really wanted to stay in school and was angry that Smith had literally pushed him out the door. They "discussed" it at the wedding and would later continue their disagreement. "Dean is the basketball coach at the University of North Carolina," Dempsey said that night. "His job is to put the best basketball team possible on the court to represent the university. His job isn't to push kids into pro basketball – especially if they don't want to go."

Smith stayed at the wedding reception for about an hour and had a similar debate with Jim Delany, who played with Fogler and had been an investigator for the NCAA before going on to be commissioner of the Ohio Valley Conference and later the Big Ten. The opinionated Delany was bullish back then about kids staying in college. But Smith was unmoved. "During the season, we ask our players to do what's best for the team," he said. "After the season, we ask them to do what is best for them as individuals. Any player – any student, for that matter – who has a chance to leave school and become financially secure for life should seriously consider it."

"An awful lot of people didn't think it was the right thing for me to do," Jordan said. "That's when I felt he (Smith) was more like a father than anything else. I wasn't going to the NBA until he advised me to do it."

As with all of Smith's players who left school early for the NBA, Jordan's contract contained a bonus clause for a substantial cash payment if Jordan returned to school to get his undergraduate degree. After attending classes for two summers, Jordan donned a Carolina-blue cap and gown and went through graduation ceremonies in December 1985. He received his bonus check from the Bulls within a week.

✪

The next player to leave Carolina early was as controversial as charismatic. J. R. Reid had been a schoolboy phenomenon for years in Norfolk, Virginia, and his recruitment proved one of the fiercest in ACC history. As a freshman, Reid stepped into the starting lineup of a team that would go undefeated in the ACC regular season for the second time in four years. By March, when the Tar Heels reached New York for the 1987 NCAA East Regional, the national press was heaping more ink on Reid than veterans Kenny Smith, Joe Wolf, and Jeff Lebo combined. Carolina needed thirty-one points from Reid to hold off David Rivers and Notre Dame in the Sweet Sixteen, but with Reid held in check the Tar Heels lost in the Elite Eight to vastly underrated Syracuse (with future NBA stars Derrick Coleman, Ronnie Seikaly and Sherman Douglas). Few figured Reid wouldn't leave UNC without a national championship.

The rumors about Reid's off-court habits had begun long before he and teammate Steve Bucknall were suspended from the 1987-88 opening game for their part in a bar fight just off the N.C. State campus in the summer of 1987. Like many star athletes at campuses across America, Reid was known to be a heavy-duty party animal. But on the court, he was producing big time. After he averaged almost twenty points the first month of his sophomore season, including thirty points and thirteen rebounds against Illinois on national television, the talk of Reid becoming the youngest player to leave UNC for pro basketball began to spread. When Smith answered a question during his weekly teleconference in January with his pat answer about "calling around to the NBA in the spring," it spawned rumors of a rift between the coach and his star player.

Most damaging was a story in *The Washington Post* by sportswriter and Carolina nemesis John Feinstein, implying that Reid and UNC were unhappy with each other. He based his theory on talks with high school stars Christian Laettner and Jerrod Mustaf, who had been recruited by Smith and had supposedly been told that Reid would be leaving early. Smith was furious at Feinstein for advancing the premise that if Reid indeed bolted for the NBA, it was due to his unhappiness at Carolina rather than his readiness for pro basketball. That certainly had not been the case with Worthy and Jordan. Reid was no angel off the court, but Smith contended his 6-9 forward worked very hard at practice and in games. Because of his basketball forte, flying dunks, and flat-top haircut, Reid got lots of attention.

The incident would be one of several in which Feinstein jumped all over rumors about Carolina players while steering clear of alleged transgressions by members of his beloved Duke Blue Devils. Years later, when Feinstein could have told the complete story about the back injury and exhaustion that led Duke coach Mike Krzyzewski to the brink of a breakdown, he chose to ignore it. The rumors about Krzyzewski ranged from physical confrontations with his own players, to cussing out their parents, to blowing up at assistant coaches in public – including even speculation that he was fired by his own athletic director and rehired after sitting out the last half of the season to get over whatever had been troubling him. Had just one of those wild stories been rumored about Smith (absurd speculation in itself), Feinstein would have been all over it in his print, radio, and TV forums. As a result of such routine bias, Smith responded to a 1994 Feinstein report on ESPN about Rasheed Wallace skipping class by saying simply, "John went to Duke."

Ironically, a disagreement with Smith did play a part in Reid leaving Carolina after his junior season, 1988-89. Smith had implemented a pro-type system of designated minutes for his starters in the first half. When Reid could not be assured that the policy would change back the next year, he and Smith started talking about his entering the NBA draft. Reid's parents, both schoolteachers, were initially opposed but were assured by Smith that Reid would have incentives built into his contract to return to college to complete his degree. Smith then went to work lobbying George Shinn, owner of the year-old Charlotte Hornets, to take Reid. The Hornets did with the fifth pick of the 1989 NBA draft.

Carolina had five more first-rounders over the next four years, all seniors. Of the five – Rick Fox, Pete Chilcutt, Hubert Davis, George Lynch, and Eric Montross – only Montross thought about an early exit following the 1993 NCAA championship. In retrospect, he should have considered it more strongly, as he was a projected top-five pick as a junior. The next season, after his averages fell and Carolina got knocked out of the NCAA Tournament in a stunning second-round loss to Boston College, Montross went No. 9 to the Boston Celtics.

Of course, Stackhouse and Wallace had little choice in 1995, when as sophomores they led Carolina back to the Final Four. Both were among the top pro prospects, and both made little secret of their desire to take care of struggling and/or ill family members. They declared for the NBA within a week of each other in May of 1995. Wallace went first after consulting primarily with his mother, Jackie, and other family members and friends back in Philadelphia. Until Vince Carter three years later, Wallace was the first and only Tar Heel player not to allow Smith to orchestrate his departure. In fact, he called a press conference at his old high school in Philly and then informed the Carolina basketball office. Either perturbed or preoccupied, Smith sent Bill Guthridge in his place.

A week later, Stackhouse turned in his eligibility, explaining that his older and ailing mother, Minnie, needed hospitalization and surgery. Stackhouse did walk the party line, however, holding his press conference at UNC like most of the others before him. In fact, after he went No. 3 to Philadelphia (immediately followed by Wallace to Washington), Stackhouse used his rookie millions to buy two houses – one for his mother and father back in Kinston and the other, a half-million-dollar mansion, for himself at the posh Governors in Chapel Hill.

Carolina had a rare three-year rest from first-round draft choices until 1998, when Carter and Antawn Jamison would both go a year early after Smith's first season in retirement. Though no longer coaching, Smith still queried the pros about Carolina's two latest stars. Like Stackhouse, Jamison and his family hung on his old coach's every word before the National Player of the Year made the obvious choice to turn pro. And, just like Wallace, Carter had friends and family involved in his hotly awaited decision – one that had actually been made for him long before he had played his last game for the Tar Heels.

CHAPTER THIRTEEN

THE GODFATHER

"Can you help me with King this summer?" Dean Smith asked a local businessman, who knew exactly what Smith was talking about. In early April, just after the 1988 basketball season had ended, Smith was in his typical scrambling mode, trying to find summer jobs for his players. While many college basketball coaches were scarcer than undefeated seasons, heading for the golf course, booster club meetings, or coaching clinics once the recruiting and signing period had ended, Smith, instead, went full-time into being the Godfather of Carolina basketball.

Smith didn't spend much time during the season lining up summer jobs for his players. If one fell into his lap, he would certainly make a note of it. But, as the son of schoolteachers, he had his Midwestern roots: family, faith, class work and practice, all with about equal priority for major college basketball players. When the season ended, summer jobs joined that list because, more often than not, they could affect players' academic standing and basketball future. Smith liked to have them attend at least one session of summer school, either to make up or get ahead in class credits and to continue building bonds with teammates by working out together in the afternoons. Unless an academic emergency required attendance at both sessions of summer school, Smith also tried to place his players in some kind of organized league, often an international tour so they would experience travel and divergent cultures. His role with the U.S. Olympic Basketball Committee, since he had coached the 1976 gold medal-winning team in Montreal, gave him some influence in landing spots for his best players on the various development teams.

Those who remained in Chapel Hill, for however long, eventually had summer employment arranged for them to meet NCAA guidelines. Players could work any jobs for which they were qualified, as long as they received pay no greater than anyone else holding the same position. This, of course, left much to interpretation and the discretion of the players' "bosses."

"What can King do?" inquired the businessman of King Rice, a rising sophomore guard who had played a reserve role on Carolina's 1988 ACC regular-season championship team.

Smith said Rice was a bright young man and could do anything asked of him. He then told the businessman that Rice would call him the next morning. Smith rarely got rebuffed at this point, even though the potential employer usually knew exactly what he was getting into. And most of the time it wound up simply being a favor to Smith and Carolina basketball. David Dixon, for example, a wealthy UNC alum who owned a successful computer business in Durham, hired Carolina players for several summers and later laughed about how he was "supporting the program" by letting them work in his warehouse for a couple of hours a day. The jobs were usual menial, minimum-wage labor, but Carolina basketball players had become accustomed to far better treatment.

Even those coming from poor, struggling, single-parent families soon basked in the good life that Smith had created for the Tar Heels. A scholarship paid for tuition, room, board, and books, and, though Smith made sure all benefits remained within NCAA guidelines, the legal perks were enough to spoil anyone very quickly. The team always traveled first class and stayed at five-star hotels, like the Essex House in Manhattan and the equally plush Park Hotel in Charlotte. They chartered planes – sometimes those cushy, private NBA jets – whenever possible to cut down on the time players would be away from class. Training table was an all-you-could-eat extravaganza. Smith also arranged that any legal gifts – whether classy traveling outfits and gear or tournament watches – were the best and most expensive permissible.

He even scheduled road games around the holidays to allow, within the NCAA rules, his players to fly home for Christmas and then to the site of the next game – all on the basketball program's tab.

So, when it came to summer school and summer jobs, Smith still worked to keep his players satisfied. After Smith applied his subtle brand of pressure, the same businessman who had once been insulted by the Carolina coach over another player's summer work schedule gave Rice a job. In 1984, the businessman had sold his share in a local establishment to a player from Smith's very first team who was looking to move his family from New York to Chapel Hill. The retail operation had been marginally successful with typical cash-flow problems for a small business. When the ex-player took over, he wound up having to sink more capital into the venture than he had expected. The story had gotten back to Smith, who filed it away in his legendary mind and, three years later, used it to benefit another of his players. When Joe Wolf, an All-ACC forward and future professional journeyman, needed a summer job, Smith sent him to see the same businessman about being a part-time salesman.

"How much can you pay Joe?" Smith asked the businessman. Then, before hearing the whole response, he added, "Well, I'll send him over, and we'll see if you screw him, too." After writing Smith a strong letter and receiving a qualified apology, the businessman had hired Wolf. Two years later, he hired Rice at Smith's urging.

Rice, it turned out, couldn't come to work most mornings because he had class until 11:00. He couldn't come after lunch because he had to lift weights until 2:00. And he couldn't come after that because the Tar Heels, present and past, always played pick-up games in the afternoon. This was a player's typical summer schedule.

"I can come at 4:30," said Rice, who like Wolf before him, and many other Carolina players, wound up working hours convenient to him.

"How's it going with King?" Smith asked the businessman during a brief phone conversation subsequent to the hiring.

"It's hard for him to find time to work because of class, weight-lifting, and playing in the afternoons," Smith was told.

"Well, then you should fire him," Smith said. "He can't get paid if he doesn't work."

The businessman, a long-time Carolina fan who received season tickets from Smith, bit his lip. "We'll work it out, Coach," he said, knowing he would eventually pay Rice something for whatever hours he could put in.

"I'll talk to King," Smith said, hanging up in the middle of his friend's next sentence.

❂

As a coach, Dean Smith was more than a nice guy to the people he cared about. He was sometimes single-minded, and occasionally ruthless, in the promotion and protection of his former players. His letters and phone calls of recommendation numbered into the thousands over the years, and those he helped ranged from the one-time jayvee manager looking for a sales job to Kenny Smith trying to hang on for another year in the NBA. Smith oversaw more than two hundred players, managers, and assistant coaches in his thirty-six years running the basketball program at North Carolina. Counting all of their parents, wives, and children, Smith's extended family reached into the thousands. Yet stories of the players he's helped off the court were so common that almost every Tar Heel has one he loves to tell.

And some they don't like to tell very much.

Kevin Madden, the youngest player to commit to Smith and Carolina, announced his intention to attend UNC after his sophomore year in high school. By the time he arrived in Chapel Hill, his body and basketball ability were more mature than his attitude. After Madden very nearly flunked out his freshman year, Smith made the kind of decision that marked his coaching career and resulted in more than 95 percent of his players graduating. He gave Madden a choice: sit out a year and study, or transfer to another school.

"I'm about to run Madden off," a perturbed Smith said in the fall of 1986, as he waited for the player, a projected starter at small forward, to report to his office. Smith was angry because Madden had not lived up to his part of the bargain: i.e., go to class and do the work. Carolina employed expert tutors, like Burgess McSwain, but they did not write the papers and take the tests for the players. Smith actually thought Madden might be better off in a less strenuous academic environment; what he didn't want was for his player to continue to slide by.

"He could have transferred but he's staying here," Smith said after playing the role of the angry father at the meeting. "He knew it would be a tough year in school and was relieved when I told him he couldn't play. It won't benefit our team, but I think it will benefit Kevin."

At times, Smith's loyalty cost him good publicity. For many years, he held a grudge toward Raycom and Jefferson-Pilot, the ACC-TV rights holders, for not hiring former Carolina players as on-air personalities. He even refused to do several pregame interviews that were required under the ACC's contract with the television producers. Other times, his acts of generosity brought him unwanted publicity. When the father of Chapel Hill native Ranzino Smith and the older brother of Durham's Curtis Hunter died in 1994, Smith paid part of the funeral costs to help out both struggling families. He was embarrassed for them – and peeved at the writer – when a magazine story reported these kindnesses a few months later.

Dale Gipple and Ged Doughton were two "walk-ons" at Carolina, unrecruited high school players who eventually earned scholarships to play for the varsity. Neither was a starter or a star, although both played some key moments as reserves on NIT and ACC Championship teams. More than fifteen years after graduating, when both were married and raising families, Dean Smith remained prominent in their lives. Their stories demonstrate how Smith formed and maintained unique bonds with all of his players, headliners or benchwarmers.

Doughton graduated in 1979 after playing reserve point guard on two ACC championship teams. For two years he backed up Phil Ford, which is to say he rarely got off the bench unless Ford was hurt or in foul trouble. In the mid-1990s, Doughton's father, a lifetime smoker, was diagnosed with lung cancer. By that time, it was common knowledge that the tremendous demands on Smith's time off the court were pushing him closer and closer to retirement. It was for this very reason that Doughton purposely did not tell Smith about his father's illness.

One afternoon, Doughton went home to visit his dad in Winston-Salem, and found George Doughton reading a two-page, handwritten letter from Smith that included inquiries, by name, about every member of the Doughton family. Smith had heard about his lung cancer from another player, found out where the elder Doughton was hospitalized, and dashed off a letter while flying somewhere on a recruiting trip.

Gipple played almost ten years before Doughton after enrolling at UNC from Burlington Cummings High School. He immediately won a starting position on the freshman team and wound up the third-leading scorer behind recruited athletes Lee Dedmon and Donn Johnston. A good shooter most of his career, Gipple's senior year was a washout. He hit only 35 percent of his shots and played less and less as the season progressed toward the eventual NIT championship. After graduating, he remained in North Carolina to work and occasionally stayed in touch with the basketball program.

In 1995, Gipple's ten-year-old son Spencer was diagnosed with cystic fibrosis and had to make periodic trips to UNC Hospitals in Chapel Hill for treatment on his lungs. Prior to one such trip, Gipple had dropped a couple of souvenir items off at the basketball office and asked Smith's secretary if she could get Smith to sign them so Spencer would have them in the hospital. A few days later, after Spencer had begun treatments to drain his lungs, Smith wandered into the pediatric pulmonary clinic at the hospital, holding a basketball, a UNC calendar, and a team picture, all signed by the players and coaches. No one from the Gipple family had called the basketball office with the date and time of Spencer's admission.

"The treatment took almost two hours, and Coach Smith waited for more than an hour," Gipple said. "He had an appointment and apologized for not being able to wait any longer, and before leaving he wrote Spencer a personal note. He took the time to find out where we were and made a special trip. He didn't have to do any of that."

In 1974, Carolina was still taking eight-millimeter movies of every game and some practices. The Tar Heels used a man named John Stokes to shoot the film, and Stokes made every trip with the team, lugging the camera and film canisters all over the country. During that summer, Stokes lost his left hand in a power-saw accident. When Stokes woke up in the hospital following the amputation, the two people in the room were his father and Dean Smith.

"Are you going to be able to keep doing our film?" Smith asked Stokes, who nodded and said his new prosthesis would work just fine. "Good. We need you."

✪

To Smith, the role of Godfather simply came with the job. He remembered, as a kid, players from his father's high school teams hanging around their small house in Emporia. Though Smith kept more personal distance from his own players than his father had, he made it clear through words and actions that he would always be there for them.

One day, in 1966, Smith had a teary-eyed player named Mark Mirken sitting in his office. Mirken had attended the same high school in Brooklyn as Billy Cunningham, and Smith had actually "discovered" Mirken one night when as an assistant to Frank McGuire he was recruiting Cunningham. When Smith took over the Tar Heel program, he offered a scholarship to Mirken, who turned out to be a college reserve whose playing time diminished as Smith brought in more talented recruits. But Mirken wasn't in his coach's office crying about his minutes.

A pre-med major, Mirken was struggling with the books – actually on the verge of flunking out after already having dropped out of school for one semester. He told Smith that his deceased father had always wanted him to be a doctor, and that on his deathbed had made Mirken promise he would study medicine. As Mirken recounted the story to Smith, and described how much pressure he was feeling, the coach was deeply moved. "You know, Mark," Smith finally said, "not all of us are cut out to be doctors. And I'm sure your father would want you to be successful in whatever you did."

Smith then suggested that Mirken visit with Dr. Chris Fordham, the dean of the UNC medical school who would go on to become chancellor of the university for eight years. Smith said there was a test Fordham gave to struggling students that not only rated their aptitude for medicine but for other careers, as well. Mirken agreed, and Smith called Fordham on the phone that day. Mirken took the test, which showed not only average aptitude for science and math but outstanding skills in the written and spoken word. At Smith's urging, and with his reassurance that it would be okay with his father, Mirken switched his major, eventually earned admittance to the UNC law school, and went on to be a successful attorney.

Almost ten years later, in the summer of 1975, Mickey Bell sat in the same chair in Smith's office. Bell had been a walk-on at Carolina who earned a scholarship after playing on the freshman team. Smith had never heard of Bell as a high school player in Goldsboro, North Carolina, but liked his hustle, if not his natural ability. Bell's playing career was over after having been a senior captain on Carolina's 1975 ACC Tournament championship team. What a glorious night that had been in Greensboro, when Bell got in for a few minutes of the Tar Heels' 70-66 win over defending national champ N.C. State. But Smith was in no mood for reminiscing.

Bell had stayed around Chapel Hill after graduating, hoping to take some additional classes, work with the junior varsity team and, eventually, break into coaching. A good-looking blond kid who liked to party, Bell had loved college and was still having a great time. Smith thought he might be wasting some of it and put him to the test.

"Mickey," he said calmly, "there's an assistant coaching job coming open at Middle Tennessee State, and I think you have a chance to get it."

Instead of perking up at the news, Bell told Smith that he didn't want to move to Tennessee. "Well, Mickey, your coaching career just ended before it started," Smith countered. In response to Bell's puzzled look, Smith explained that if he had really wanted to be a coach he would have jumped at the opportunity to get a full-time job. Smith also said he would no longer make any calls to help Bell in the coaching profession, that if he still wanted to coach he'd have to do that on his own.

"Now, since I'm not going to help you be a coach, what else are you interested in doing?" Smith said, knowing exactly where he was going. The week after the tough-love meeting, Smith made several other calls on Bell's behalf. Eventually, Bell landed a local sales job with Converse, the athletic shoe company that Smith's program endorsed at the time, soon got promoted to regional manager, and, in 1986, moved to Boston after being named president of Converse.

Smith had actually ended that meeting with Bell abruptly after a glance at his watch. He went out the back door of Carmichael Auditorium, jumped into his beige Cadillac, and drove across campus to Memorial Hospital. Making his way through the construction site of what seemed like an ongoing renovation of the medical complex, Smith asked at the front desk how to get to the recovery room. Walking down the sterile hallways, passing patients on stretchers and in wheelchairs, doctors in white coats and attendants in light blue scrubs, Smith found himself growing uncomfortable. He disliked hospitals and had spent relatively little time in them. He had known virtually no sickness in his family; in fact, his parents were well into their seventies, still living in Kansas and working every day.

But this was something he had to do, wanted to do. Mitch Kupchak, his star center and one of his favorite players, had undergone an operation to repair a ruptured disk in his chronically bad back. The 6-10, curly-haired Kupchak had made All-ACC as a junior and would anchor another top-ten Carolina team the next season – if his surgery worked and he could rehabilitate his back in time. Smith wasn't thinking about the eighteen points and eleven rebounds Kupchak had averaged the prior season, though. He was there because Kupchak's working-class parents could not make the trip from Brentwood, New York, in time for the operation. They hoped to be at their son's bedside in the recovery room, but Smith wanted to be there, too, in case they didn't make it by the time their son opened his eyes.

He had made such visits for many players, had even witnessed surgical procedures. After a game against Clemson the previous season, Kupchak needed to have an epidural block to ease the pain in his ailing back so he could make it through the rest of the ACC schedule and, hopefully, the NCAA Tournament.

"They were going to inject my spine with a long needle," Kupchak recalled years later. "I'm in the operating room, and Coach Smith walks in wearing a gown and a mask. He seemed pretty squeamish. But he was there, first thing Sunday morning, and kept his hand on my shoulder the whole time . . . . It was comforting to have him in there."

Usually able to influence his players' fate, Smith felt helpless when it came to injuries. Besides visiting the hospital, he asked probing questions of doctors and trainers to learn as much as he could about an injury and to get their most specific guesstimate on when a player might return. He had to make plans for practices and games.

"He never pressured us to get an injured player back before he was ready," said team physician Tim Taft. "But he was very insistent on knowing when the player would be back, and if we missed he wasn't happy about it."

★

Prior to the start of each season, Smith invited an attorney, police officer, or an NCAA official to speak to his team about the variety of potentially compromising situations high-profile college athletes could find themselves in – and how to avoid them before they happened. Typically, the early lectures would cover shoplifting and traffic violations, the later ones alcohol and substance abuse. Almost every year, someone outside the program warned the Tar Heels of the wiles of sports agents and the "runners" or gamblers interested in fixing games.

On the few occasions when his players stepped over the line, Smith was supportive – but never subversive of the legal system. Though he helped his players find a lawyer and always asked to be kept informed, he almost never used his power and influence to get them out of trouble. Of course, as the most prominent citizen in a small town that idolized its college athletes, Smith did not have to make any midnight phone calls in order for his players to get the benefit of the doubt. He might return a favor months later with a couple of courtside tickets, but Smith was too smart and too principled to intervene in the legal process. There were plenty of traffic tickets and an occasional DUI, and those offenders had their days in court.

Smith did use his influence when he believed an incident to be symptomatic of a bigger problem. On at least one occasion, he arranged for a player who was a binge-drinker to see a doctor who prescribed the medication that caused severe illness if mixed with alcohol. A few years later, when Tar Heel star Rick Fox found himself being stalked by a fanatical female, Smith enlisted the help of friends in the police department to try to protect Fox from harm – and to take action before the bizarre story hit the local newspapers and TV stations.

Rarely did Smith get involved in the domestic affairs of his players. He had, in 1979, after learning of Mike O'Koren's secret marriage to UNC cheerleader Kim Cline. O'Koren and Cline had dated for almost two years, but only family and closest friends knew they had run off to South Carolina one weekend during the summer. After meeting with O'Koren's older brother and Cline's father, Smith went along with the charade because the marriage had been an impetuous one and O'Koren and Cline never actually lived together before they divorced. Even though the turbulent relationship occasionally affected O'Koren's play on the court, Smith continued protecting him right through the night police brought divorce papers to his apartment in the summer of 1980. Cline had waited until O'Koren, picked in the first round of the NBA draft, had signed with the New Jersey Nets. (She later received a modest settlement.)

O'Koren was on Franklin Street at the time, so his roommate called Smith to ask him what to do with the subpoena. "We'll deal with it in the morning," Smith said, adding, "don't tell Mike when he gets in tonight. Let him have a good night's sleep before he finds out."

Perhaps his program's most highly publicized incident occurred in the fall of 1987, when J. R. Reid and Steve Bucknall wound up in a Raleigh nightclub called "Shooters II" and, as Smith later rationalized, were "pushed and provoked" into an altercation with several rowdy N.C. State fans. A Raleigh man who claimed to have been an innocent bystander charged both Tar Heels with assault, Reid for spitting on him and Bucknall for punching him in the face. When the story hit the media, Smith couldn't resist a bit of spin control. "If spitting is assault," he said, "I've been assaulted many times at Reynolds Coliseum." He nevertheless suspended Reid and Bucknall for the season-opener against Syracuse in the Hall of Fame game in Springfield, Massachusetts, saying he was sitting them down not so much for their part in the fight as for their poor judgment in hanging out at a Wolfpack watering hole.

Reid and Bucknall's teammate Rice had an unfortunate stretch during his career, during which he was first charged after scuffling with his girlfriend and later busted for drunk driving. Rice's lawyer had arranged to spirit him in and out of a court appearance through the back door, but Smith preferred that Rice not duck the hovering reporters. Never disengaging from his role as his players' surrogate parent, Smith felt bad later when he learned that Rice was actually just restraining his angry girlfriend during an argument. He tried calling Rice several times before reaching him.

"I was embarrassed and didn't want to see him," Rice recalled. "Finally, I went to his office. He said, 'King, don't you understand, I'm here for you in the good times and the bad? If anything, I'm here for you more in the bad times.'"

Of course, these relatively few scrapes with the local authorities pale in comparison to the overwhelmingly positive effect Smith and his teams have had on society over the years, beyond the thrills and enjoyment they delivered from the basketball court. There were the hundreds of visits the players made to hospital wards around the state, the thousands of birthday and Christmas cards Smith wrote to families of players (and recruits he did not get), and the hundreds of thousands of autographs signed by Tar Heel players and coaches that, in the 1990s, required hiring two "autograph managers" and implementing a new system.

Smith, himself, signed everything that arrived at the basketball office seeking his coveted inscription, although books and posters often remained in a pile next to his desk for as long as two years. The players, however, had carefully orchestrated sessions to sign selected items and, beyond that, could give out autographs after games only if they felt like it. This often angered fans, who occasionally got snubbed by players.

While Smith was lenient about the amount of time his team spent signing autographs, he adamantly opposed his former players' writing checks back to the university once they had become successful professionals. He believed they had already made their contributions to UNC through basketball and were only being hit up for their notoriety and, in the case of pro stars, their instant wealth. He had been most insistent that they not donate to building the Smith Center in the early 1980s because, in his words, "they were the ones who created such interest in our program" that the school needed a bigger arena. Besides, they all got complimentary tickets from the coach and did not have to give in order to buy season seats.

Smith even discouraged Brad Daugherty, one of his All-Americans and later an NBA all-star, from helping in the campaign to raise $3 million to build the school's Black Cultural Center, even though Daugherty volunteered to take part – after making a $100,000 donation. Ever protective, Smith feared what he saw as the exploitation of successful black athletes, and he knew that others from his program would ultimately be asked to contribute as well.

Smith remained the godfather figure to the great majority of his players long after they left Chapel Hill, particularly those who encountered tough times. Take, for example, the case of Bill Chamberlain, one of the few former Tar Heels caught criticizing Smith during and after his career at Carolina in the early 1970s. A proud, petulant player from New York City with extraordinary talent, Chamberlain had followed

Charlie Scott to Carolina as the school's second black scholarship basketball player. He had an up-and-down career – injured as a sophomore, MVP of the NIT as a junior, then out again during several games early in his senior season when the team reached the 1972 Final Four in Los Angeles.

There, Chamberlain was late for the pregame meal and, according to Smith's consistent policy, lost his starting job and sat out as many minutes of the game as he had been late joining the team. After a devastating upset loss to Florida State, Chamberlain and Smith exchanged heated words in the locker room.

Smith used the word "boy" innocently while addressing Chamberlain, who stood up defiantly. Smith snapped, "Bill, I don't have to defend myself on that issue and you know it. We're not talking about anything here except breaking a team rule."

Over the next few years, while Smith was working hard on his behalf, Chamberlain had moments of disloyalty, when his immense pride got the best of him. He claimed that Smith had held him back as a senior – in favor of talented sophomore Bobby Jones and transfer Bob McAdoo – and that it cost him money on a pro contract. The truth was that Smith had encouraged Chamberlain to turn pro after his junior year – when his stock was highest following the great NIT performance in front of the New York press. Now, reputed to have a bad attitude, the silky, 6-7 Chamberlain was no longer considered a can't-miss pro.

Drafted by both the NBA and old ABA, Chamberlain picked the fledgling league and played for the Kentucky Colonels until suffering a serious back injury. He recovered from disc surgery to play briefly for the NBA Phoenix Suns, but basically his basketball career was over at age twenty-five. He turned back to Carolina and to Smith, who knew very well of Chamberlain's critical remarks. Under the circumstances, many coaches would have been disinclined to help, but Smith felt all the more responsible for Chamberlain. After a meeting in Chapel Hill to clear the air, Smith recommended Chamberlain for an assistant coaching job at Duquesne and later a state job with the North Carolina Department of Crime Control and Public Safety.

While working in Raleigh, Chamberlain assisted the Shaw University coaching staff and eventually, again with Smith's backing, took the job as athletic director and head basketball coach at Laurinburg Institute, where Scott had prepped before his historic enrollment at UNC.

"It's worked out," Chamberlain said in 1997. "I pretty much owe everything I have to Carolina basketball."

❂

Even though Smith had five children of his own, he parented more than 250 players, team managers, and assistant coaches over his forty-plus years in the business, not to mention the secretaries, athletic department staff members, and friends who dropped by in various states of distress to seek his advice.

The annual UNC basketball media guide carried five full pages listing all of Smith's lettermen, when they graduated, and where they currently worked. According to the summary box, 229 of 237 lettermen graduated and ninety-three earned graduate degrees. Fifty-four of them played in the NBA or old ABA, and another fifty-two played semi-pro ball or in Europe. But the much larger breakdown included 114 businessmen, thirty-seven coaches and teachers, fifteen attorneys, eleven physicians, three dentists, two pastors, one pharmacist, and one cop. Eight were retired and four deceased, Smith having attended every one of the funerals.

Smith began each of their careers by making promises he could keep, that they would get an opportunity for a college education and a chance to play big-time basketball. He ended most of their careers by letting them start their last home games, popularizing the concept of "Senior Day" that many college programs later adopted. In between, he suggested books to read and had them learn significant passages and quotes. He exposed them to prominent people and special strategies, such as the statistical analyses of the team and upcoming opponents sent in by old friend and 1942 UNC grad Louis Harris, the famous political pollster.

And he watched with pride as they gave plenty back to society and to the game of basketball – from the incomparable Michael Jordan, to the dozens of pro players, coaches, and administrators, to retired black stars like Daugherty, Kenny Smith, and James Worthy, who finally landed high-profile broadcasting jobs for which Smith, the Godfather, had lobbied through the years.

CHAPTER FOURTEEN

THE FATHER OF INVENTION

Dean Smith was speechless for one of the few times in his coaching life. The Tar Heels had just returned from New York, where they had lost to Georgetown in the ACC-Big East Challenge at the Meadowlands. It was 1989, and after nearly thirty years on the job Smith thought he knew how to react to anything that might be said about his team.

He would not have been upset about criticism over the twelve-point loss to the Hoyas, who with Alonzo Mourning and Dikembe Mutombo were better than a Carolina team trying to rebuild from losing Steve Bucknall and Jeff Lebo to graduation and J. R. Reid to the NBA a year early. He wouldn't have even minded flack over the Heels' ragged play, which kept them on the verge of being blown out most of the game. Smith knew it might be a tough season, given graduation losses and the lack of an experienced shooting guard. (His fears proved correct, despite the continued emergence of Hubert Davis, as Carolina wound up winning only twenty-one games.)

But this was not about how the Tar Heels played. It was about how they looked before they began the game. Smith had just learned that some Carolina alumni and fans from New York were saying his players' uniforms, particularly their bell-bottom warm-up pants, were seriously out of style. In North Carolina, where the Tar Heels could dress out in burlap sacks and be cheered, team clothing was never an issue. They had had the same style of uniform for more than fifteen years, and no one cared because, after all, it was Carolina. But in New York, style did matter. And when the word got back to Smith that his uniforms were so far from the cutting edge as to be obsolete, he took it to heart. The master of detail had somehow failed to notice that almost all basketball warm-ups, college and pro, were now made more like casual jogging outfits with elastic ankle cuffs. The straight-tailored leg with the flare bottom was outsville.

This was no small concern to Smith, who had been the first coach in the ACC and among the first in the country to put his team into V-neck jerseys and colored shoes. In the early 1970s, Carolina donned blue Converse sneakers with its home white uniforms and wore white shoes with road blues. The Heels also went through a period of wearing stretch knee socks with their numbers on one leg – except for George Karl, whose old gym socks hung over his shoes and seemed to flop along with his blond hair. Yes, Carolina taking the court with its white, velvety warm-ups and the blue shooting shirts under the jackets was the rage back then.

It was also an integral part of Carolina's image as a first-class program, along with the cashmere travel blazers and Smith's insistence that his teams stay in five-star hotels and eat at the best restaurants. The coach, himself, was always impeccably dressed, either in stylish sport jackets or expensive, Italian-cut suits. And when, between the 1972 and 1973 seasons, former players Larry Brown and Doug Moe convinced him to lose his hair cream and go for the blow-dry look, he willingly acceded to the dictates of fashion.

"Well, we haven't changed our uniforms in a long time; maybe we should think about it," Smith said after a long pause. Wondering aloud how they should go about it, his eyes lit up at the suggestion that North Carolina native Alexander Julian give the Tar Heels a complete makeover. Julian, by then a well-known fashion designer in New York, had grown up in Chapel Hill, where his family still owned and operated a clothing store on Franklin Street. A UNC grad and lifelong Tar Heel fan, Julian returned to North Carolina often and, two years before, had gained notoriety for having designed the uniforms for

Charlotte's new NBA team.

"If we use Alex, I'll need his word that he doesn't do this for any other college team," Smith said. "It wouldn't mean as much if other teams were wearing his uniforms as well."

Later that day, Smith's secretary, Linda Woods, placed a call to Julian in New York City. She found out that Julian was traveling overseas and was told he would be extremely difficult to reach. "Make sure he knows that it's Coach Dean Smith calling," Woods said before hanging up.

Within an hour, Julian had returned the call. "Dean Smith is a great hero of mine, and I've been a Carolina fan since before I could talk," he said later. Then he added with typical dramatic flair, "Having Dean Smith ask you to redo the Carolina uniforms is like having God ask you to redo the uniforms for the archangels."

Julian went through an elaborate process, including having Michael Jordan test different fabrics while practicing before the next season. Claiming that "some of the most beloved fabrics in America are Carolina blue," Julian experimented with chambray, oxford cloth, and faded denim in his design studio. His associates said Julian was part kid in a candy store, part mad inventor.

Julian introduced the first version of Carolina's so-called "designer uniforms" in the fall of 1991 at a press conference that featured Hubert Davis and George Lynch as models and attracted media from around the state and the nation. Julian, himself, was in Europe and could not attend. Although the denim warm-up jacket and shooting shirt have changed since then, and the original nylon uniforms did not take to being washed so many times in one season, the staple of the new design became the famed argyle striping down both sides of the jersey and shorts. The diamond-stitched pattern consisted of several shades of Carolina blue and defined the Tar Heels' contemporary designer look.

Champion Products, a division of North Carolina-based Sara Lee Corporation, worked with Julian to produce the prototype but was eventually cut out when Nike signed a multimillion-dollar contract with UNC in 1993. Since then, Nike has marketed authentic and replica Carolina uniforms, shooting shirts and warm-ups to retail outlets all over the world. Well into the 1990s, licensed apparel carrying the various Carolina trademarks remained in the top five sellers among all colleges and universities. Some of the most popular items were the oversized replica jerseys and baggy basketball shorts, worn by teenagers all over the country.

Julian, who donated his work for "love of the university," eventually overhauled the UNC women's uniforms, as well, trimming their jerseys and shorts in Carolina blue with a paisley stripe down both sides. When the Lady Tar Heels broke out their new togs following their own national championship season in 1994, it was yet another example of the many innovations credited to Smith over the years.

✪

Long before the advent of Carolina's designer uniforms, Smith's innovations on the court were contributing to his growing legend. Most famous, of course – or notorious, from the perspective of opposing teams – was the offense that changed the game.

Larry Brown, Johnny Yokley, Bobby Lewis, Larry Miller, Dick Grubar, Eddie Fogler, Charlie Scott, Steve Previs, George Karl, Jimmy Black, and Kenny Smith all took turns running Four Corners with success over twenty years. But the spread offense was redefined by Phil Ford from 1975 to 1978 and continued to be associated with the All-American guard long after he graduated and moved on to pro basketball. Ultimately, as the biggest single reason for the implementation of the shot clock 1986, Four Corners changed the rules of college basketball. The 1982 ACC Championship game, when the Tar Heels held the ball against Ralph Sampson and the Virginia zone, began a national furor that ultimately led to a clock.

"We had very little chance of getting a rebound with Sampson sitting under the basket," Smith explained. "We had five excellent passers and ballhandlers in Black, Doherty, Jordan, Perkins and Worthy. And we wanted them to come out and chase us. We were playing to our strength just as Virginia was playing to its strength."

Critics predicted Carolina couldn't survive without its pet offense, the pet peeve of all opponents. But the naysayers turned out to be dead wrong. Ironically, Smith had lobbied for the shot clock, plus the three-point shot, for years. When both were instituted, Carolina became one of the highest-scoring and best three-point shooting teams in America. As the college game changed forever, once again

Smith had been thinking ahead and making his plans.

Two decades earlier, he was watching a tennis match on the Carolina campus when he came up with another novel idea. Tennis players wore sweatbands on their wrists to keep their hands dry. Why couldn't basketball players do the same thing in hot, sweaty gyms? Smith asked his equipment manager to order wristbands, in white and Carolina blue, and instructed the student team manager to always have extras for the players, home and away.

On a 1968 road trip to Charlottesville and College Park, manager Randy Forehand courted disaster by forgetting to pack the team's wristbands. "Know my fright when I forgot them," Forehand said. "I went all over Charlottesville. Nobody had wristbands, the tennis stores, the athletic stores, sporting goods stores. Nobody had wristbands.

"By now, all of our players liked them and wanted to wear them, and it's either everybody wears 'em or nobody wears 'em," Forehand said of Smith's team-oriented dress code. So with nowhere else to go, Forehand did the unthinkable: He bargained with the enemy, since Virginia had already copied Carolina's idea. Forehand went to Norm Carmichael, the center for Virginia, and begged him to loan Carolina enough wristbands for the entire team. Carmichael agreed – with one stipulation. He wanted Tar Heel All-American Miller to autograph his wristband before giving it back.

"Carmichael saved my butt," Forehand said. "Coach Smith never found out I had forgotten them."

Another innovation stemmed from a difference of opinion between Smith and his legendary college. Phog Allen had always maintained that players who couldn't stay in the game for forty minutes weren't in shape, but Smith believed otherwise, especially with the kind of pressure defense the Tar Heels deployed. Instead of worrying about playing the whole game, Smith wanted his players to go as hard as they could when they were on the court and then willingly tell him when they were tired. So, during preseason drills in 1961-62, his first year as head coach, he invented the "tired" signal. By raising a fist to the bench, any Tar Heel could take himself out of the game and then put himself back in by saying, "Coach, I'm ready."

Not that the system was flawless. Smith still remembers with amusement that in the very first game of the season he forgot about the ploy.

When Larry Brown gave him the "tired" signal running by the bench, Smith stood up, thrust a fist back at Brown and said, "Yeah, Larry, way to go!" A few years later, reserve Ricky Webb tried to increase his overall playing time by taking himself out every time he got in the game and then putting himself back in. Smith wised up to the maneuver and made Webb run laps at practice.

Two other Smith innovations that became common practices in college basketball were the foul-line huddle and the time-out after a basket to stop the clock. In the age of changing defenses, Smith had various ways to make sure his players knew exactly which defense they were going to use on the opponent's next possession. After missing a shot, they always ran back and played man-to-man defense. Generally, after making a basket, they sprinted back and got the defensive call from the point guard through a hand signal – yet another "Deanovation." However, if a Carolina player got fouled, the next defense was anybody's guess, so Smith had his team huddle around the free-throw shooter to get the defensive call. He considered following a made free throw a good time to set up a full-court press, because at least four of his players were close to the baseline where the ball was to be inbounded and could quickly implement a man-to-man defense.

Carolina was also the first team to utilize time-outs after made baskets to set up the defense for the next inbounds pass. Until a rule change that automatically stopped the clock after each field goal in the last minute of a game, precious seconds were often wasted before the other team put the ball in play. Smith, the master of time management at the end of close games, had his teams stop the clock to make certain they were in defensive position. That became commonplace at all levels of basketball – with all five players making the time-out sign over their heads in the final, frantic seconds.

Smith made changing defenses an art form. The Tar Heels loved to surprise opponents with different defenses that all looked the same at the beginning of a possession. Once an opponent crossed midcourt with the ball, Carolina teams might play tough man-to-man defense, spring a double-team on the ball handler, or by overplaying one side force a pass into the corner where two Tar Heels would trap the panicky receiver into a time-out or a turnover. Of all his beloved "hybrid" defenses, one of Smith's favorites was the match-up or "point" zone, which he developed in the 1970s. Unlike a traditional zone defense, where players covered certain areas of the floor and only those opponents who came into their areas, Smith's point zone combined zone and man-to-man principles. Opponents who moved through the various zones were picked up in a man-to-man style defense, while the other Tar Heel defenders remained conscious of where the ball was. The point zone got its name because, if executed correctly, three defenders were in a line between the ball and the basket at all times.

Credit Smith with another innovation that has become routine throughout basketball – a scorer pointing to the man who passed him the ball. Smith began that practice in his early years at Carolina, hoping to draw attention to the player who committed the selfless act of giving the ball up to a teammate with a better shot. Tar Heel fans sitting in the arena were quick to adopt the signal, adding another measure of congratulation to the playmaker.

✪

Once Carolina starting winning ACC championships in 1967, losses at Carmichael Auditorium were so rare that, when they occurred, stunned fans left the building silently. In twenty-two years of games in Blue Heaven, Smith's teams lost only twenty times, posting six and a half undefeated seasons and staging some of the most memorable victories and comebacks in Carolina history. One of the greatest was the monumental upset of unbeaten and top-ranked South Carolina on January 4, 1971, when the Tar Heels held the ball and forced Frank McGuire's Gamecocks out of the zone, ran them ragged, and posted the stunning 79-64 win. That game ushered in a new era of invincibility for Smith's program – and paved the way for a number of other "unforgettables."

On March 2, 1974, fifth-ranked Carolina had actually played pretty well against a ragtag Duke team performing way over its head. With seventeen seconds left in the game, the Heels trailed by eight points, and their fans were not-so-silently streaming for the exits. In the time-out huddle Smith smiled and said, "Wouldn't it be fun to come back and win this game? Here's how we're going to do it." Then, in what was to become legendary succession, Bobby Jones made two free throws and converted a steal, Walter Davis scored following another Duke turnover, and then, after the Blue Devils' Pete Kramer missed a free throw, Davis banked in a thirty-foot prayer at the buzzer to force overtime. Thousands of fans poured onto the court in a victory celebration that was only a few minutes premature. Carolina eventually won, 96-92. The biggest comeback in the shortest time in the history of college basketball cost interim Duke coach Neill McGeachy any chance of getting the job on a permanent basis.

Among the greatest games played at Carmichael were the two comeback wins over Sampson and Virginia, the first of which added considerably to the drama of the second. By this time, Smith had rallied his team so regularly from second-half deficits that it was no longer a question of whether the Tar Heels would make a run, but when. That inevitability often preyed upon wary opponents trying to protect a lead.

In 1982, Carolina roared back from sixteen points down to beat the Cavaliers, 65-60. That narrow win, coupled with a sixteen-point loss at Charlottesville later in the season, helped convince Smith to hold the ball against Virginia's zone in the third meeting between the two teams in the ACC Tournament. That was the controversial game, won by the Tar Heels, 47-45, that allowed them to play in the East Region of the NCAA Tournament on the way to the national title.

Virginia, after having been sent to the Southeast Region and getting knocked out, was determined to win the national championship in Sampson's senior season, 1983. And the Cavaliers looked like national champions when they again surged to a sixteen-point lead in Carmichael Auditorium. But that was before Michael Jordan capped a Tar Heel rally in the last minute with a follow shot, a steal and dunk, and a game-ending rebound over Sampson. The 64-63 win was UNC's eighteenth straight and sent Jordan on to win his first of nine different national player of the year awards.

Smith was sometimes so cool and predictable in late-game huddles that he even irritated his own players. On January 19, 1986, the day after the Smith Center had opened in the middle of the season with a weekend of festivities and an emotional, nationally televised win over Duke, the Tar Heels were in Milwaukee trailing Marquette by seven points with less than four minutes to play. The team was 18-0 and ranked No. 1 in the country, but it hadn't been easy.

Smith, his players, and his entire program had been under tremendous pressure, trying to stay focused while the countdown continued to the grand opening of the building that bore his name. The morning of the Duke game, workers were hurriedly hanging the oversized honored jerseys from the girders of the Deandome when Smith walked onto the court. "Hey, move them to the left," Smith had shouted up to the guys on the catwalk. "Mr. Swofford wants them here," one of them yelled back, referring to UNC Athletic Director John Swofford. "IT'S MY BUILDING!" shrieked Smith, his nasal voice piercing the air.

But now Smith was smiling in the face of a poor performance by his team. Carolina was heavily favored to beat Marquette but had played sloppy and uninspired basketball. "Okay, we've got them right where we want them," Smith said, winking at senior center Warren Martin. Jeff Lebo, a freshman and yet to be a believer, stood behind Smith in the huddle and rolled his eyes at a teammate. "We looked at each other like, 'What the hell, that's not where we want them. Seven down is where we want them, not seven up.'" Smith continued, "Let's not panic; we can still come back and win, and this is how we're going to do it. We've been here in practice before, so let's go out and do it." The Tar Heels sprung a surprise defense on Marquette, forced two turnovers and kept fouling the Warriors, who nervously missed several free throws down the stretch as UNC won 66-64 to stay unbeaten.

Come-from-behind wins were so common under Smith that the Carolina media guide had a six-page section called "Fantastic Finishes" depicting famous rallies from 1967 through 1997. Sophomore Charlie Scott capped a seventeen-point comeback over unbeaten Utah in December of 1967 with the winning shot and, fifteen months later, scored twenty-eight points in the second half against Duke to revive the Tar Heels in the ACC Tournament title game. Dudley Bradley, a Charlie Scott of defense, committed high thievery in 1979 at N.C. State, stripping Clyde Austin of the ball in the open court and dunking at the buzzer to bring the Tar Heels back from the dead. Smith pulled off miraculous finishes against two different schools coached by old rival Lefty Driesell, several when he was at Maryland and perhaps the most memorable against Driesell's James Madison Dukes in the 1989 Maui Classic. When King Rice hit the buzzer-beater to complete the nine-point rally in the final minute of play, Driesell did not act surprised or particularly upset. He had been there before. Carolina comebacks under Smith actually became more prevalent as each new generation of players bought into the tradition. In the "Fantastic Finishes" section, almost half of the legendary rallies occurred in Smith's last ten years on the job.

In reality, they were not miracles after all. Smith's practices were so thorough and so precise that his teams rarely found themselves in a late-game situation for which they had not prepared. Smith reserved the last half-hour of practice for different scenarios – six down with three minutes to play, four behind with thirty seconds left, trailing by two with two seconds showing on the clock.

"It's incredible," said Lebo, the coach at Tennessee Tech who as a Carolina player learned firsthand that the Tar Heels were never out of it until mathematically eliminated (too many points to make up with too few ticks left on the clock). "We were drilled for those situations and practiced them over and over. It's what separated his (Smith's) from a lot of programs. The time and score and what kind of shot you needed, and then what defense we were going to play. His teams were there so many times, and it was amazing how often we confronted something that we just happened to have practiced that week."

✪

Smith even prepared his players for situations over which they had no control. At the end of the day, everyone on the team had a designated time within which he had to complete his wind sprints from one end of the court to the other. The players had to touch the baseline with their toe each time down – or else run the sprints again. Occasionally, Smith would blow his whistle, claim a player had missed touching the baseline, and send him back, even if the player had done it correctly the first time. He wanted to demonstrate that all teams were going to get bad calls during a game, and the last thing he wanted from his players was a temperamental outburst. Players who complained, who popped off during practice, stayed late to run the arena stairs wearing a weighted vest.

The two hours late in the afternoon during basketball season were sacred for Smith. "I have never taken a phone call during practice in all my years of coaching," he said. "I have also refused to talk to anyone during our practice time. This would include alumni, the chancellor, or the athletic director. There are twenty-two other hours in the day when I can be reached." Likewise, out of the nearly four thousand practices he conducted, Smith never missed one to go recruiting, no matter how badly he needed new players. His first obligation was always to the players he had in school. His own self-excused absences from practice were few and far between: a few for the funerals of close friends and those four days in 1987 when he literally could not stand up because of severe nosebleeds.

Smith was in complete control of his practices, whether conducting drills himself or watching his assistant coaches work with the players at their individual "stations," and he seemingly knew everything that was happening in the gym. Since 1966, all practices had been closed, and all visitors needed prior permission to attend. Only Smith's closest coaching friends and former players could watch from courtside; all others had to sit in the upper arena. Smith said that he did not want visitors to be a distraction, but he also did not want them to be able to see and hear exactly what went on.

In October of 1989, UNC's rookie radio announcer, Mick Mixon, wanted to watch his first Tar Heel practice and thought he had followed instructions perfectly. He had called the basketball office that morning to request a pass, stated his reasons, and was told to come by for the index card that would allow him access to the Deandome's upper deck. Mixon entered the balcony early in the practice and, noticing Smith teaching offense at one end of the court, moved around to take a seat on the baseline high above the basket. Because Carolina practices were like delicate chemistry labs, where only one voice was heard at a time, Mixon carefully placed his briefcase on the concrete floor and began to sit down. A split second before his fanny hit the cushioned chair, the high-pitched reverberation of his own first name stunned him.

"Mick!" Smith yelled up to him, "over there, between the baskets!" Mixon gathered up his stuff and moved around to midcourt, where the sight and sound lines down to Smith were farther. In his proper place, Mixon watched the rest of the practice uninterrupted.

Smith insisted that he and his assistant coaches always be lively and energetic during practice, and demanded the same of their players. "Each player must make a great effort to appear enthusiastic," he once wrote. "By acting this way, the player will often become enthusiastic even if it was not his inclination when he first took the court." Though mechanical, that concept proved marvelously efficient in accomplishing the goals of every practice session. Those goals, along with the minute-by-minute schedule, were printed on a neatly typed sheet and given to each coach and player. Such meticulous preparation was the result of off-season meetings and player evaluation sessions, leading to a master practice plan, then to a weekly plan, and, ultimately, to the daily practice plans tailored to the twists and turns of the season.

Reams have been written about Smith's practices and his seniority system: the tight schedule; the thought and emphasis of the day; freshmen chasing loose balls and carrying the gear; water breaks by class, seniors first. Whether upper- or underclassman, the quickest way for a player to get into Smith's doghouse was to complain or offer any excuse to a criticism leveled by one of the coaches. That was a gross waste of precious practice time and threw the schedule off. Every team member was required to make direct eye contact with Smith and his assistants while they were speaking, and even the slightest facial gesture could draw a rebuke from the coaches. "We're here to help you become better basketball players," Smith was known to say.

In his last few years as a coach, Smith's favorite part of preseason practice was altered considerably by the encroaching schedule. Official practice usually began around October 15, and whereas teams once had a full six weeks to prepare for their first game – known as "boot camp" to the players – they began playing in holiday tournaments as early as mid-November. These games took away Smith's vaunted teaching edge, which had traditionally made Carolina the best-coached team in the country in the first month of the season and had almost always resulted in a fast start.

A mathematician by training, Smith was often ridiculed for the incessant record-keeping of his student managers, who recorded every movement made in practice and shot taken warming up for games. For example, a player missing a layup in the weave drill at the beginning of practice always knew to fall out of line and run a single lap around the court. Not only were there dozens of awards – charges taken, screens set, loose balls collected – on a daily and weekly basis, the managers kept track of a "plus point" system in which the players could reduce the number of sprints they had to run at the end of practice. Generally, the players who were spared sprints were the best athletes who didn't mind running them. Plus points could also be carried over from season to season or bequeathed by departing seniors to underclassmen – a wonderful means of building continuity.

Peer pressure became an integral part of Smith's practice structure in the 1960s when his golf partner and local psychiatrist Earl Somers told him that soldiers in combat were more likely to perform well out of loyalty to their cohorts than in response to a set of rules or ideals. Thus, never letting a buddy down became a teaching focus for Smith, who often punished the entire group for an individual's infraction. "When a player breaks a rule or fails to do what is expected of him, it hurts the entire team," Smith explained. At his most extreme, Smith was known to make the offending player take a water break while watching the rest of the team run sprints.

One drill that fostered togetherness and interdependence came at the free-throw line at the end of a hard practice, where every player had to make two consecutive foul shots before the entire team could hit the showers. The pressure of letting teammates down in this situation was presumably comparable to that of hitting free throws late in a close game with a hostile crowd screaming at the top of its lungs. The exercise also helped fatigued players retain their focus and concentrate on the fundamentals and their own personal rituals at the foul line.

In the late 1960s, after Smith had recruited a number of star players, competition between the "white" and "blue" teams began in earnest. The blue team consisted of reserves who rarely got into games and, consequently, understood that their season would be played in practice. Scrimmage scores between the whites and blues were recorded daily and tabulated as the season progressed. Smith was always upset when the blue team had whipped his starting rotation, but in the 1970s the blue team got so good that Smith began inserting it into games as a unit to play scrappy defense and wear out the opposition by moving the ball without really looking for a shot. Occasionally, a blue team player – such as Mike Pepper in 1980 – won a permanent promotion to the top eight men and sometimes even started.

Practice was considered the tough part of playing for Smith, and the games came so easily because of what the players had been so expertly taught. In 1981, against a Duke team that prided itself on aggressive man-to-man defense, Smith called a play during a time-out that everyone knew would work. As the huddle broke, assistant coach Eddie Fogler turned to a spectator sitting directly behind the Carolina bench and said almost giddily, "Watch the backdoor layup." Seconds later, Sam Perkins took the inbounds pass, held it over his head and faked a toss into the corner. Jimmy Black had been going that way for an instant, but was now reversing his direction toward the basket. Perkins hit him for a wide-open layup.

A few years earlier, Maryland had arrived in Chapel Hill for a practice in Carmichael Auditorium the day before the game. Fogler sneaked a peak at the Terrapins' workout just as Driesell was imploring his big men, Lawrence Boston and Chris Patton, to watch for the lob to Walter Davis when Carolina took the ball out under its own basket. This was a routine play, one Smith had called often in that situation, and one that was easily scouted. But it underscored the difference between his practices and those of other programs.

Sure enough, early in the second half, the Tar Heels missed a shot, and in the rebounding scramble Maryland knocked the ball out under the basket. Down at the Maryland bench, Driesell and his assistant Dave Pritchett stood up, waved, and hollered to Boston and Patton, "Watch the lob to Davis!" The whistle blew, the ball was slapped, and here came Davis from the top of the key into the lane, where he easily caught the soft inbounds pass from Mitch Kupchak and laid it in at the top of his jump. Fogler couldn't help but glance down the sideline, where Pritchett had dropped to his knees, head in hands, and Driesell stomped the court like he was killing ants. Fogler elbowed Smith. They both smiled.

CHAPTER FIFTEEN

THE DUKE RIVALRY

Long-time rival Duke hovered over the darkest day of Dean Smith's coaching career with almost devilish delight. On March 30, 1991, Smith became the only coach to ever get thrown out of a Final Four game, and it happened as thousands of Duke fans cheered wildly from their section of the Hoosier Dome in Indianapolis. Their team was there, too, and would win the school's first national championship two nights later.

Smith's long war against Duke began inauspiciously. During his reconstruction of the Tar Heel program, he lost his first seven games to the Blue Devils. Smith then compiled a 59-28 record against the archrivals from twelve miles down the road. Vic Bubas won those first seven and proved the lone Duke coach to have a winning percentage over Smith. But Bubas won only five of the last thirteen games between the two men and, perhaps because he saw the writing on the wall, left coaching at the relatively early age of forty-two to become a vice president at Duke and eventually the commissioner of the fledgling Sun Belt Conference.

Bucky Waters, Bubas's successor, posted a huge upset over the third-ranked Tar Heels in 1972, and Neill McGeachy, who coached Duke for a year after Waters resigned suddenly in 1973, blew the infamous "eight points in seventeen seconds" lead to Carolina at Carmichael

Auditorium in 1974. In his six seasons, Bill Foster's most memorable win over Smith was the bizarre 47-40 game in which Duke held Carolina scoreless in the first half.

Mike Krzyzewski took the rivalry to a new level in his seventeen years of coaching against Smith. Not only did Krzyzewski's program pull even with and briefly surpass Carolina's, the intensity on the court, in recruiting, and even in the banter between the two coaches and their respective constituencies reached an all-time high. After Krzyzewski had resurrected Duke in a time frame eerily parallel to Smith's at Carolina in the early 1960s, the two coaches developed a personal antagonism that remained virulent until Smith's retirement. The Duke students, for years a nemesis of and a target for Smith, inflamed the controversy in a game on January 18, 1989, at Cameron Indoor Stadium.

Smith was generally reluctant to be critical after his team had lost, for fear his message would be interpreted as sour grapes. He had made an exception after an eight-point loss in 1978, when he scolded the Duke students for their ridicule of Mike O'Koren's facial acne. This time, however, Smith had the benefit of a marvelous upset win over the top-ranked and previously unbeaten Blue Devils. Carolina carried a 14-3 record to Duke but had lost two of its last three games and was reeling from a 23-point pounding at Virginia. And the Tar Heels were without their senior leader Jeff Lebo, who stayed back in Chapel Hill with a severely sprained ankle to watch on TV. Ironically, this scenario usually meant trouble for Smith's next opponent. "A team is most dangerous," he liked to say, "the game after it has hit rock bottom."

While no one gave Carolina a chance, Smith believed his team's superior size could neutralize Duke, and with good games from guards King Rice, Steve Bucknall, and freshman Hubert Davis the Tar Heels indeed could win. In fact, Smith had cut short an afternoon radio interview for a rare appearance at the team's pre-game meal to make sure the players were staying focused. Behind twenty-one rebounds from J. R. Reid and Scott Williams, Carolina clobbered Duke on the boards, broke it open midway through the second half, and won going away, 91-71.

Early in the game, Smith had noticed a placard in the student section across from the Carolina bench that read "JR CAN'T REID." Smith stifled his outrage and continued to coach as hard as he ever had. But in the post-game press conference, he went after the Duke students again. He charged that the sign was racially motivated, asking pointedly whether the students would have been similarly creative if Reid, his star forward, had been white. He added that the sign was absurd, anyway, since Reid was an excellent student with high SAT scores and good grades.

Later that season, Smith still had not let the incident go. Prior to the teams' rematch in Chapel Hill, which Duke was to win, Smith made reference to the sign again in his teleconference, observing that the combined SAT scores of Reid and black teammate Williams were higher than those of Duke's white stars Danny Ferry and Christian Laettner. "I know," Smith said, "because I recruited both of them." A week later, during team workouts the day before the ACC Tournament in Atlanta got under way, Smith found himself in the middle of a controversy that would underscore the tension of the entire weekend.

To many observers, Smith had crossed the line of privacy and decency by talking about the test scores of players from another program. But he disagreed and continued to make his point that holding up the "JR CAN'T REID" sign fostered racism throughout the country, and that Duke should take steps to control its crowd behavior. Virginia sportswriter Bill Brill, a Duke graduate and long-time Blue Devil sympathizer, argued with Smith in the runway of the Omni in Atlanta. "You can't talk about the SATs of another school's players!" Brill charged. "Why not?" Smith countered. Inside the arena, Krzyzewski was holding court with a small group of sportswriters that included, among others, pro-Duke journalists such as John Feinstein. "It really pisses me off that he would talk about my players," Krzyzewski said of Smith.

Years later, whenever reminded of the incident, Smith insisted that he had not reacted out of anger. "I knew exactly what I was doing," he said, and indeed Dean Smith rarely hesitated to make a point of a principle in which he believed regardless of who might be affected. Referees, NCAA officials, TV moguls, or members of the media – it mattered little. Smith had become a prominent enough figure in collegiate sports that he could pick his battles and garner plenty of publicity.

This particular controversy was the backdrop for the 1989 ACC Tournament, one of the most contentious in history. Carolina had lost the last two games of the regular season and, having not won the tournament since 1982, wasn't being given much of a chance. Before their first game against Georgia Tech, the players called a meeting among themselves to get their heads straight. After beating Tech, they did it again before the semifinals against Maryland. When they advanced to Sunday's championship game, Smith called a team meeting, walked in and said, "You guys are doing a good job" and walked out.

The atmosphere resembled a heavyweight championship fight on Sunday afternoon, March 12, so stifling were the excitement and anticipation. When the teams came out to warm up, the tension that hung in the atmosphere of the Omni was so palpable that some spectators were actually having a hard time breathing. Not only were their teams playing for the ACC title on national TV, but in this rubber match of the season between the schools, Tar Heel and Blue Devil fans had been assigned tickets in adjacent sections of the arena.

A single aisle separated the two fanatical groups, and the crowd noise was punctuated by their often-obscene razzing of each other. Krzyzewski's own family members, by this time well known as emotional and animated, sat at the front of the Duke section and engaged in the taunting. Krzyzewski's wife, Mickie, their daughters, and their friends divided their time between cheering for their team, yelling at the officials, and countering the Carolina cries coming from the next section. From that point on, right through Smith's retirement and beyond, Krzyzewski's family would often be at the center of controversial incidents at Carolina-Duke games.

The Tar Heels won this epic battle, claiming their first ACC Tournament championship in seven years, as Smith and Krzyzewski competed as hard on the sideline as their players did on the court. Early in the second half, Krzyzewski said something to Carolina's Williams for committing a hard foul in front of the Duke bench, and Smith yelled down to Krzyzewski, "Don't talk to my players!" Late in the game, Reid tangled with Ferry for a rebound and knocked down the Duke All-American, who the week before had been nominated for the Naismith Player of the Year Award in college basketball. "How's that, Mr. Naismith?" scowled Reid, an All-American who had not been nominated.

Following the 77-74 victory, Smith was at it again. His team had been relegated to the Southeast Regional of the NCAA Tournament, while Duke inexplicably had been assigned to the East Regional and two games at the Greensboro Coliseum. Noting that Duke Athletic Director Tom Butters was on the NCAA basketball selection committee and convinced the Blue Devils had been given the favorable draw because if it, Smith kept the needle hot for two weeks. After his team had advanced to the regional semifinal to play Michigan for the third straight year, Smith pointedly commented, "I'd rather be playing Minnesota," referring to Duke's opponent in the East.

When eventual national champion Michigan, which Carolina had defeated the prior two years, knocked off the Tar Heels, Smith mentioned the NCAA assignments one more time. And, of course, it rankled him that Duke easily beat Minnesota and then upset Alonzo Mourning-led Georgetown to reach another Final Four, Duke's third in the last four years. In fact, for the seventh consecutive year, Smith attended the annual coaches' convention at the Final Four while Krzyzewski was there to play ball.

✪

With Duke now the "in" team in college basketball, the 1990 season proved to be another turning point in Smith's career. Reid turned pro after his junior year, the third Carolina player in the 1980s (after Worthy and Jordan) to leave early for the NBA, and a solid recruiting class got overshadowed by two New York-area guards Smith had recruited and lost. Carolina's top choice had been Kenny Anderson, a long-time schoolyard legend from Queens who supposedly was following his second cousin Kenny Smith to Chapel Hill. Coach Smith had also recruited Bobby Hurley of nearby Jersey City and told him he was his second choice behind Anderson.

For years, that system of prioritizing recruits by position – and telling them where they stood – was a staple of Smith's method. Likewise for many years, high school players and their parents respected that kind of honesty, and in many cases so coveted a scholarship to Carolina that they were willing to wait. But college coaches had become much more aggressive in the pursuit of prep stars, and the increased media coverage of recruiting had swelled the heads and egos of many top prospects. If they weren't the first choice, to hell with that school.

Anderson had been everyone's top priority, because the lithe, left-handed wizard could really play. Georgia Tech coach Bobby Cremins, a native New Yorker, had recruited him hard and gradually learned through his street sources that Anderson was not sold on UNC. Cremins called Anderson almost daily and, in the early fall of 1988, dropped the phone when Anderson told him, "I'm not going to Carolina." Anderson committed to Tech before the November signing period, canceling his scheduled visit to UNC, and would lead the Yellow Jackets to their only Final Four appearance the following March. He stayed at Tech two years before turning pro.

Like many kids in the Northeast, Hurley had grown up a fan of the Tar Heels after watching them so often on television in the early 1980s. Hurley's father, Bob, was also his coach at St. Anthony's High School and admired Smith's program for its success on the court and its image off the floor. During the summer of 1988, however, both father and son felt let down by Smith's request that they hold off their decision on a school until Anderson made up his mind. Anderson and Hurley had been rival stars for several years, the best black player in New York versus the best white guard in New Jersey.

Krzyzewski seized the opportunity to tell the Hurleys that Duke wanted them in its program more than Carolina did. Using the high-pressure style that was so successful at the time, Krzyzewski got his point guard by promising Hurley that the starting position was his to lose from his first day on campus as a freshman. When Hurley announced he was going to Duke before Anderson committed to Tech, Smith had already figured out his plan had backfired and he would lose both guards. While his critics called his methods old-fashioned, Smith philosophically saw the outcome as one of the times when honesty didn't pay off.

It looked like he might have gotten a last laugh when, in their first meeting of 1990, Carolina blew out Duke and harried freshman Hurley into ten turnovers. In the rematch at Duke on the last day of the regular season, Carolina won again to post its third victory in four years at Cameron Indoor Stadium. A frustrated Krzyzewski lashed out at his team for backing down to the bigger Tar Heels, as his record against Smith fell to 8-16. In the two games, unheralded junior King Rice had initiated Hurley into ACC basketball – outscoring him by eleven points, handing out ten more assists, and winning the trash-talking undercard.

Still, Duke got hot in the post-season and made it all the way to the national championship game before getting crushed by UNLV. Carolina, meanwhile, pulled off the upset of the NCAA Tournament by stunning top-seeded Oklahoma in the second round, but Smith's team again failed to survive the Sweet Sixteen. His kingdom getting restless, Smith faced some pointed questions during his tour of booster club meetings that summer. Aware that Duke's four trips to the Final Four in five years had hurt Carolina fans, Smith was ready when asked if he believed that defeating Duke twice in a season was more important than reaching the Final Four.

"I don't know, let's see," Smith answered quickly, calling for a show of hands. He had checkmated the crowd, which Smith knew could never minimize his dominance over Duke – at least not in front of him. But Smith, himself, was far from satisfied with just beating the Blue Devils. In fact, he had returned to the recruiting road in order to put together an incoming class that would be called the greatest assemblage of high school talent ever signed by one school. Eric Montross, Clifford Rozier, Pat Sullivan, Brian Reese, and Derrick Phelps were not quite that good, but Smith missed out on one player who might have put that class over the top.

Of course, that player went to Duke. High School All-American Grant Hill had liked Carolina growing up and would have made an outstanding UNC freshman class truly extraordinary, but Krzyzewski landed the 6-8 forward in the fall of 1989 with his typical recruiting rush. Having already been to the brink of the national championship several times, Krzyzewski told Hill there were talented players in his program and promised he would continue to sign great athletes to play alongside him. Dazzled and pressured for the rest of the weekend, Hill surprised himself by shaking Krzyzewski's hand, verbally committing to Duke and agreeing to cancel his scheduled visit to Carolina the following weekend.

Upon getting the bad news, Smith wondered what Krzyzewski could have said to make Hill pass up his other recruiting trips and commit to Duke on the spot. In the years to come, it remained a source of frustration and irritation for Smith and his staff that part of the Duke strategy was to pressure high school players into cutting off the recruiting process cold before they could see for themselves what all the other schools had to offer.

✪

Smith's resurgence as a recruiter and coach in the 1990s may not have been as motivated by Duke's success as some people theorized. Nevertheless, he seemed determined to break the string of bad luck that had kept his team out of the Final Four since 1982 and cost his program some key recruits it might well have signed. Danny Manning, Danny Ferry, Billy Owens, Anderson, and Hill – all heading to Chapel Hill at one point – wound up elsewhere. And, in 1988, a gifted sophomore power forward named Kenny Williams announced he would attend Carolina, effectively scaring off recruits who were considering UNC. By the time Williams failed to graduate from high school, most of the other prospects had made different plans.

Though Smith denied it, he clearly was on the road more frequently than he had been in years, reconnoitering high school games and all-star camps, usually with Phil Ford by his side. He did acknowledge one change in Carolina's recruiting system, which historically had contacted prospects for the first time in earnest after their junior years in high school. Smith moved the calendar up, beginning the sales pitch to potential recruits during their junior years and sometimes earlier. At the same time, Smith made it clear they would not be hearing from him or his assistants every day.

With Ford learning the ropes, Smith again had his recruiting staff in place. The affable and charismatic Ford served as the front man, the first person to see prep stars. Veteran assistant Bill Guthridge, considered a wily talent scout, had the second opinion. If both agreed to go after a certain player, Smith got heavily involved and eventually was the ultimate closer. While recruiting had become more difficult, because minutes played and pro potential were now as important as academics and campus life, Smith had an advantage going after the big freshman class of 1991. He could offer almost all of his high school targets the promise of playing time, in some cases immediately.

During the 1990 season, in fact, Carolina was so thin in the backcourt that Smith pulled out what was to become one of his most famous analogies. A registered Democrat who contributed money and support to his party, he likened the fact that he did not have a qualified substitute for his point guard to the situation in the White House. "King Rice is our Bush," Smith said cagily to the press one afternoon early in the year. "I'd hate to have to find out who our Quayle is."

He encountered a different problem early in the 1991 season, when many Carolina fans wanted Smith to impeach senior Rice in favor of freshman Phelps. During the ACC-Big East Challenge game against Connecticut in the Deandome, the home crowd booed Rice after he turned the ball over repeatedly against the Huskies' pressure defense. When he put Phelps in the game to a large roar from the fans, Smith could not hide his irritation and commented on it after the 79-64 victory. The next morning, he had Rice in his office assuring him that he, and not Phelps, was his starting point guard for the rest of the season.

Far better known than Rice during their respective recruiting periods, Phelps was the latest in a long line of highly touted guards to migrate to Carolina from New York City. Way back in 1957, former coach Frank McGuire had tacked a cartoon from the old *New York Telegram* to the wall in his office, depicting his famed Underground Railroad: three young lads with suitcases emerging from a city subway stop and walking toward South Building on the UNC campus. The sign on the subway stairs read, "Uptown Bronx, Downtown Chapel Hill." Tommy Kearns, York Larese, Larry Brown, Eddie Fogler, and Kenny Smith had all come from the Big Apple before Phelps.

Reese, more of a perimeter player than Phelps, also came from New York City, although he never would have been signed had Smith gotten Hill. Reese was more familiar with North Carolina than his classmates, since his older brother had moved South eight years earlier and was working in Roanoke Rapids, two hours north of Chapel Hill. During one visit to North Carolina, the sixteen-year-old Reese had stopped by the UNC basketball office and introduced himself to the coach. Smith asked him if he would be interested in attending Carolina and talked to him about his schoolwork without ever mentioning basketball. That impression lasted.

Sullivan was the so-called small forward of the recruiting class, and for him it was an easy decision. Having grown up in New Jersey without a father in the house, Sullivan once asked former Tar Heel Mike O'Koren, who had played for the New Jersey Nets, about the family atmosphere at Carolina. When Sullivan heard that Smith was, in fact, a second father to his players, he turned down the Duke scholarship offer and signed with UNC. O'Koren also told Sullivan that he had been part of a large Tar Heel freshman recruiting class, and that was the best way to go in.

The seven-foot Montross was the surprise gem of the group; recruiting analysts had ticketed him for Indiana or Michigan. But the top player in Indianapolis prep basketball didn't like the often-abusive style of Indiana coach Bob Knight and wasn't sure about Michigan, his father and grandfather's alma mater, and its unproven new coach, Steve Fisher. Unbeknownst to most fans and recruiting services, Montross ultimately decided between Duke and Carolina, only this time the high-pressure tactics backfired on the Blue Devils. "Eric's family comes from old money, and he was going to take his time," Smith said the year after Montross signed. "Already having played in gyms bigger than Duke's, he was impressed with the size and quality of our place."

Ironically, the player in the class with the most natural ability turned out to be the biggest disappointment. Clifford Rozier, a 6-9 forward from Florida, whose grandmother lived a few miles from the Duke campus, was not a particularly hard worker and did not accept sitting on the bench behind sophomore George Lynch, senior Pete Chilcutt, and Montross. Rozier never meshed with the other players, stayed to himself, and quickly became the subject of transfer rumors. Rozier came from the same Florida area as ESPN announcer Dick Vitale, and it did not help matters that Vitale would implore Smith during TV broadcasts to play the talented but temperamental youngster. On several occasions during that year – and others – Smith had to tell Vitale tersely to "let me coach my team." After the season, Smith suggested the idea of transferring to Rozier, who wound up at Louisville.

With this highly regarded class in the fold, Carolina did finally break its Final Four drought in 1991. However, the freshmen had very little to do with it. Seniors Rice, Chilcutt, and Rick Fox led the Tar Heels to the ACC and NCAA East titles and a trip to Indianapolis, where waiting were Kansas, UNLV, and Duke. At the Thursday night CBS dinner, honoring the competing coaches, Smith teasingly asked Krzyzewski for his autograph. Coach K, participating in his fourth consecutive Final Four and fifth in the last six years, had become the toast of college basketball. Some saw Smith's mock gesture as an admission that the torch had been passed.

Three weeks earlier, their teams had played another spark-filled game in the finals of the ACC Tournament in Charlotte. Duke had narrowly won both regular-season games, but the third match-up was all Carolina. The Tar Heels broke on top early and led by as many as twenty-five points in the second half, while players from both teams traveled well beyond the bounds of self-control. Fox, playing off a widely circulated rumor that Duke star Christian Laettner dated both men and women, turned to Hurley at one juncture and said, "When are you guys gonna put the fag back in?" Laettner, frustrated with how the game was going, jawed at officials all afternoon and finally got a technical foul when he told ref Gerry Donaghy to fuck off.

Two days later, Duke alumnus and Carolina antagonist Feinstein enraged Tar Heel fans with a column in the now-defunct *National* sports daily entitled "Dean Smith, a Winner and a Whiner." Ignoring the deplorable conduct of both teams during the ACC final – including Krzyzewski's explaining away Laettner's behavior by calling him "an asshole" – Feinstein dredged up time-worn clichés about Smith's manipulation of the press and hung his article on a comment Smith had made to Krzyzewski during the post-game interviews. Aware that the outcome of the ACC title game had thrown the NCAA seeding into limbo, Smith had asked Krzyzewski if he had "talked to Tom" about where either team might be assigned. To Feinstein, of course, Smith was subtly implying that Butters would again help the Blue Devils gain a favorable draw in the NCAA Tournament.

Even after Carolina was awarded the No. 1 seed in the East and Duke was sent out to the Midwest, hundreds of letters and calls flooded into the *National*'s offices in New York, forcing editor Frank Deford to answer many of them personally. Naturally, he defended Feinstein's right to pen his own column and chalked it up to healthy partisanship. Deford received several other letters after the Final Four, where Feinstein was seen blatantly cheering for Kansas from his seat on press row during the Jayhawks' semifinal win over Carolina. Of course, after the game, Feinstein led the charge of reporters covering Smith's ejection on his second technical foul in the last minute of play.

Obviously baiting official Pete Pavia, Smith had walked a substitute to the scorer's table after Fox fouled out, yelling, "Pete, how much time do I have" to put in the sub? A stickler for the rules, Smith knew how much time he had and was essentially daring Pavia to give him another technical. No official in his right mind, with a national television audience watching and the game's outcome already decided, would have thrown out an icon such as Smith under those circumstances. But Pavia was not in his right mind and did not walk away. Taking medication for the cancer that would eventually kill him, the short-fused Pavia "t'd" up Smith. There was a brief delay as Smith walked ignominiously to the locker room, passing the Kansas bench and shaking hands with former assistant Roy Williams. As he exited, Duke fans, hundreds of them students, chanted "Go to hell, Carolina, go to hell!" and continued it all weekend as the Blue Devils upset UNLV and then defeated Kansas for the NCAA crown.

After the horn sounded, Guthridge followed Pavia and fellow officials Donaghy and Ed Hightower off the court into the runway. "That wasn't right, Gerry! That wasn't fair!" shouted Guthridge, intending Pavia to hear him. Guthridge was so agitated that two security officers, fearful of an altercation, stepped in front of him and blocked his path. Members of the Carolina team rushed to Guthridge's aid, although none of the Tar Heels touched the officers. The crowd dispersed without incident, and Smith headed for his post-game press conference, where he apologized for "taking the attention away from a great victory for Roy Williams and Kansas."

✪

What should have been a very satisfying season for Smith ended with that regrettable incident, as depressed Tar Heel fans trudged home from dank Indianapolis. By then, Michigan had already signed up its "Fab Five" – the new "best ever" recruiting class – and Carolina's freshmen were all but forgotten. In fact, the Tar Heels went on to be just ordinary by UNC standards in 1992, losing eight games in the regular season and four straight at one juncture. They entered the ACC Tournament in Charlotte again the subject of rumors that Smith had lost his touch and Duke would have the dynasty for years to come.

On paper, the team was far better than it performed. Phelps, Reese, Montross, Sullivan, Lynch, and freshman Donald Williams were all highly recruited. And senior Hubert Davis had emerged as one of the best pure shooters in college basketball. Sophomores Kevin Salvadori and junior Henrik Rodl were capable back-ups. But after a big upset win over top-ranked Duke in January, the team seemed to get worse as the season wore on. And virtually no one gave Carolina, or anyone else besides Duke, a chance to win the ACC Tournament title.

With the Tar Heels trailing Wake Forest in the first round and playing pitifully, Guthridge got a tip at halftime from a local writer that the pressroom banter had been less than kind to Carolina. "Tell Dean that everyone's saying you guys are through, going nowhere this season," the writer urged, "maybe it will fire up the team." Guthridge leaned over to Smith just before the second half started and told him what the media was saying. Smith put his hand over his mouth and replied, "For once, they may be right." Both coaches shared a chuckle.

Carolina came back to defeat Wake Forest and then went on to avenge two regular-season losses to Florida State in the semifinals. Even though their team wasn't playing, Duke fans – including Krzyzewski's family – were really into this one, cheering for the Seminoles and joining the FSU crowd in its famous tomahawk chop. The next day the Blue Devils crushed Carolina by twenty points to win the ACC title on their way to a second straight national championship. Smith rallied his team to a pair of NCAA wins, but a mistake-prone performance against Ohio State in the Sweet Sixteen sent the Tar Heels home and Smith into the videotape room.

He analyzed game after game, trying to figure out why his team had played so poorly the second half of the season. He determined they all hadn't worked hard enough in practice and decided to take a different approach the next season. Meanwhile, Montross and Lynch, sick of hearing about Duke all summer long, were making plans of their own. The players held impromptu team meetings and spent more time together in the off-season than they had in the past. When the 1993 season opened, Carolina came out with laser focus and, for once, wasn't afraid to talk about its ultimate goal, winning the national championship. With the Final Four scheduled for New Orleans, Smith placed a doctored photo of the Superdome in each player's locker on the first day of practice. The overhead message board read "1993 NCAA Champions North Carolina."

Despite Laettner's graduation, Duke remained the team to beat in the ACC and the nation. Hurley and Hill were still around, and Krzyzewski had risen to Smith-like status on campus and among his fans – but without the same humility. Over the summer, someone identifying himself as a Carolina fan had approached him. "I don't give a shit what you are," the coach had said with a smile. Inundated with requests for personal and professional appearances, Krzyzewski faced the grueling demands that Smith had for years, and he tried to do it all. In contrast to Carolina's approach that season, the Blue Devils and their coach appeared worn out. They beat the Tar Heels at home in early February but got drubbed in the rematch in Chapel Hill and were knocked out of the 1993 ACC Tournament in their first game. Duke also failed to make the Final Four for the first time in six years, losing in the NCAA second round to Jason Kidd and California.

Smith, meanwhile, had put together one of his most prototypical teams. With virtually the same players, except the sweet-shooting Davis, Carolina carefully improved in every statistical category. They shot a higher percentage from the floor, including three-point range, had a far better assist-turnover ratio, and absolutely killed people on the boards. Defensively, they developed an old-fashioned Tar Heel tenacity – not great quickness but always in the right place at the right time and utilizing their most effective zone in years. After losing at Duke, Carolina finished first in the ACC and tasted defeat only one other time for the rest of the season – to Georgia Tech in the conference tournament final, when Phelps sat out after getting injured the day before against Virginia.

At his masterful best during the NCAA East Regional, Smith stayed cool as his team fell far behind and then rallied to win two pressure-packed games at the Meadowlands in New Jersey. In the crucial moment against Arkansas, Smith suckered the Razorbacks with a back-door play for Donald Williams. Then, before the Elite Eight game, Smith unwittingly motivated his team against Cincinnati, whose players infuriated the Tar Heels by claiming in print that Smith should have won more than one national championship with all the talent he had had over the years. "Michael Jordan and James Worthy won't be playing for them tomorrow," said Cincy's Nick Van Exel smugly. Phelps shut down Van Exel in the second half, and Carolina won in overtime when Williams drilled two jumpers from three-point land to bury the Bearcats.

Never in Smith's storied career had the Carolina constituency come together like it did in New Orleans the following weekend. Tired of Duke's recent domination and irked by the sentiment that it had been acceptable to lose to Kansas and Roy Williams in the 1991 Final Four, Tar Heel fans renewed their commitment to Smith and their determination to help him win his second national title. That the Jayhawks were again the semifinal Saturday opponent mattered little. This time, nothing but a victory and advancement to Monday night's championship game would do.

The years had taught Smith when to tinker with his team, and this time he knew his players were ready to go. Arriving late to the locker room because he had forgotten his pass and had to talk his way into the Superdome, Smith said simply, "If you don't know how to play basketball by now, there's not much time to teach you." Led by Lynch, an unselfish warrior who had turned himself into a pro prospect, Carolina manhandled Kansas underneath and won behind twenty-three points from Montross and twenty-five by Donald Williams. Among loyal Tar Heels, who had watched Roy Williams grow into a great young coach, there was little sympathy when Kansas went down by ten.

The rumor that Jordan, Worthy, and the rest of the 1982 starting five had flown into New Orleans to give the team a pep talk before the Monday night game was fun but far-fetched. A creature of habit who regarded his pregame locker room as a sanctuary, Smith wouldn't dare try such a dramatic move. Besides, he knew his team was anxious to take on sentimental favorite Michigan and its Fab Five, which had beaten the Tar Heels by one point the previous December in Hawaii. This was his most cohesive team in years, and Smith had demonstrated that the day before when he ignored the NCAA policy of taking only his five starters to the major press conference. Smith had brought along his top eight to reward all of them and further emphasize basketball as a team game.

Late in the second half against Michigan, Smith flaunted his strategy again by putting his sixth, seventh, eighth, and ninth men in to play with Montross. While that group committed a shot-clock violation and CBS announcers Billy Packer and Jim Nantz openly questioned Smith's move, four fatigued and banged-up starters were resting on the bench. When they returned, Carolina went on the run that won the game; Final Four MVP Williams rained down two more majestic jumpers,

Phelps knifed in for a layup, Lynch hit a turnaround in the lane, and Montross added the exclamation point with a flying dunk.

Of course, much has been made since of Chris Webber's infamous time-out (and resulting technical foul) with Michigan trailing by two and eleven seconds left to play. But Smith knew it was hardly an unforced error, as great defense by Phelps and Lynch had forced Webber to panic and call a time-out his team didn't have. It was no different from harassing him into a travel or a bad shot. Following the 77-71 victory, Smith cared little about the fuss over Webber's mistake. Instant comparisons were being made to 1982, when Fred Brown had thrown Georgetown's last chance away in the final seconds of Smith's first NCAA title in the same building. "Okay, call us lucky," he said, "but also call us national champions."

After his press conference, Smith walked down the hallway where Krzyzewski, working as a CBS commentator, had symbolically just passed by in the opposite direction. After thirty-one years of coaching, Smith was enjoying this feeling only for the third time – winning a championship in the last game of the season. Back on top after people had again written him off, he went to find his family and have a late-night dinner.

The next morning, while his team headed home and much of North Carolina slept off the championship celebration, he and Ford boarded a plane for Philadelphia to sign up a high school player named Rasheed Wallace. Smith knew well from experience that staying on top would be harder than getting back there.

CHAPTER SIXTEEN

THE COACHING TREE

"I'm looking for a new basketball coach," Mike McGee said midway through the 1993 season. "Ask your friend who he recommends. While you're at it, ask him if he's interested."

That had become a standard line for McGee, the athletic director at the University of South Carolina, who like so many others used Dean Smith's program as a barometer. When McGee held the same position at Cincinnati and Southern Cal, he had fired and hired basketball coaches. Each time, he had asked Dean disciple Eddie Fogler for suggestions and, kiddingly, asked him if he wanted the job. This time Fogler was interested. After thirteen years on Smith's staff, Fogler had left Chapel Hill in 1986 to resurrect the once-proud Wichita State program. He took the Shockers to two NCAA Tournaments and one NIT, then moved to Vanderbilt in 1989. Fogler's Commodores won the NIT title his first year and, in 1993, captured Vandy's first Southeastern Conference championship in ninety years. That's where this story really gets interesting.

Smith had urged Fogler to go to Wichita State, where the basketball program was coming off probation and there was little downside to the move. The Shockers were simply looking for respectability after former coach Gene Smithson had spent years dragging the program down and through the mud. Three years later, Smith and Bill Guthridge discouraged Fogler from going to Vanderbilt, seeing little upside at a school with good tradition but tough academic standards and limited money for athletics. They suggested Fogler stay put until something else came along, but the one-time Carolina point guard went anyway.

With basketball the primary sport at Vanderbilt and new athletic director Paul Hoolahan having arrived from UNC, Fogler appeared to have it made in his new job. Memorial Gym sold out for every game, and Fogler's reputation as a fair and fun coach to play for lured key recruits right away, including Duke transfer Billy McCaffery. But Fogler grew unhappy with his financial package after a story in the *Atlanta Journal* reported he was the second lowest paid coach among his peers in the Southeastern Conference. He went to Hoolahan for a raise, arguing that basketball generated more revenue for Vanderbilt than football – a statistic only Kentucky could match in the SEC. But Hoolahan, who had accepted chancellor Joe B. Wyatt's mandate to reduce the $3 million annual subsidy the university provided the athletic department, refused. Thus, when McGee sent out his feeler, Fogler had already decided to listen to any offers.

McGee had fired Steve Newton, effective after the 1993 season, and was trying to bring Bobby Cremins back to South Carolina. Many of Cremins's old friends and cronies from his playing days with the Gamecocks still lived in Columbia, and they believed they could entice Cremins to "come home." Despite pursuing Cremins aggressively, McGee remained skeptical. "He goes back and forth on it every day, but I just don't believe he'll leave Georgia Tech," said McGee, whose back-up list now had Fogler's name at the top.

A football All-American and later head coach at Duke, McGee had gotten to know Dean Smith, ironically, while earning his Ph.D. from UNC. McGee had been fired at Duke in 1978 with two years left on his contract, which stipulated he would not be paid if he took another coaching job. So McGee had enrolled in Carolina's doctoral program in education with a focus on sports administration. He always laughed about how "Duke put me through Carolina." After four years at Cincinnati and five at Southern Cal, McGee had returned to the East Coast to try to save the struggling South Carolina program. As he had done in his previous stops, McGee made bold moves quickly, canning football coach Sparky Woods in 1993 (during McGee's second year there) and letting Newton know that the 1992-93 season would be his last on the bench. Pressured to go after the wonderfully wacky Cremins, but convinced he would never get him, McGee started calling around. He admittedly knew little about basketball and needed help finding the best candidates. When he called Smith, McGee received further confirmation that Fogler wasn't happy at Vanderbilt and might well be interested.

Meanwhile, Homer Rice was making his plans in case Cremins left Tech. Unlike McGee, Rice had a strange feeling that he was going to lose his coach. "I don't know why in the world he would do it, but I think he's going," Rice said. Ten years before arriving at Georgia Tech as athletic director, Rice had held the same position at UNC. During his tenure there, he had gotten to know Fogler and had followed his coaching career. While Vanderbilt was still playing in the 1993 NCAA Tournament, Rice called a friend of Fogler's to check out his possible interest in the Tech job. This practice of using intermediaries is popular among athletic directors looking for new coaches; they can exchange private information with their candidates, and the candidates can still declare to the press, "I have not talked to anyone from so-and-so university."

By this time Fogler knew of South Carolina's interest and had told McGee that he would like to talk to him as soon as the season ended. McGee had passed the word on to Fogler that the $600,000 annual package he had put together for Cremins would be available for the school's second choice, as well. But Georgia Tech – in the ACC where Fogler had cut his teeth as a player and coach – was the more attractive position. He knew that Cremins made almost $700,000 annually between salary, TV and radio, and his Nike contract, and he asked his friend to find out whether Cremins's successor would earn at least that much. "Yes, he will," said Rice, who faxed an outline of the coach's salary, outside income, and benefits to Fogler's friend. "Tell Eddie I think Bobby's going and that I want to talk to him as soon as possible."

After learning how much the next Tech coach would earn, Fogler sent this message to Rice: He was interested, but only if he were assured he could have the job. He did not want to be listed with other candidates in the newspaper and did not want to interview with a

committee. Rice understood Fogler's desire to stay out of the speculation and reiterated that he was his man. "Tell Eddie that, for political
purposes, I am going to have to interview Kevin Cantwell and Perry
Clark, and their names will be in the paper. But they aren't getting the
job. Eddie's the person I want." Cantwell, Cremins's long-time assistant, was said to do much of the actual coaching at Tech while Cremins
was the great recruiter. Clark was a popular black coach and former
Tech assistant who had quickly turned the Tulane program around.
Both men had considerable support.

Late Tuesday night, March 23, Cremins called McGee and told him
he had decided to stay at Georgia Tech. McGee turned his attention to
Fogler. "Bobby's a little goofy," McGee said the next morning. "Even
though he kept telling me he was coming, I never thought he would.
Now I want Eddie." McGee was interrupted to take another call. It was
Cremins, who told him that, after staying up all night, he had changed
his mind and decided he wanted to "come home." McGee sent a private plane to Atlanta to pick him up, and Cremins was introduced at a
press conference in the Frank McGuire Arena that afternoon.

The next day, Rice left for his vacation home in Marco Island, Florida,
to spend the weekend planning the details of hiring a new basketball
coach. He would interview Cantwell and Clark as quickly as possible and
then, as soon as Vanderbilt finished NCAA Tournament play, offer the job
to Fogler. About 6:00 A.M. Friday, Rice was awakened by a phone call
from Cremins, who was in tears and could barely speak. He told Rice he
had made a terrible mistake and asked if he could have his old job back.
Rice was both flabbergasted and frustrated. "I've got to let him come
back; he's part of our family," Rice said later that morning. "But I'm not
sure Bobby will be able to coach anymore. I think he's having a very hard
time and may need to take some time off."

Fogler was already in Seattle, where Vanderbilt was preparing to play
Temple in the Sweet Sixteen. McGee spent most of Friday talking to
Cremins, trying to convince him to stick with his commitment. By the
time Cremins left his office and headed back to Atlanta for good, the
game in Seattle had tipped off and Temple was on its way to ending
Vandy's season.

"I'm bullshit about this," McGee said Saturday morning. "I'm glad
Cremins is gone. He's a flake, and I don't want him. I'd rather have

Eddie. How can I find him?" Fogler was in his hotel room packing to go home when he heard the news about Cremins. He and his wife, Robin, had already grown excited about moving to Atlanta, but he started laughing. "I knew, when all was said and done, Bobby wouldn't leave," Fogler said. "Tech is too good of a job. And he makes too much money."

Three days later, after Fogler had visited with McGee in Columbia and called Smith for advice, he said yes to South Carolina. He went to New Orleans where his alma mater would win the national championship, but only stayed briefly before flying back to Nashville to begin another move – this one a step closer to Chapel Hill. His latest job change further fueled rumors about who would succeed Dean Smith.

✪

Smith's multibranched coaching tree, by now an old oak, had produced Billy Cunningham and Larry Brown; Fogler and Roy Williams; small-college coaches Bill Chambers, Dudley Bradley, and Tony Shaver; high school teacher/coaches Clyde Lynn, Warren Martin, and Jeff Wolf; and most recently 31-year-old Jeff Lebo, beginning his head-coaching career at Tennessee Tech. And so many more in between.

Kevin Madden was among dozens of players who never thought about coaching until he was around Smith. After his professional playing career ended in Europe, Madden returned to his hometown of Staunton, Virginia, to coach where he once starred. With Smith's guidance and influence, even former managers Rick Duckett and Mike Ellis landed college coaching jobs. Duckett was named head coach at Winston-Salem State after five years at Fayetteville State. Ellis has been an assistant at Virginia Commonwealth since 1988. While some of his ex-players have earned jobs on their own, Smith's pull has helped more times than not.

It's virtually a legend in Kansas that he badgered KU Athletic Director and old friend Bob Frederick into hiring the unknown Williams, who was just two years removed from part-time status. After Larry Brown left Kansas with an NCAA probation in 1988 as well as an NCAA championship, it would seem that the last thing the Jayhawks needed was one Tar Heel alum to bail out another. But when Brown fled back to the NBA, Smith somehow convinced Frederick to hire

Williams. Frederick, whose wife accused him of being crazy the night before he introduced Williams, was merely desperate: six head coaches had already spurned his overtures.

Only weeks before being named at Kansas on July 8, 1988, Williams was ready to accept an offer to coach George Mason. But Smith told him to wait: "I think we can get you something better." Williams, who had left Owen High School in Swannanoa, North Carolina, to take a part-time position on Smith's staff in 1977 for twenty-seven hundred dollars a year, indeed waited; he wound up making a million a year coaching the Jayhawks. An almost overnight success, Williams took Kansas to the Final Four in only his third year and won more games in his first ten seasons than any college coach in history. His Jayhawk teams averaged twenty-eight wins between 1989 and '98, including seven Big Eight/Big Twelve championships.

"I don't think I would have considered any assistant other than Roy, or one from another program than the one he was in," said Frederick, who recognized he was putting his own job on the line with such a controversial hire. "But we have a great deal of respect for Dean and what he thinks. He told me Roy Williams was soon going to be one of the best coaches in America. His last recommendation (of Larry Brown) resulted in a national championship for Kansas."

"The one reason I'm here is Dean Smith; I have no hesitation saying that," Williams said upon being hired. "A big factor was the way he's respected around the country and here in Kansas. Bob Frederick and the committee evidently were impressed with what I had to say, and the only reason for that is the great training I got under Coach Smith. Every day, for the last ten years, he was preparing me to be a head coach, telling me to think like a head coach in every instance."

Yet Fogler and Williams were just the tip of the iceberg. For the last twenty years of Smith's coaching career, at least fifteen of his disciples held pro, college, or high school jobs at any given time. And the tree had taken root long before that. The late Kenny Rosemond left Smith's staff in 1965 to take the head-coaching job at Georgia, where he lasted eight seasons. John Lotz spent eight years by Smith's side before taking over at Florida, where he won SEC coach of the year in his fourth season. (Lotz was fired after his sixth year, and Smith helped him return to UNC as an assistant athletic director.)

When college coaches started getting big money and recognition in the late 1970s, the profession suddenly had great appeal. That's why Williams left a comfortable high school job to take the newly created part-time position, and why so many youngsters started setting long-term goals to become coaches. Duckett, a good high school athlete growing up in Winston-Salem (his deceased brother, Kenny, played in the NFL), wanted to stay involved with sports when he got to UNC. Ellis could have been a Division III player but instead went to Carolina, applied to be a team manager and began his on-the-job training.

"I knew I wanted to coach, but I wasn't sure the best way to get into it," Ellis said. "Then someone suggested managing at Carolina would be something to consider. Was it worth it? An assistant at a Division I school once told me he'd trade places with me for a year just to be near the Carolina program. That's when I knew I had a great situation. The main thing Coach Smith ingrained in me was that the game was more important than the score, and that life was more important than the game. I've tried to apply that every day since then."

Smith has moved his men around like chess pieces, helping them at the beginning, middle, and end of their careers. After Larry Brown replaced Rosemond, Bill Guthridge replaced Brown in 1967. Fogler replaced Lotz in 1972. Fogler left, Williams moved up, and Smith hired part-timer Dick Harp, Smith's 69-year-old former freshman coach at Kansas. Already on the staff was graduate assistant Randy Wiel, an ex-UNC player.

When Williams went to Kansas, Phil Ford was hired with no experience, and, after Harp retired, former player Dave Hanners returned from East Tennessee State. When the NCAA cut coaching staffs back to three assistants, Hanners got an "administrative" job in the athletic department (he continued to share an office in the basketball suite) until Wiel took the head-coaching position at UNC-Asheville in 1993. After Smith stepped down, Guthridge, Ford, and Hanners moved up, and Pat Sullivan, an office aide and graduate student, became a part-time coach in a top-five program. When wannabe coaches from around the country have called, asking for his help in landing certain jobs, Smith has told them candidly, "Only if one of our guys doesn't have a chance."

Other programs look to Carolina guys, as well, to fill vacancies. After four years on the East Tennessee State staff, Hanners told head coach

Les Robinson, a former N.C. State player and future Wolfpack coach, that he'd been asked back to Chapel Hill. "Les said, 'You've got to go. You'd be crazy if you didn't take it. But before you go, I want to sit down and talk about who we can get to replace you,'" Hanners recalled.

"Coach Smith was talking to him a few days later and asked, almost off the cuff, 'Who are you getting to replace Dave?' Les said he didn't know. Coach Smith said, 'You know, Buzz Peterson might be interested, and I think he'd do a fine job.'" (Peterson, who played for the Tar Heels from 1981 to 1985, was a part-time assistant at Appalachian State, where he eventually returned as head coach.) "That minute, Les made up his mind. I tried to get him thinking about other names, not because I didn't want Buzz to get it, but what if Buzz wasn't interested? But it was over. The interview was a formality. And, you know, Les played at N.C. State."

On the other hand, Smith's influence hasn't always worked. He was frustrated, for instance, when Hanners could not land the head job at UNC-Wilmington in 1994 – even though he had been an assistant there. The school balked because Hanners had not been out on the road recruiting for several years and instead hired former Wake Forest assistant Jerry Wainright. Smith was particularly perturbed because UNCW chancellor James Leutze had once been on the faculty in Chapel Hill, and Smith thought that should have given Hanners the edge.

Smith also tried mightily to get Texas to hire Phil Ford over Clemson's Rick Barnes in 1998. Ford had not been aggressively seeking head-coaching positions, but Smith got him an interview at Texas by calling Longhorns' Athletic Director DeLoss Dodds. Former Carolina football coach Mack Brown, who had moved to Texas only months before, also pushed Ford. However, although he was a legend in North Carolina, Ford was just another coach applying for a job in Texas. And compared to that of the experienced, super-slick Barnes, Ford's interview was an uncomfortable disaster. Committee members asked him about his long-time battle with alcohol, about his separation from his wife, Traci, and even about the controversial on-court behavior of the 1998 Tar Heel team. Ironically, the Texas committee thought the way Carolina's players had celebrated during the 1998 season showed a lack of discipline. Under former coach Tom Penders, Texas had been one of the least disciplined teams in the country. Because all six Tar Heel "starters" were black, and Ford was black, Texas seemed to hold their behavior against the UNC assistant coach.

Ford shrugged off the experience as just that. "It was good to go on an interview to see what it was like, and next time I'll be more prepared," he said. Then he added with a laugh, "My penalty for not getting the job was that I had to stay at Carolina."

✪

While Smith has sent more coaches into the college ranks, pro basketball also has had a healthy share of his disciples wearing $4,000 outfits and pacing the sideline, or watching from the front office. Cunningham coached the 76ers to an NBA title in 1983 and later owned part of the Miami Heat for seven years. Donnie Walsh, a guard on Smith's first Carolina team, coached for six years in the NBA before moving up to general manager and eventually president of the Indiana Pacers, where he hired Larry Bird to succeed Larry Brown as coach.

And then there's Brown's own story. Back in 1977, UCLA had tried to hire Smith away for a second time. He seriously considered going (his second wife, Linnea, a California native, had family on the West Coast), before eventually declining and telling UCLA Athletic Director J. D. Morgan that Brown was tired of pro basketball and wanted to coach college again. Brown stayed long enough to lead the Bruins to the NCAA title game in 1980, then returned to the pros following the next season. Two years later, when Kansas was looking for a coach to replace veteran Ted Owens, athletic director Monte Johnson made his perfunctory call to Jayhawk alumnus Smith. Settled in Chapel Hill for the duration, Smith told Johnson that Brown had again grown weary of the pro grind and wanted another college coaching job. Somehow Smith convinced Kansas to take a chance on the unpredictable Brown, who had once accepted the head-coaching job at Davidson only to quit before his first game. "He may not stay forever," Smith told Johnson, "but he'll win while he's there."

George Karl sought Smith's counsel in his turbulent early days as an NBA coach, when he ripped locker doors off their hinges and threw violent tantrums in front of players. Once thought to be in permanent coaching exile – whether in the CBA or Europe – Karl got another chance in the NBA when then-Seattle general manager Bob Whitsett tracked him down in Spain after calling Smith. Following six and one-half seasons and four Western Conference titles with the Sonics, Karl enlisted Smith's help to get the head-coaching job at Milwaukee.

But, ironically, the biggest debt of gratitude is owed by a man who never played for Smith, the head coach, and who has treated him more irreverently than any other Tar Heel alumnus. "The thing about Smitty," Doug Moe said in 1989, "is that he does more for people without wanting anything in return. He doesn't even want people to know." Moe had already been at Carolina for a year when Smith arrived in 1958. Frank McGuire and Gunar Moe had decided in the Moe family's Brooklyn flat where young Doug was going to college. "That was fine with me, I didn't care," recalled Moe. "I was one of those goofy kids. All I cared about was playing ball."

His grades reflected that, four Ds and one F the first semester of his freshman year. After attending two sessions of summer school, Moe joined the Tar Heel varsity in 1958. The rugged 6-5 forward averaged twelve and one-half points and seven rebounds a game and, largely due to his defensive reputation, made the All-ACC team. But the next time around, not even summer school could save Moe, who flunked out and missed the first twelve games of his junior year. Smith was already splitting time between the basketball office and South Building, where he assisted chancellor William Aycock in answering the NCAA inquiries into McGuire's program. Probation would be leveled on UNC a year later in January 1961.

That was during Moe's best collegiate season, when he averaged twenty points and fourteen rebounds as a unanimous All-ACC selection. But the NCAA probe cast a shadow and led to some of McGuire's darkest moments. A wild melee at Duke resulted in suspensions for Brown, Walsh, and Duke's Art Heyman, and then McGuire convinced the athletic council at UNC to let his team skip the ACC Tournament because of the probation. After the season, Moe was suspended from school for having failed to report a contact with New York gamblers, who were paying players to fix games all over the country. Moe also forfeited his contract with the Chicago Packers of the NBA and was eventually banned from the league. He went into the Army Reserve and then wound up selling insurance in Durham, his basketball career apparently over.

By now, McGuire had resigned under pressure and been replaced by Smith, who had a mandate from Aycock to clean up the program. Moe was out of school and his reputation was clearly linked to McGuire. But Smith continued to regard all of McGuire's players as his own and reached out to help Moe.

"Smitty called me one morning and said, 'You've got an interview at Elon College with the coach and president of the school,'" Moe related. "He said, 'Meet the coach at two o'clock in the gym, be on time, and wear a coat and tie.'" Moe impressed Elon coach Bill Miller enough to land an assistant coaching job for two years while he finished up his degree. By the time he graduated, Moe had spent six years, including two summers, in school and was already twenty-five years old.

Meanwhile, Smith continued to work on Moe's behalf during his first two seasons as the Tar Heel head coach. When two professional scouts showed up in Chapel Hill, angling to persuade Carolina star Billy Cunningham to leave college and play in Italy, Smith did not see red – he saw an opportunity for Moe. Summoned from Elon to talk to the scouts, Moe wound up signing a contract to play overseas, where he became an Italian hero in two seasons. When the ABA was formed in 1967, Moe returned to star for four different teams in the new league, thrice as an all-star. He then rejoined former Carolina teammate Larry Brown as an assistant coach with the old Carolina Cougars and Denver Rockets and eventually spent twelve years as head coach for NBA teams in San Antonio, Denver, and Philadelphia.

Moe was fired from Philly in 1993 with four years left on his multi-million-dollar contract and returned to Denver as a rich retiree who split his time between the dog track, the golf course, and a fifty-and-over baseball league. Long ago, he had been a kid in trouble going nowhere. "I owe most of it to Smitty," said Moe, who continued to call his old coach by the old nickname. "He stuck with me when I had nowhere to go. He's done that for a lot of guys since then. I guess all of them, really."

★

Dean Smith received grudging praise from his closest rivals, mainly because he made their lives so difficult. He dominated them on the court and sometimes opposed them in coaches' meetings, when he believed his point of view was right, if not popular. Over the last thirty-three years of his career, Smith owned the so-called Big Four with a 181-78 overall record against Duke, N.C. State, and Wake Forest, winning 84 percent of his home games (eight undefeated seasons) and an astonishing 59 percent on the road.

Except for going 8-12 against former Duke coach Vic Bubas, Smith did not have a losing record against any of his ACC foes. He won twenty-four of thirty-eight games with Mike Krzyzewski, including eight of the last nine, thirteen of nineteen from Wake Forest's Dave Odom, and a surprisingly close seven of twelve over Les Robinson of N.C. State. The late Jim Valvano had upset Carolina in his last try but overall went 7-18 against the Tar Heels. Outside the state, Rick Barnes won one game in eight tries against Smith, Cremins ten of thirty-eight, Jeff Jones four of eighteen, and Gary Williams six of twenty-one. Pat Kennedy beat Smith the first two times their teams played, then lost nine straight and wound up with a 4-10 record against UNC.

Of the previous "generation" of ACC coaches, Carl Tacy went 10-29 against Smith during his thirteen years at Wake Forest, winning all but one of those games in a seven-season stretch. Lefty Driesell beat Smith only ten times in forty-one tries but did win his last two games against Carolina, including the Tar Heels' first-ever loss in the Deandome. Both Bill Fosters (Clemson and Duke) were a combined 9-31 against Smith. Cliff Ellis, Foster's successor at Clemson, was 4-17. Virginia's Terry Holland lost eighteen of twenty-eight games to Smith, including six of ten during the Ralph Sampson era. Norman Sloan, who competed against Smith for fourteen seasons at N.C. State, finished 13-25 against Carolina despite having won nine straight in one stretch.

"If Dean would quit beatin' people all the time, he'd be a whole lot more popular," Driesell once snorted. His refusal to shake Smith's hand after a game one year spurred assistant coach Bill Guthridge to chase Driesell off the court and, later, led to a confrontation between the two head coaches at the annual ACC meetings that spring.

Of course, the last confrontation between Smith and a rival coach began in 1994, when Barnes decided he wanted to make a statement that Clemson basketball would not be pushed around by the established programs in the ACC. He intentionally got thrown out of his first game against Carolina after complaining that the officials had helped the Tar Heels by calling thirty-two fouls on his team compared to nine against UNC. Smith stayed out of it but, after reviewing the tape of the Tigers' aggressive defense, confided that his team probably deserved even more than the fifty-one free throws it had shot at Clemson.

The Tar Heels blew out Barnes's team in the rematch in Chapel Hill and, in a third meeting at the ACC Tournament, won easily again. But in the second half, Barnes went after Smith, who had complained when Clemson's Iker Iturbe committed a hard foul on UNC's Jerry Stackhouse. "Iturbe! Iturbe!" Smith yelled, pointing a finger at the rugged Spanish forward. On the other bench, Barnes grew incensed and demanded the officials call a meeting at the scorer's table. Smith sauntered over, hands in his suit pants' pockets.

"I don't want him talking to my players!" Barnes fumed, then looking at Smith said, "I ought to kick your ass for talking to one of my players." Smith, now smirking, said softly, out of the side of his mouth, "You want to hit me, Rick? Go ahead, throw the first punch." Barnes lunged toward Smith and was easily stopped by officials Frank Scagliotta, Rick Hartzell, and Steve Gordon. Scagliotta then slapped Barnes with a technical foul.

The Smith-Barnes feud continued into the next season when Barnes again complained to the ACC about Smith's talking to his point guard Bill Harder. Smith acknowledged that he had told Harder to stop holding Dante Calabria's jersey by saying, "You're a better defensive player than that, Bill, move your feet!" The controversy ended when ACC Commissioner Gene Corrigan called Barnes and Smith to his home for a private meeting and basically told both of them to knock it off. Barnes finally beat Smith in the ACC Tournament that year, as Clemson rallied from nine points down to win on a dunk at the buzzer. In 1997, Smith's last season, Carolina upset nationally ranked Clemson twice without incident. A year later, after Clemson had set an ACC record by committing forty-one fouls in Chapel Hill and finished the game with only four players on the floor, Barnes had had enough of UNC and the ACC. He took the Texas coaching job.

Although he was depicted as a gentleman by the press and Carolina fans, Smith's fierce competitiveness had drawn the ire of his fellow coaches since the early days – or at least since his Tar Heels became a force in the ACC. Like Smith, former Virginia coach Bill Gibson had struggled in his early years and grew resentful when Carolina built a powerhouse in the late 1960s. Smith had already lost one game at UVA in 1966, when the winning basket went in suspiciously close to the final horn going off. Three years later in Charlottesville, Smith questioned the clock operator in the tense, closing minutes and drew an angry rebuke from Gibson. Storming to the scorer's table, Gibson railed at his opponent, "Don't come up here with all of your talent and then accuse us of cheating."

LET'S MAKE A (NIKE) DEAL!

Although his basketball program never came close to any kind of probation, Dean Smith was accused of breaking an NCAA and institutional rule in 1993, an episode that led to a serious rift with then-UNC chancellor Paul Hardin. And Smith, one of the most loyal, supportive employees the university has ever had, exacerbated the situation with what Hardin considered insubordinate comments to the press and public.

When Smith's personal contract with the Converse Athletic Shoe Company came up for renewal in 1993, he seriously considered having his players wear another brand of sneaker for the first time in his coaching career. Smith's relationship with Converse had begun in the early 1960s when Chuck Taylor came to town, took him to dinner, and asked him to buy Converse All-Stars for his team. "You got a free meal, and that was about it," Smith said. The relationship grew through the 1970s and 1980s, when current LSU athletic director Joe Dean was the Converse national sales rep and competing companies began giving major colleges free shoes and apparel, hoping the exposure would result in retail sales.

After Nike burst onto the scene with its Coaches Club, which handed out cash and Nike stock to college coaches, the financial numbers grew to staggering proportions – and continued to escalate in the race to "sign up" the most prominent programs. As college basketball exploded on television, the corporate strategy became to take the money normally spent on traditional advertising and give it to the highest-profile coaches so their players' shoes would be seen on TV and in still photos.

Carolina, with nearly all of its games on the tube, was among the most coveted schools. Smith resisted Nike's overtures for several years until Converse decided it also had to pay certain coaches to keep their programs under contract. In the early 1990s, Smith and Kentucky's Rick Pitino were the highest-paid Converse coaches, each making well into six figures in addition to the apparel provided for the Tar Heels and Wildcats. By this time, one of Smith's former players, Mickey Bell, had risen to the presidency of Converse, and conventional wisdom had Carolina and Converse together forever – or at least as long as Bell was there.

In reality, however, the relationship was showing signs of strain. For one thing, customer service had deteriorated. In 1987, for example, when freshman star J. R. Reid had fractured his foot early in the season, Converse had special support shoes to Chapel Hill within days. But in recent years Bell had been personally embarrassed to have to call his old coach on the phone and apologize for slow or inaccurate deliveries. "Coach Smith was always polite, but he did make a strong point that things needed to improve," Bell recalled in 1995, two years after losing the UNC account. The last straw came when Rick Fox and several other Tar Heels complained about blisters and discomfort from their Converses. Some of the players even wore their own shoes at practice, donning the required Cons for games. Only Michael Jordan, who loved Adidas when he was in school, had done that in the past.

Aware that Smith's contract was coming up for renewal, Nike and Reebok asked to make presentations following the 1993 season. Smith agreed and flew out to visit both shoe giants in Oregon and Massachusetts, respectively, after his Tar Heels had won the national championship in New Orleans. However, if the Tar Heels were to switch from Converse, Smith wanted his players to make the decision. He asked both Nike and Reebok to send a supply of shoes for his team to wear over the summer. If, after trying both, the votes were even all-around, Carolina would stick with Converse. Another supplier would have to win a solid majority.

Most of the players voted for Nike, which had become the shoe of choice for millions of teenagers and young adults. From that point on, Smith entered serious negotiations with the company that, ironically, had recently signed Duke coach Mike Krzyzewski to a fifteen-year personal service contract worth as much as $6 million. Given the controversy generated by that arrangement, many people thought it odd that Smith was trying to be like Mike.

But Smith presented several ideas that would clearly distinguish his own agreement with Nike from the one Krzyzewski had made – first and foremost that Nike could not have Carolina basketball unless it supplied the other athletic programs at the school with shoes and apparel. Plus, the basic contract would be between Nike and the UNC athletic department. Smith would still have a "personal" shoe deal, as he had with Converse, although he did not realize at the time that his ability to "privatize" the almost $2 million he would receive had been hampered by a new NCAA ruling on the outside income of coaches.

In the past, the president or CEO (in this case, the chancellor) of a school had to merely give the coach permission to negotiate any endorsements. However, at the 1992 NCAA Convention, the rule had been changed so that the terms and conditions of such contracts required the consent of the school's top officer. Smith had been able to keep his personal endorsements private because the Open Records Act did not apply to non-official university actions. But the new rule meant that Hardin was required to know the specifics of the contract and approve them.

"I interpreted that as meaning this would be a matter of record that would be entitled to public disclosure," recalled Hardin, who stepped down as chancellor in 1995. In other words, because he coached at a state university, Smith's shoe deal could no longer be kept to himself.

Hardin knew that athletic director John Swofford and Smith were considering a truly brilliant contract with Nike. But he had not signed off on the details when Swofford gave a short statement to the UNC Sports Information Office for release to the media on July 20, 1993. The statement, which did not disclose financial terms, said that the twenty-six UNC varsity athletic teams would receive Nike shoes and apparel and that Smith had severed his 31-year relationship with Converse. The quotes from Swofford made the statement read as if the athletic department had made the deal "after talking" with Smith, who had consulted with his players.

"This agreement will provide . . . tremendous savings . . . (and) better serve our entire department and not just the basketball program," said Swofford, whose charge was to balance an annual $20 million athletic budget that had to be self-sustaining – with no supplement from the university and no taxpayers' dollars. Nike would provide shoes and apparel for all of the programs that chose to participate and also make four-year cash payments to football coach Mack Brown ($500,000), women's basketball coach Sylvia Hatchell ($255,000), track coach Dennis Craddock ($75,000) and baseball coach Mike Roberts ($50,000).

Only Anson Dorrance, head of UNC's soccer program, decided not to go with Nike, because he already had a long-term contract with Adidas from which he received about $25,000 annually. (When the Nike deal was renewed in 1998 for a total benefit to UNC of $11 million, Dorrance did switch for $600,000 over five years.)

Leveraging Nike's burning desire to have his Tar Heels wear the "swoosh," Smith had managed to save the athletic department $2.2 million in annual equipment and travel costs, plus get another $420,000 for the other head coaches. Even though Smith had his own contract worth $1.7 million, he should have been considered a hero to UNC athletics. It worked out quite to the contrary. In fact, Smith was forced to disclose everything about the Nike contract, plus what he was going to make personally from the deal, at a press conference he likened to being placed in the stocks in the town square of Salem, Massachusetts.

❂

Smith and Hardin were never particularly close. For one thing, Hardin had graduated from Duke and Smith regarded him as a "Dookie" at heart. "Dean and I had a cordial relationship, but from his standpoint not a warm one," Hardin said. "I wasn't one of the good ol' Carolina boys." Second, Hardin was thought by some to be such a stickler for the rules that he did not overly support athletics. Although he attended all home games and traveled to post-season bowls and tournaments, he stayed away from the locker rooms and sidelines where other chancellors and presidents have been known to prostrate themselves before their coaches and top athletes.

Fifteen years before going to UNC, Hardin had been run off as president at SMU. There, he had fired the athletic director and put the football coach on probation for cheating. In a power struggle with wealthy and influential alumni, Hardin had lost his job at the expense of his integrity. After Hardin left, SMU received the strongest possible NCAA sanction, the death penalty, and had its football program disbanded for two seasons. So, following thirteen years as president of Drew University (a Division III school with no athletic scholarships), Hardin accepted the UNC job for, among other reasons, its squeaky clean record in intercollegiate athletics. "Nobody had a stronger stake in integrity in athletics," Hardin said. "Dean's character and long record of integrity had a lot to do with it. I would not have gone to any school where the coach was gossiped about as being a little slick."

Although it later appeared to some that Smith was trying to pull off the Nike deal behind an inattentive chancellor's back, he was simply acting with the same autonomy he had for years. Only this time, Hardin believed a rule had been broken and a university policy violated. When members of the Board of Trustees heard about the Nike agreement and contacted Hardin, he said tersely, "I have not seen and approved any contract. So there is no contract."

Hardin called Swofford to his office and reminded him of the rule change at the most recent NCAA Convention. After Swofford and Smith worked out the details of what was a plum deal for his department, Hardin claimed they had simply forgotten about the new rule and allowed the terms of the agreement to be released. It touched off a furor that lasted for months. The media had a field day with Carolina. Because Krzyzewski's personal arrangement with Nike had caused so much controversy, Hardin, Smith, and Swofford received equal coverage. Several newspaper editorials asked how Smith could have acted so independently, without knowledge of the chancellor or the trustees.

"It was a blunder," Hardin said. "Coach Smith made a mistake in negotiating a contract without conferring with the university. The total explanation was that John, and I suppose Dean, had lost sight of a very important rule change, which was very unusual because both of them were always so meticulous about those things. It was not necessarily wrong to begin negotiations. Dean and John were wrong to announce a contract had been entered into because they had no power to do that without my approval. And I was out of town."

Smith balked at Hardin's assertion that all terms of Nike's deal with the university had to be disclosed. So Hardin checked with UNC System president C. D. Spangler, who after consulting university attorneys confirmed Hardin's interpretation. "Dean was on edge because I guess no one had ever put his knowledge of the rules up against Dean's," Hardin said. "I was right and he was wrong and he was embarrassed by that. In private conversations, he went along with it by saying, 'Well, you're the boss.' But it was plain that he was uncomfortable having a boss who was an activist."

Hardin further angered Smith by telling him that, in light of the controversy, any purely personal provisions Smith made with Nike would have to be disclosed as well. At this point, Hardin was determined to leave nothing behind closed doors that might subject the university and him to further criticism. Smith contended that he should not have to go public with his personal agreement because no other UNC faculty members were required to disclose the terms of their independent consulting contracts. On the other hand, although he acknowledged strong sentiment in some quarters for "no shoe contract at all," Hardin said he never considered penalizing an exemplary coach and his program by squelching the deal completely. "I would be changing the rules to the detriment of the most integrity-filled, character-laden coach in the country," he said. "Why shouldn't this most honest and incorruptible man benefit from something that was perfectly legal? It did not suit me to make a case for no shoe contracts using Dean as the vehicle. Everyone knew of his success, and his graduation rates were stunning. There had never been a taint on his program of any kind. And he was never going to let Nike tell him that he had to wear a lapel pin or where he was going to take his team."

Thus, after several months of revised negotiations between UNC and Nike amidst swirling speculation, Hardin approved the four-year deal, and Smith begrudgingly appeared at a news conference on Saturday, October 2, at the inconspicuous hour of 6:00 P.M. Hardin, in absentia, had instructed Smith to distribute copies of the school's 26-page contract with Nike to the media. An accompanying statement said that details of any personal service pacts made with UNC coaches would be released once they were signed. "I didn't want to be here, I didn't want to be here, it's unfortunate," Smith said from the podium, shaking his head. When asked about Hardin's statement that he, Smith, and Swofford had made a mistake, Smith gave what his boss later construed as an insolent answer. "Paul made a mistake in thinking I couldn't negotiate," he said. "I can negotiate. It's been in my contract since 1981."

Hardin did not immediately know about Smith's remarks, but later reiterated his position. "Dean's not a lawyer, I am," he said. "And his contract cannot be superior to an NCAA rule."

In retrospect, Hardin saw the incident as the result of a rare gaffe by an otherwise impeccable man caught between his own pride and embarrassment over the amount of money he was being offered. "Dean is a very proud man, and also a modest man," Hardin said. "He combines modesty and pride in a baffling kind of way. Dean doesn't really feel that he needs to be presided over because he's honest and he's good and he'll do the right thing. It's stunning to see that he actually called me 'Paul' in that press conference and said I was the one who was wrong. I didn't remember that he was that blunt. That's insubordination. That really is."

The unfortunate episode obscured what may have been the most magnanimous gesture of Smith's career. He not only saved the university millions, he gave away much of the personal money he received from Nike. He divided an annual $300,000 payment among his assistant coaches, administrative staff, and a fund to help those former players who did not finish school get their degrees. He donated his $500,000 signing bonus from Nike to various charities, including a large gift to the university's bicentennial fund-raising campaign in the names of Mr. and Mrs. Dean Smith. Of course, as he might have feared, cynics pointed out that Smith merely had Nike pay off the bicentennial pledge he and his wife had made more than a year earlier, thus saving them the money.

The full disclosure and the months of press coverage also provoked the ire of some students and faculty members. This contingent was outraged that the UNC athletic department would "sell out" its freedom of choice – and, worse yet, to a shoe giant that was under heavy criticism for unscrupulous labor practices in Asia. Before and after he retired, Smith met with student members of the "Nike Awareness Campaign" to explain the university's position and learn more about their grievances. Though it did not affect his personal legacy, Carolina retained the stigma of being "a Nike school."

At his retirement press conference in October of 1997, Smith praised several chancellors for whom he had worked. Predictably, Hardin was not among them.

✪

A far less-publicized contract over which Smith also exercised great influence was UNC's multimedia rights to, among other things, broadcast Tar Heel games on the radio and produce the weekly coaches' shows. This contract put more than $1 million annually into the athletic coffers (it has since grown to $2-plus million), further supplementing the financial packages of the head football and head men's basketball coaches. Above the $175,000 annual salary Smith made when he retired, he also earned $255,000 from his Thursday night radio call-in program and his Sunday morning television show. His summer Carolina Basketball School netted several hundred thousand more, although he was known to share that generously with his assistants who ran the camp. Combined with the Nike contract, his total income placed Smith among the highest-paid college basketball coaches in the country, but far from the very top.

Krzyzewski and Smith's former assistant, Roy Williams, each made about $1 million, a figure Smith could have easily matched had he kept the Nike money for himself and regularly chosen to make paid personal appearances or accept commercial endorsements. Perhaps chafing under his own policies, Smith would occasionally comment on the money he could have made from this speaking engagement, that product endorsement.

Prior to 1992, each of Carolina's athletic media properties had been contracted separately, essentially leaving UNC athletics with several different partners that each paid a rights fee. This played nicely into Smith's godfather philosophy, because he could "throw a carrot" to a number of people who had been loyal to him and his program. For example, Woody Durham had been the play-by-play announcer – the "Voice of the Tar Heels" – since 1971. Although Smith's relationship with Durham's boss, Jim Heavner, deteriorated over the years, he remained devoutly loyal to Durham. They were golf buddies who often took trips together after the basketball season.

On the other hand, Smith had also developed a fierce allegiance to John Kilgo, who like Durham was a UNC graduate and had covered the Tar Heels for years as a local columnist and commentator in Charlotte. When Jefferson-Pilot Communications bought the rights to produce the coaches' weekly television show from Heavner in 1983, Smith allowed J-P employee Kilgo to replace Durham as host of his shows.

Though Smith did not mind having "two sons" and ostensibly treated them equally, the arrangement created growing controversy and fractious feelings within the Carolina camp. Durham and Kilgo were rivals who each wanted the other's job. Plus, while having to bid out the rights to the radio and TV properties separately and accepting smaller rights fees from several other companies (game-day programs and magazines covering the Tar Heels), Carolina had little leverage or synergy with any of them.

Meanwhile, Heavner and Swofford had begun to develop a friendship that allowed them to share ideas about the future of Carolina athletics. Heavner, already a millionaire from buying and selling radio stations, sat on the board of directors of Host Communications in Lexington, Kentucky. Host had developed the concept of "one-stop shopping" with several universities and won the exclusive multimedia rights to represent their athletic departments. Heavner told Swofford about the approach that would give UNC one media rights holder with whom it could build a true partnership and, through closer involvement from the athletic department, drive the sponsorship dollars higher than they had ever been. In 1992, Swofford agreed that the Tar Heels would put all of their media properties under one umbrella.

When he heard about the idea, Smith objected. He knew it could mean that either Durham or Kilgo would be out of a job, and he liked the routine he had developed with both of them. Smith had become a creature of habit and, as his workload increased, abhorred any change that required more of his time. He did virtually no preparation for his weekly shows, walked in, taped the interview or took the calls, and walked out. And he preferred it that way.

As unquestionably the most powerful man at the university, Smith could kill the multimedia concept before it ever got off the ground, and he threatened to do so. Still unclear why what he considered to be a good system had to change, he reluctantly agreed to let Swofford proceed with the bidding out of the exclusive, packaged rights – with one very specific stipulation: nothing would change for Smith unless he agreed to it. That meant, no matter which company won the rights, Kilgo would be retained as host of his radio and TV shows. And that, regardless of who now owned the shows, Kilgo would continue to produce them in exactly the same manner. Kilgo would have the same budget as always and be able to travel to any away basketball games he deemed important.

After Heavner, as expected, won the multimedia rights in 1993, Smith often reminded employees of the Village Companies that everything would remain the same as it applied to basketball. Meanwhile, football coach Mack Brown dumped Kilgo and, with Durham now hosting, agreed to a more contemporary format that livened up his shows. Not so for Smith. He turned a deaf ear to Heavner's argument that paying the athletic department more than a million dollars a year in rights fees meant, among other things, a smaller travel budget for the TV show in favor of flashier production costs. When Kilgo heard that Heavner did not want to send him and the TV crew all the way to Hawaii for a single game during Christmas week of 1994, he complained to Smith. Running into Heavner's sports division manager at lunch a few weeks later, Smith walked by his table and snapped, "I said no changes."

Heavner took that literally and refused to pay Kilgo more than the $30,000 salary he had received from Jefferson-Pilot to host and produce the shows. When Smith began to divvy up his Nike money, he earmarked an additional $30,000 for Kilgo, who then became the highest-paid host of the twenty-one weekly radio and TV college coaches' shows in the country.

Smith's unyielding loyalty to Kilgo puzzled the many fans of Carolina athletics who considered Durham their true umbilical cord to the Tar Heels. Kilgo had made some money for Smith in the early years and blatantly supported him in his *Carolina Blue* sports tabloid.

After Smith retired, Bill Guthridge also retained Kilgo as his host for the first year. Then, when Heavner won renewal of the multimedia rights in 1997 for more than $2 million a year, he put his foot down.

By virtue of his own contract with Durham, he was already paying him to host the coaches' shows and saw no reason that he should continue to pay Kilgo, especially now that Smith was gone. Citing language in the multimedia contract that UNC merely had "approval rights" over the radio and TV announcers, Heavner submitted Durham's name. Carolina certainly could not refuse to approve its own radio play-by-play man. Guthridge, who by this time had developed his own strong distaste for Heavner, finally agreed to a compromise: Durham would take over the TV show and Kilgo would stay on as the radio call-in host, receiving no money from Heavner's company.

Kilgo hardly had to worry, though. In the summer of 1998, Smith signed a contract with Random House to write his autobiography for a reported $850,000 advance. He immediately hired Kilgo as his ghost-writer and inquired with the publisher about the standard fee for such a surrogate author. The answer he got was between 20 and 30 percent of the advance.

✪

Almost obsessively protective of his empire, Smith wanted to control who had access to Carolina basketball and, especially, who made money off his program. If he could have had his way, only his former players and coaches and closest friends would be able to derive any profit from the vast interest that had grown in the Tar Heels over the years. That was the source of his growing dislike for Heavner, whom he saw as feeding sumptuously off of Carolina and particularly the bas-ketball program. Heavner, a lifetime supporter of UNC who had con-tributed upwards of $1 million to the university, had known Smith since paying him five dollars per daily radio show in the 1960s. But they were no longer friends.

Once, while taking his exercise by walking the concourse in his own arena, Smith saw several new, illuminated signs for Coca-Cola on the walls and found out they were part of the multimedia deal. Citing the athletic department's self-imposed policy against signage in the football and men's basketball venues, Smith had those signs removed with one phone call. He also believed, rightfully so, that it was Carolina basketball – much more than any other school – which was responsible for the

ACC's escalating television rights. Thus, when the conference decided the letters "ACC" would appear on every school's home court for TV promotion, he had the letters on the Deandome floor outlined in very light paint for the first season of the mandate.

Smith was also fiercely vigilant about the bastardization of his own name and, especially, his likeness. In 1982, a local bar owner sought his permission to hold "the first annual Dean Smith Lookalike Contest." Smith not only denied the request; he said he would call his lawyer if the event took place. Years later, a Chapel Hill radio station ran some commercials for a dry cleaner, using an impersonation of the distinctly nasal-voiced coach. Months after the spots had stopped airing, the general manager of that station introduced his wife to Smith at a university function. While shaking her hand, Smith smiled and said slyly, "I could have sued your husband for those commercials."

By the time he broke Adolph Rupp's record for career victories in 1997, word had gotten through to most merchants around the state not to put Dean Smith's name, face, or any distinguishing characteristic on anything for sale without his permission. Scott Smith, who started with Converse, had worked in the athletic apparel business for years and helped spread his dad's concerns. After a local apparel store had gotten their okay to produce a commemorative T-shirt for Smith's 879th career win, Dean had to reverse his field when Nike informed him that they owned the rights to his name and likeness. Smith called the store owner, asked her to cease selling the T-shirts, and offered to pay for any of the sales that would be lost.

However, where it did not concern him or his program, Smith was far more open to lending his name and influence. Every so often, he championed a cause that, ironically, placed UNC athletics or Tar Heel basketball in an embarrassing light. If he cared strongly enough, it did not matter. His wife, Linnea, had turned activist against child pornography in the 1980s, launching a one-woman assault on *Playboy* magazine for its alleged depiction of young girls as sexual objects. Her campaign influenced Kenny Smith (in 1986) and Reid (1988) to decline their selections to the *Playboy* preseason All-American Team and the expenses-paid trip that came along with the honor.

Dean Smith helped Linnea get in front of the National Association of Basketball Coaches (NABC), where she asked her husband's counterparts to boycott the *Playboy* gala by having their players also refuse the recognition. (Ironically, Smith had been the *Playboy* preseason Coach of the Year in 1976, and he and Linnea had taken the trip together.) Some coaches were sympathetic, but others were annoyed that the first lady of America's most-publicized basketball program would ask them to give up what might be their teams' best chance for national publicity. Still others used her campaign to get an advantage in recruiting the same high school players Carolina went after.

In fact, after years of writing letters to *Playboy* and confronting the magazine's top brass, Linnea Smith finally had to back off. She found out that certain competing coaches were portraying her as a "kook" who had an influence on the players in her husband's program. "Don't go to Carolina," became the cry of several rival recruiters. "Dean Smith's wife has this thing about women and sex. She won't let any of their players have sex."

Dean Smith's own record on social causes is long and distinguished. Besides helping to integrate the restaurant where his team ate pregame meals in the 1950s, he attended student sit-ins during the Vietnam War in the 1960s and appeared in ads for a nuclear freeze in the 1970s. After his retirement, Smith actively campaigned against the death penalty in North Carolina, once appealing to governor Jim Hunt to commute the sentence of a two-time killer.

However, in the last few years before his retirement Smith's cause célèbre had become the beer industry's support of college athletics. He waged a war that cost his own school hundreds of thousands of dollars, sent him to Washington to testify in Senate subcommittee hearings on the subject, and even spilled onto the practice floor on the eve of the ACC Tournament.

Recognizing underage drinking as the number-one killer of teenagers in the country, Smith campaigned vigorously for the elimination of beer advertising during college sporting events. Beer was not sold at most college arenas and stadiums, and the NCAA did not accept beer advertising during television coverage of its own men's and women's basketball tournaments. But Smith strongly objected to what he often referred to as "our good friends at Budweiser" airing commercials on regional telecasts of ACC football and basketball. And for years he attempted to get beer advertising off the Tar Heel Sports Network radio broadcasts of Carolina football and basketball games.

Smith was particularly annoyed in the fall of 1995 when Woody Durham appeared standing next to an oversized Coors Light can on a basketball schedule card produced by Heavner's radio network. He believed that, while the university did not produce that specific schedule card, it created an unwanted association between Carolina basketball and the beer industry. Before Coors became a radio advertiser with the Tar Heels, Budweiser had been an advertiser for years. Both companies had annual six-figure sponsorships and felt betrayed after reading public statements from Smith criticizing beer advertising on college games.

"You expect me to keep spending money with you when your basketball coach runs his mouth all day long about our products," said Coors distributor Rodney Long. "We spend thousands of dollars on moderation advertising. We think we're very responsible, but we're in the business of selling beer."

Eventually, pressure brought by Smith caused UNC to prohibit beer and liquor and tobacco advertising with any of its sanctioned media. One of the half-dozen or so major sponsorship categories, beer ads could bring the multimedia rights holder (and thus the university) a million dollars over the course of a five-year contract.

Before he was successful in knocking out the beer ads, the apparent hypocrisy of Smith's stand had not been lost on his rivals and enemies. In March of 1996, Duke's Krzyzewski called Smith on it before the opening round of the ACC Tournament in Greensboro. A week before, Carolina and Duke had played an especially heated game in Durham, with the Tar Heels posting their seventh straight win over the Blue Devils. In the second half, volatile UNC guard Jeff McInnis had been ejected after receiving his second technical foul. The Duke crowd chanted "ASS-HOLE!" as McInnis left the floor.

As he had done several times in the past, Smith criticized the Duke fans for their vulgarity and sarcastically said the "esteemed Duke faculty" must be proud of their behavior in creating such a hostile atmosphere. The way he saw it, his player had merely complained after having been fouled intentionally and knocked against the press table. "If I were McInnis, I would have reacted a lot more strongly than he did," Smith said.

When asked about Smith's comments during the practice day for the

ACC Tournament, Krzyzewski defended his own fans by saying, "They were only making an accurate statement about one of (UNC's) players." And then, changing the subject, he called Smith a hypocrite. "If you're going to criticize beer advertising, you ought to get your own house in order first," Krzyzewski said, referring to the ads still running on the UNC radio network.

Smith bristled when he heard those comments. The next season, the ads were history.

ROLLER-COASTER
TO THE RECORD

For years, Dean Smith maintained that how his team played one year made no discernible difference in the amount of attention paid to the UNC program the next. But the surge of support leading up to the 1993 NCAA championship, which solidified Smith's place as the elder statesman and grand pooh-bah of college basketball, took the fascination for the Tar Heels to yet another level. This time, Smith acknowledged the difference – certainly in requests for his time and attention – and the fact that he had reclaimed ACC preeminence while seemingly building another dynasty made it crazier than ever.

So many letters of congratulations flooded the Carolina basketball office that Smith was still answering the last of them four years later. Tar Heel fans, tired of Duke's recent domination, rejoiced in the reaffirmation that Smith's philosophy of team over individual could still win a national championship. Mike Krzyzewski had grown less subtle in knocking Smith's style over the years. His thinly veiled reference in a *Sports Illustrated* article to how much more a plant can grow outside of a bottle than inside particularly perturbed Carolina fans, many of whom crowed when Duke got knocked out of the 1993 NCAA Tournament short of the Final Four for the first time in six years.

After winning his long-awaited national championship in 1982, followed by James Worthy's early departure for the NBA draft, Smith did everything he could to downplay the Tar Heels' chances to repeat. Worthy was gone, and so was point guard Jimmy Black, whom Smith considered the most valuable player on the team. He succeeded in convincing fans and the media that incoming recruits Brad Daugherty, Steve Hale, and Curtis Hunter wouldn't be much help the next year. Sam Perkins and Matt Doherty were coming back, but Smith had no idea that Michael Jordan would improve as much as he did between his freshman and sophomore seasons.

Likewise, Smith tried to emphasize how much the 1994 Tar Heels would miss George Lynch, the team's MVP and the glue that held the 1993 national champs together. But the loss of Lynch, who had become a sentimental favorite of UNC fans since they learned he had been declared legally dead at birth, did not seem insurmountable. After all, Carolina had the other four starters back and had signed up two of the most heralded recruits in the nation, Jerry Stackhouse and Rasheed Wallace. And the speculation that center Eric Montross would turn pro (he was rated a top-five pick after his junior season) was defused right away when Montross's father, Scott, said, "Are you kidding? And miss another year of playing for Dean Smith and Bill Guthridge?"

Smith was so swamped after the win over Michigan that even Guthridge had a tough time getting in to see his boss. Smith declined most of the requests for his time but did appear in several charity golf events, a willing concession since he loved golf so much and had such precious little time to play in the off-season. Another wave of proposals for him to write his autobiography came along, and while he rejected those overtures, he did find himself in the middle of book controversy within the UNC family. John Kilgo, the host of his weekly radio and TV shows, was writing the story of Carolina's championship season for a Charlotte publisher, which had proposed a deal to the UNC Alumni Association for marketing and distribution of the book. But Jim Heavner's Village Companies also wanted to do a commemorative book under the umbrella of its multimedia partnership, with the athletic department making money off the venture. "What's this all about?" Smith asked wearily in early April. Finally, he agreed to make Heavner's book the "official" version by writing a foreword, and in turn the Alumni Association got a cut in exchange for turning down the other proposal.

Then, in June, Michael Jordan called Smith to see if he had heard from Jordan's father, James, who had been incommunicado for several days. News reports about James Jordan's disappearance quickly followed, and then came the story out of South Carolina that a body believed to be Jordan's had been fished out of a creek. Dental records confirmed that it was indeed Jordan, who had been kidnapped, robbed, shot, and left for dead by two black youths who would eventually be convicted for murdering the father of the world's most famous athlete.

Smith, of course, had known James Jordan for years and had heard the rumors about the philandering, gambling, and bad business deals that had squandered a relatively tiny portion of his son's fortune. Just the prior May, when the Chicago Bulls were on their way to their third straight world championship, Smith had read all about Michael and James taking a night off from the New York Knicks series and gambling until the wee hours in the nearby Atlantic City casinos. Tales of Michael's own gambling excesses were familiar to Smith, who remembered that the ultracompetitive player liked to wager on pool, cards, "Horse," almost anything, way back in college. Before his senior year, after finding out the squad that won the scrimmage in practice each day would not have to participate in sprints, Jordan announced, "I'm not running one time this season." He figured he'd win every scrimmage and was willing to bet on it.

But despite all the wild stories, James and Deloris Jordan had remained the closest of friends to Smith. James, of course, was the main character in that rollicking story outside the victorious Carolina locker room at the Superdome in 1982. Others waiting for the players to emerge looked curiously at Jordan and James Worthy's father, Ervin, as they kicked an imaginary object down the hallway. Asked what they were doing, Jordan said, "We've knocked that monkey off Coach Smith's back and now we're kicking it the hell out of here!" Long after their son's shot had sealed Smith's first NCAA title and Michael had left Carolina, the Jordans were regular guests of Smith at Tar Heel games.

Now, Smith was in Wilmington to help bury James Jordan. He and Ed Ibaguen, Jordan's long-time friend and original golf teacher, met Michael at the Raleigh-Durham airport, watching as Jordan's Lear jet touched down. Dressed in an elegant dark suit, his bald head gleaming in the summer sun, Jordan looked composed behind his sunglasses as he stepped off the plane. Then he walked into his old coach's arms, put his head on Smith's shoulder, and cried like a baby. Dean Smith had yet another responsibility. He was now Michael Jordan's surrogate father.

✪

"Coach Smith had the uncanny knack of knowing what every player needed and giving it to him," said Dave Hanners, who played for the Tar Heels in the 1970s and joined Smith's coaching staff in 1989. "Some players needed confidence and some needed a reality check. He was tougher on certain guys, but he was never unjust or illogical. Coach Smith was a great solution finder. Although he might have yelled at one person more than another, at the end of the day it seemed like he treated everyone the same."

Despite Smith's famous seniority system, he always maintained that the best players got most of the minutes. "It amuses me that some people think I wouldn't put the best basketball team on the court," he said once. Of course, that team generally consisted of the more experienced players, not only because of their ability, but also because they had had the training to execute Smith's freelance offense and complicated, changing defenses. When freshmen played, and there were a lot of them who did, it was because they were clearly better than any upperclassmen at their position. That could be said for Phil Ford, the first freshman to start his first game under Smith in 1975, and Ed Cota, who twenty-two years later was the last freshman to start an opener with Smith still on the bench. "No one behind them in those particular years was any better than they were," said Hanners of Ford and Cota.

Never was Smith's system put to a greater test than in 1994, when Stackhouse was clearly outplaying senior Brian Reese during the preseason and Wallace was simply more talented than fifth-year senior Kevin Salvadori. Stackhouse, Wallace, and the third freshman that year, Jeff McInnis, were also the first Tar Heel players under Smith who seemed unwilling to wait their turns. They came to Carolina with reputations and attitudes, and soon they had written "Young Guns" on their Nike shoes. Ironically, a year before, few people would have imagined any of the three in a Carolina uniform.

Considered too much of an individual star to conform to Smith's system, Stackhouse was linked early with Duke, N.C. State, and Florida State, where his half-brother, Tony Dawson, once played for the Seminoles. But after apparently eliminating the Tar Heels from consideration, he called Ford late in the summer of 1992 and said he wanted to come to Chapel Hill for an unofficial visit. He committed to Carolina soon thereafter, saying he had always been a UNC fan. "I knew the words 'Dean Smith' before I could ever put a face to them," he noted.

Wallace, in turn, appeared ticketed for either Georgetown or one of the Big Five schools in his native Philadelphia. However, Jackie Wallace, who coordinated her son's recruitment, was impressed by the detail with which Smith answered the questionnaire she sent out to Rasheed's final ten schools. Then, when Smith visited her home, Wallace said she "just about fell in love with him." She also liked that Ford phoned often but never violated the designated period of time she set aside for recruiting calls. Smith and Ford went back to Wallace's home the day after the 1993 national championship game, but only to pick up the signed letter-of-intent. Wallace had told them weeks earlier that he was coming.

McInnis had played with Stackhouse at Oak Hill Academy in Virginia their senior year, but would have never been at Carolina had Randy Livingston followed through on his lifelong dream to play for the Tar Heels. The brilliant 6-4 guard from New Orleans excited Smith as much as any recruit ever had with his defensive potential and overall command of the game. But Smith was leery of Dale Brown, who had made Livingston's older brother a manager on his LSU basketball team and was applying heavy pressure to Livingston's mother to keep her son close to home. Much the same thing had happened five years earlier with Shaquille O'Neal, who shook Smith's hand and said, "Coach, I'm coming." That was the last Smith heard from O'Neal, but at least Livingston called to say he had changed his mind and was going to LSU. That's when Carolina offered a scholarship to McInnis, the gold-toothed kid everybody called "Touche."

At practice, Stackhouse's physical superiority over the oft-injured Reese and his power moves around the basket quickly became the talk of campus. Of course, Smith noticed that after thunder-dunking on one end, Stackhouse often lost the man he was supposed to be guarding on defense. Likewise, Wallace, one of the best pure talents to ever don Carolina blue, generally dominated his daily battles with Salvadori, but his problem was a short fuse. It earned him more technical fouls than any other Carolina player, and it cost him the reward of being named a starter. Although McInnis had little chance of displacing senior starter Derrick Phelps at point guard, he knew how fragile Phelps was and figured an injury would get him in the game sooner than later.

From an early season loss to Massachusetts through a blowout at the hands of Wake Forest in February, Carolina was a team with too many good players. While injuries can sometimes help sort out a crowded lineup, Reese's slow recovery from a preseason sprained ankle and Donald Williams's leg and shoulder injuries only served to complicate matters. When Reese heard rumors that he might lose his spot to Stackhouse, he said with a shrug, "I guess being a senior at Carolina doesn't mean what it once did." But Reese wound up starting thirty-four of thirty-five games after Stackhouse told Smith he was comfortable coming off the bench. Meanwhile, Dante Calabria, who had made more than 50 percent of his three-pointers as a starter subbing for Williams, lost minutes and his outside touch when he returned to a reserve role.

Finally, two weeks before the ACC Tournament, Smith named Wallace the permanent starter at strong forward over Salvadori and assigned certain roles to other players. The team banded together to win the regular-season finale at Duke, finishing second to the Blue Devils in the standings, and then took the tournament in Charlotte. But there was little celebration and no net-cutting ceremony after the 73-66 win over Virginia in the finals. By this time, Carolina was widely rumored to be a team in turmoil. The Tar Heels had given Smith his twelfth ACC Tournament title, had been awarded the top seed in the NCAA East Regional, and had reclaimed the No. 1 national ranking, but much of the talk was about how Salvadori sulked on the bench during the Virginia game. Peppered with questions about alleged dissension at his pre-NCAA Tournament press conference, Smith sighed and said, "What are we talking about here? Young people, all of whom want to do well." It was an acknowledgment that things weren't exactly rosy. And when assistant coach Bill Guthridge, who had always believed that a team that didn't have it together by February was probably not going to get it together, was asked if this team could be an exception, the best he could offer was, "I hope so."

A lackluster performance against sixteenth-seeded Liberty portended what was to come in the NCAA Tournament. If the Tar Heels could not pound the small and skinny Flames, how would they deal with rough-and-tough, eighth-seeded Boston College in the second round at Landover, Maryland? Watching films of the Eagles before the game, Smith not only saw excellent three-point shooting and rugged center Billy Curly, he noticed BC's No. 23 throwing elbows and playing what Carolina had long considered dirty basketball. Sure enough, with the Tar Heels down ten points the next day, Phelps stole the ball and had a breakaway layup when, while airborne to the basket, he was toma-hawked from behind by Danye Abrams, No. 23. Phelps suffered a con-cussion and did not return, as Smith implored the officials to eject Abrams for a flagrant foul.

Enraged the rest of the game, Smith was not his steel-trap self after Carolina rallied to tie the score on two pressure-packed free throws from Montross. When BC missed a shot, the Tar Heels had the ball with two minutes left and a chance to take the lead for the first time since early in the game. But instead of calling a time-out, telling his players "we have 'em right where we want 'em," and diagramming a high-per-centage shot or sure foul, Smith let them play on. Williams, who had already failed on ten of eleven shots, fired up an ill-advised three-point-er that missed. BC got the rebound, scored at the other end and pulled off the season's biggest upset, 75-72. After the game, a shaken Smith was still complaining about Abrams's allegedly flagrant foul and was less complimentary to Carolina's conqueror than usual.

This was a bad loss, given the Tar Heels' potential to repeat as NCAA champions at the Final Four scheduled for the Charlotte Coliseum. It also snapped one of Smith's most amazing streaks – thirteen consecu-tive years reaching at least the Sweet Sixteen of the NCAA Tournament – and magnified several decisions Smith had made during the season: not starting Stackhouse and Wallace; not going back to Calabria when Williams couldn't find his outside shot; not telling a couple of surly seniors to like it or lump it for the sake of the team. Rarely had Smith found himself the subject of such second-guessing, but to him the choice of values over victory was no choice at all. He might have won more games, but he might have also lost the confidence of the entire team by breaking some well-known traditions. And to Dean Smith, winning his way was the only way.

✪

The 1994 Tar Heels had proved prophetic a preseason story in *Basketball Times* magazine, which while picking them No. 1 had asked and answered the rhetorical question: "Who's going to beat them? Only themselves." Indeed, the season had confirmed Smith's long-time adage that having too many good players on one team could be dangerous. The perfect squad, he theorized, consisted of five clear-cut starters, three solid substitutes, and five other guys who worked hard in practice and were just happy to be there. So prior to the 1994-95 season, Smith liked the fact that his lineup was virtually set. Four players had graduated, leaving sophomores Stackhouse, Wallace, and McInnis, and seniors Williams and Pat Sullivan as expected starters. The 6-7 Sullivan, who had come in with the Montross-Phelps-Reese class, had voluntarily taken a red-shirt season in 1994 in order to break the logjam of players and to give himself the chance to shine the following year.

Calabria, the smooth-shooting junior from Joe Namath's hometown in working-class western Pennsylvania, could come off the bench to play either guard position. And there was good competition for the other two spots in Smith's eight-man rotation between senior Morehead Scholar Pearce Landry, sophomore seven-footer Serge Zwikker and underrated freshman guard Shammond Williams. However, Sullivan suffered a bulging disc before the season opener that required surgery, sidelining him for at least ten weeks and causing a domino effect on the team. Calabria, the most talented of the reserves, moved into the starting lineup as a 6-4 small forward, which in turn pushed the 6-5 Stackhouse to the post position opposite Wallace. Landry wound up the only other sub with significant playing time, leaving Smith with a six-man squad fraught with as many perils as the overloaded team he had fielded the year before. "Sullivan has to go under the knife; he's probably out for the season and it could be disastrous," a distraught Smith said just before the opening game against Texas.

Nevertheless, the Tar Heels were 9-0 and ranked No. 1 in the country when their lack of depth began to tell. Calabria sat out the January 4 game at N.C. State with a sprained ankle and Carolina lost by ten. Still, in one of Smith's finest coaching jobs, his athletic but thin team managed to finish the regular season in a first-place tie with Wake Forest, Maryland, and Virginia. And the Heels were on the verge of winning the ACC Tournament when Wallace went down with his own turned ankle in the last five minutes of the championship game against the Deacons. Following the two-point loss in overtime, Carolina was seeded No. 2 in the NCAA Southeast Regional. But Zwikker came off the bench to replace a hobbling, ineffective Wallace and help secure tough wins over Murray State and Iowa State.

Now, they were two games from returning to the Final Four. With Wallace fully recovered, they dispatched Georgetown from the regional semifinal in Birmingham and faced a favored Kentucky team for a trip to the Kingdome in Seattle. As thousands of Kentucky fans poured into the Alabama city, Smith and his staff were working overtime trying to figure out how to beat the tall, talented, and tenacious Wildcats of Rick Pitino. Eddie Fogler, who while coaching at Vanderbilt and South Carolina had faced Kentucky a dozen times, spent some time going over the scouting report with Smith and Guthridge. Given that part of Pitino's system was to shoot a lot of three-pointers, Carolina decided to sag inside on big men Walter McCarty and Andre Riddick and give up some wide-open looks to long bomber Tony Delk.

The strategy worked well early and got better as the game progressed, as Delk wound up hitting only seven of twenty-one shots from the field. Frustrated by their inability to go on their habitual scoring runs, the Wildcats kept shooting quickly and missing. Meanwhile, Carolina played brilliantly in the second half, getting back on defense and patiently waiting for the right shots. McInnis and Stackhouse repeatedly took the ball to the basket and, after Kentucky committed, fed Wallace for dunks and layups. The 74-61 win, practically a blowout, stunned Pitino, who was so confident of victory that he had reserved a room at a Birmingham restaurant for a private party later that night. After the loss, Pitino canceled the room.

Smith had again one-upped himself by taking a team to the Final Four that really had no business being there. Overmatched on defense, he begrudgingly scrapped his pressure, man-to-man schemes in favor of a match-up "point zone." In the 75-68 semifinal loss to defending national champion Arkansas in Seattle, bigger Razorbacks Corliss Williamson and Dwight Stewart manhandled Stackhouse, who sustained a deep thigh bruise on the opening tip, and Wallace, who was inexplicably lethargic in the second half. When the front line had been outplayed during the season, Calabria, Williams, and McInnis were usually reliable from outside. In this game, they combined to make only eleven of thirty-eight shots.

Though Smith had now taken three teams to the Final Four in the 1990s, after critics had predicted he would never get back there, he found himself taking the blame for the Tar Heels' failure to win it all. The exhilaration of the Kentucky upset was blown away by the loss to Arkansas, considered an inferior team to the Wildcats. Another blow landed when Stackhouse and Wallace decided to turn pro – the first time Smith had ever lost two sophomores. And if this were not enough, rumors began to circulate in the spring of 1995 about an alleged affair between McInnis and Phil Ford's attractive wife, Traci. The story, spread wildly over chat rooms on the Internet, would dog Carolina through the next season. It certainly didn't help that the Fords were having marital problems and had separated. As with most point guards in the program, Ford had taken McInnis under his wing and made him part of his personal family. While acknowledging a close friendship between McInnis and Traci Ford, no one in the Carolina program ever confirmed that anything inappropriate had taken place.

❂

The roller-coaster ride that marked Dean Smith's fourth decade on the job continued through the 1996 season and into 1997, his last year. Continually bombarded by off-court responsibilities, including player problems that seemed to grow more complicated every year, he contemplated retirement more and more. Those closest to him noticed the increased strain, the unhappy weekends away from his family, and, frankly, the pressure to keep coaching until he broke Adolph Rupp's record for all-time victories for a major-college coach.

That subject had irritated Smith for years, so much so that he had on several occasions guaranteed the media it would never happen – once joking that he would quit the day before the game to tie the record. But as Smith closed the 1995 season forty-six wins shy of Rupp's mark, his concern for the condition of his program became inextricably bound up with the approaching record. He had always promised he would step aside before the next season as opposed to after the last one – implying that he wouldn't know until the start of practice whether or not he would have the enthusiasm to begin a new year. Of course, waiting for that "next season" to start would also allow Smith to hand the reigns to his own chosen successor.

Such a scenario could never materialize, however, if the Tar Heel program was in trouble. And entering the 1996 season, Smith had no earthly idea if he could ever restore his team to national prominence. Two NBA first-round draft choices and 1993 Final Four MVP Williams had been replaced by three freshmen of whom he was uncertain. Vince Carter, a high-flyer from Daytona Beach, was the most heralded of the group. But Smith knew Carter would have to learn more than how to jump, that his basketball savvy was sketchy, and that his immense athletic ability had never forced him to play hard. Antawn Jamison had been a highly rated recruit his sophomore and junior years in Charlotte but had dropped in the recruiting rankings during a sub-par senior season. Also in question were Jamison's SAT scores, and in June Smith was already resigned to Jamison's spending a year in prep school before enrolling at UNC. Ironically, the recruit Smith felt best about was a 6-8 German named Ademola Okulaja, who been recommended to Carolina by former Tar Heel and American exchange student Henrik Rodl. Okulaja was a year older than most college freshmen, physically mature, and mentally tough from having competed on German club teams.

Furthermore, junior center Serge Zwikker, a five-year project, had never played more than a few minutes a game on the college level. Did Zwikker, at 7-2, 250 pounds, and not overly athletic, have the stamina to be the starting center? If not, who would be? Sure, McInnis and Calabria returned, and Smith believed that having experienced guards would help early in the season while the newcomers inside got acclimated. Maybe McInnis could penetrate and dish to Dante for open jumpers. If Calabria could hit a few, perhaps that would stretch the defense and create some open shots closer to the basket. But Smith really wasn't kidding when he said with a laugh at an early summer alumni function, "We'll have our worst team in thirty years!"

Then Jamison passed the required SAT score on his last try, and two months later Smith and Guthridge couldn't believe the 6-9 freshman's quickness during three-man drills the first week of classes. Jamison had spent much of his high school career facing the basket, but in Carolina's low post offense he could easily lose his man, catch entry passes with his suction-cup hands and lay the ball in. His first go-around the ACC, while opponents indeed were worrying more about Calabria and McInnis, Jamison averaged eighteen points and almost twelve rebounds a game. Okulaja proved to be a solid contributor as well; however, as Smith had feared, Carter did not want to do much more than take alley-oop passes for spectacular dunks.

After wondrous comeback wins over Wake Forest and Duke, the Tar Heels finished the first half of the ACC season with a 7-1 record. Then, things got nasty on and off the court. There were now rumors of a rift between Calabria and McInnis, proud players from different worlds who both liked to have the ball in their hands when Carolina no longer could get in inside. Convinced Jamison was the real deal, opponents geared their game plans around stopping him, and Smith battled officials who allowed Jamison to be pushed and shoved and moved away from the basket. Antawn's averages dropped by five points and three rebounds, as Carolina lost three straight conference games and stood only 9-6 going to Duke for the regular-season finale. A loss in Durham would surely relegate the Tar Heels to fourth place in the ACC, breaking yet another Smith mark of finishing no lower than third every year since 1965.

The atmosphere at Duke was even more venomous than at Wake Forest four days earlier, where the Deacons had romped by twenty-four points. There, wicked Wake fans had waved signs and yelled in unison at Ford and McInnis, as Carolina basically quit playing late in the second half. Smith was upset with his players but realized their sinking confidence was in peril. He also remembered his old adage that the worst time to play a team was after it had been embarrassed, and that's one thing he could say about the Tar Heels' performance at Wake Forest. Duke fans were juiced to break a six-game losing streak to Carolina, dating back to 1993, and they too got on McInnis from the opening tap.

What happened late in UNC's 84-78 upset victory said much for Smith the coach and the man. Smith, for sure, heard the vicious taunts hurled at his point guard, and he defended McInnis for overreacting to a hard foul by Duke's Jay Heaps and picking up his second technical for an automatic ejection. He even understood when he told an emotional McInnis to settle down and heard his player spew a rash of obscenities. Some people believed McInnis was swearing at Smith, but that was not the case. Smith's point after the game, and into the next week, was more about the society we live in than his player losing his cool in front of a hostile crowd. He contended that McInnis's in-your-face style of play and his chest-thumping gestures were part of the black culture that – like it or not – had taken over the game of basketball. It was clear to Smith that white players who danced and waved their arms and talked trash were seldom criticized and, more to the point, were treated differently by the referees. He cited Duke's Chris Collins, who grinned and grabbed his teammates and bantered with the man guarding him just as much as McInnis, as an example of how white players were perceived as gutsy and tough, while blacks were considered belligerent.

Those were the battles Smith found himself fighting as the 1996 season ended with a first-round loss to Clemson in the ACC Tournament and a second-round beating by Texas Tech in the NCAA East Regional, the second such quick exit for the Tar Heels in three years. McInnis essentially quit going to class after the team returned from the regional loss in Richmond, and speculation quickly began that he would enter the NBA draft in June. Even after Smith told McInnis he was, at best, a late first-round pick, and then when Denver took him in the second round, McInnis could have changed his mind and returned for his senior year. But he had no intention of doing so; he stayed away from Chapel Hill and let the incompletes in the classes he blew off turn into Fs.

McInnis had grown up near a drug- and crime-ridden section of Charlotte, basically distrusted white people, and, as a result of that upbringing, was something of a scam artist. Smith understood all that and didn't blame McInnis for his problems as much as he blamed himself for Carolina's having failed in its mission. He believed McInnis to be a good kid and hoped the peer pressure of the Tar Heel program could keep him in line and eventually reform him. Even after McInnis got cut by Denver, for attitude as much as ability, Smith denied he had flunked out of school and helped him get placed on an overseas team, later into the CBA, and eventually back into the NBA.

❂

Before the 1996 season, Smith had said sarcastically of the Rupp record, "When we win eight games this season, and eight the next, I'll be a little closer." Despite losing four of its last six games, Carolina still managed to win twenty-one and move Smith within twenty-five victories of tying Rupp's 876 as he entered the 1997 campaign. Yet Smith found himself in another quandary; winning at least twenty games was a given at Carolina (UNC had done it for twenty-six straight years), and only slight improvement over the previous season would mean Smith might be upstaging his own team by tournament time. "I don't want the attention on me, I want it on the team," he said tersely before the opening game. "That's why I said several years ago I'd get out before I break the record. Luckily, it shouldn't be a problem this year . . . you can't count on twenty-six wins with any team."

Dean Smith's thirty-sixth, and last, winter on the bench turned out to be one of his strangest. While winning nine of its first ten games against a soft schedule, his team continued the uneven play that had marked the last half of the last season. Much of it came from a new backcourt of Ed Cota and Shammond Williams, who had taken over for Calabria and McInnis and made a lot of mistakes early. Cota, a twenty-year-old freshman whom Smith had discovered three years earlier, had arrived in Chapel Hill after attending three public high schools in New York City and a prep school in Connecticut. Williams had also taken a prep year, after no major college had offered him a scholarship coming out of high school, and got tagged as only a shooter before landing at Carolina. Smith, in fact, had hurt Williams's feelings and confidence after his freshman year when he said, "Shammond scares me to death" when he has the ball.

The front line had three sophomores, and while all had had their moments, none were considered superstars in the making. Jamison had made All-ACC as a freshman, but a so-so second half of the season and 52 percent free-throw shooting were hardly signs that he would develop into a dominating All-American. Okulaja was clearly a role player, at best, and Carter had been so disappointing in his first year that unfounded rumors had him transferring to a school back in Florida. Senior Zwikker had been better than expected in his first starting role, but his single-digit scoring and rebounding averages weren't making anyone forget about Eric Montross.

The situation was so tenuous that a controversial transfer student who had yet to play a game for the Tar Heels – and began the season under suspension – was looked upon as a savior by some desperate Carolina fans. Makhtar Ndiaye, Smith's first transfer from another four-year school, had been penalized for taking illegal travel expenses to a summer basketball camp from sneaker impresario Sonny Vaccaro. Smith and Carolina maintained that Ndiaye had done nothing wrong, but the incident foreshadowed the continuation of a jaded career for the 6-9 African from Senegal.

Ndiaye had spent a year at Oak Hill with McInnis and Stackhouse, accepted a scholarship offer from Wake Forest, and never played a game for the Deacons after the NCAA ruled he had been illegally recruited. Allowed to transfer without penalty, Ndiaye stayed a year and a half at Michigan before he decided to leave there as well. Kansas coach and former Smith assistant Roy Williams, who had watched Ndiaye play for Michigan, encouraged his old boss to change a 35-year policy of not taking major-college transfers. Claiming he had always wanted to play at Carolina, Ndiaye visited Chapel Hill and, in his words, "had to convince" Smith to give him a scholarship. After succeeding, he had practiced with the team in 1996 while sitting out his NCAA-mandated red-shirt year.

Ndiaye was certainly not the answer to Carolina's apparent front-court problems, and Smith knew it. In fact, he had taken Ndiaye against the recommendation of recruiting analyst and friend of the program Bob Gibbons, who told Bill Guthridge that Makhtar was overrated as a player and considered a troublemaker by people who knew him well. Smith had felt differently after meeting Ndiaye and, perhaps influenced by his need for depth up front, broke with tradition. McInnis, who was still in the program, and Ndiaye had roomed together during the 1996 season.

Ndiaye turned out to be a seldom-used back-up his "junior" year, and Carolina played the 1997 ACC season with basically six men. When they lost their first three conference games for the first time under Smith, including blowing a 22-point lead to Maryland at home, fans feared and critics claimed that, once and for all, the game had passed the 65-year-old coach by. The rap was that he hadn't recruited players to replace Stackhouse and Wallace and couldn't coach the guys left in the program. Despite widespread criticism of Carter as "soft" and of Williams as a selfish shooter, and despite a players-only, obscenity-laced shouting session after a twelve-point loss at Virginia, Smith stayed poised and positive about his team in public.

Privately, he admonished the Tar Heels to play harder and to stress teamwork, but, worried about the whole season collapsing, Smith stayed more even-handed than he might have been in the past. Somehow, they rallied from nine points down in the last two and a half minutes to beat N.C. State and avoid an 0-4 start, then managed a mild upset of Clemson to go 3-5 the first time through the ACC. Ironically, the turning point might have come in a seven-point loss at heavily favored Duke. Almost winning this game seemed to give the players renewed confidence. Smith, who worked longer and later into the night watching tape, figured out a few things to do but confessed during a subsequent sixteen-game winning streak, "They had more confidence in themselves than I had in them."

In a remarkable turnaround, Carolina went undefeated over the second half of the season, reached the ACC Tournament finals by knocking off twice-defending champion Wake Forest for the second time in seventeen days, and, in defeating N.C. State for his thirteenth tourney title, brought Smith within one game of Rupp's record. Smith, who had decided to bring Cota off the bench in the first few minutes of every game, was flabbergasted by his team's offensive efficiency during the storybook stretch, as it shot better than 50 percent in fifteen out of the sixteen games. But it had been his persistent planning and teaching that enabled Cota, now the ACC assist leader, to get Jamison the ball at the low post, Zwikker on the baseline, and Carter above the basket. When opponents gave up and sagged inside to stop the layups, short jumpers and dunks, Williams nailed one big three-pointer after another.

A team that seemingly couldn't beat anybody good, literally couldn't be beat in February and March. The Tar Heels were so into their own successful run that they easily handled the pressure of their coach's impending all-time record. After blowing through the ACC Tournament in Greensboro, they defeated Fairfield and crushed Colorado in the first two rounds of the NCAA East Regional in Winston-Salem to give Smith the most major-college wins in history. Smith then notched career victories 878 (over California) and 879 (over Louisville) in the Sweet Sixteen at Syracuse and, while he was at it, earned his eleventh trip to the Final Four – second only to John Wooden's twelve.

Despite the strained back of newly named All-American Jamison and a late rally by Louisville, Smith maintained his wit and wisdom in the final minutes of the Final Eight game. After the Cardinals had cut a twenty-point Carolina lead to three, Smith called a time-out and said matter-of-factly, "Well, they might catch up and win, but we've had a good season." Okulaja screamed in his face and led the starters back on the court to take care of business, as the Tar Heels went on to win easily, 97-74. Once going nowhere, they took a 28-6 record to the RCA Dome in Indianapolis for UNC's fourth Final Four in the 1990s.

The 1997 season solidified the myth of Dean Smith perhaps more than any other during a career that spanned four decades, eight presidents, and thirty-five opposing ACC coaches. Faced with his own increasing age, the attitude of fans with short memories, and the encroachment of pro basketball into the college game, how could he have had the energy, patience and resilience to pull off yet another turnaround? While so many successful coaches go out, and go down, doing what they've done for years, Smith scrapped his favorite plans in favor of what worked. He junked his pressure defense, stopped his incessant substituting, and let the first point guard since Phil Ford dribble more than pass. He "raised the roof" with his celebrating team, signed more autographs than ever, and recovered yet again from two players whom he had sent out of his program early to the NBA. The sport had changed for the umteenth time since a skinny, slick-haired Smith had forgotten to bring out a game ball for his head-coaching debut in 1961. But there he was, thirty-six years later, heavier, grayer, and as sharp as ever with a play call here or an official's call there. In many ways, things hadn't changed at all.

What was to be Smith's last Final Four as a coach ended as his first had, exactly thirty years and five days earlier, with a disappointing loss after looking great in the early minutes. Just like his sixth UNC team had done against Dayton in 1967, his thirty-sixth team led Arizona by double digits in the first half. Then, the shots stopped falling, the other guys got hot and, suddenly, the magic spell was broken. Smith kept coaching until the final, frenzied seconds, but he had been in his profession long enough to know this particular game was over.

Also at an end was a legendary career that had taken a one-time aspiring math teacher all the way to the head of his class. For the 1,133rd time, Dean Edwards Smith shook hands with the opposing coach, found something appropriate to tell his players, and then met with the press – one final time taking the high road by complimenting the other team. Then the most successful college basketball coach of all time went home to watch the game all over again, wondering what he might have done differently.

STILL IN CHARGE

A worn-down Dean Smith left the bench, moved out of his office, and gave up his personal parking space, but he hardly walked away from the notoriety and sovereignty he had achieved. That he still came to work almost every day and did not meddle clearly indicated he had no regrets over his decision. That he continued to be inundated with personal requests meant he had underestimated what his retirement would bring. At least now Smith had an excuse to just say no.

As the last coaching days of Dean Smith moved further away in the rearview mirror, friends and associates remarked at how good he looked. Remaining tanned from after-October 15th golf, a relaxed Smith relished not having to begin the same routine he had endured through the last forty years. He and his wife spent one early November weekend at the beach, and Smith made good on his pledge to see his grandchildren more often. When informed he had been selected *Sports Illustrated*'s Sportsman of the Year, he even allowed photographers to shoot him and grandson Luke at the home of his daughter, Sandy Combs, in Charlotte.

Returning to Chapel Hill, he heard that Mack Brown had resigned as Carolina's football coach to take the Texas job. Asked for his advice, but aware that Dick Baddour had already made contact with Georgia's

Jim Donnan, Smith recommended Carl Torbush if Carolina chose to "stay inside." Donnan ultimately declined the UNC offer and Torbush was introduced late Monday afternoon, December 8, after Smith had been in Baddour's office that morning. Torbush called the next day to thank Smith and pledged to help Bill Guthridge in the continuing recruitment of football-basketball star Ronald Curry, who would eventually sign with UNC in April.

Trying to maintain a low profile, Smith remained the major force behind Carolina basketball. He gave over his elegant office to Guthridge and moved down the hall into a smaller room once occupied by the restricted-earnings coaches on his staff, and he stopped parking in the space with the "reserved" sign that had been placed there for him ten years earlier. Smith had not asked for the space, but athletic director John Swofford gave it to him after continually seeing Smith's car parked at the far end of the large Smith Center lot. The old space stayed empty for more than a month following Smith's retirement – no one dared park there – until the sign was taken down. Somehow believing he no longer rated special privileges, Smith went back to walking across the parking lot.

He attended only a handful of games in person, watching the rest at home on television while "cheering so hard. I'm like a fan. My heart beats faster. I've been yelling at them – the players and coaches – through the television set." He made a surprise halftime appearance during the game with Hampton Institute on December 16 to be honored as *SI*'s Sportsman of the Year. With no prior announcement that he was coming, the crowd greeted him with a huge roar and stood cheering during the short presentation. The team had remained on the court to watch the ceremony, and cognizant that the Tar Heels had not played well together in the first half, Smith motioned with his hands at several players to pass the ball.

Smith had hoped the Sportsman of the Year honor and first-person interview he agreed to do for the December 22 edition of *Sports Illustrated* would bring closure to his public career, since he covered a number of issues about the game of basketball and his personal beliefs. But it had the opposite effect, spawning more requests for his comments from the media. The public wasn't satisfied, either. So many copies of the edition with Smith on the cover and accompanying poster of him were sent in or dropped by the Deandome that the basketball office finally posted a sign on the door that said no more would be accepted for autographs. Smith's suddenly smaller office remained cluttered with dozens of items seeking his signature.

While he occasionally reviewed game tapes with Guthridge and the other coaches, Smith attended few staff meetings and spoke with the players only in passing. Behind the scenes, however, he remained influential, positioning the team for the highest exposure and the players for the best opportunities once their careers were over. He was still in charge of scheduling, using his considerable clout with CBS, ABC, and ESPN to get Carolina prime television dates. Smith was reticent about accepting the prestigious Arthur Ashe Award for Courage (for his support of integration and other social issues) at the annual ESPYs until Ashe's widow, Jeannie, called Smith personally and told him how much her late husband had respected him. Up to that point, the ESPN brass had teasingly tried to twist Smith's arm with some "back-scratching" banter about all of the cable network telecasts the Tar Heels enjoyed every season.

Usually an off-the-cuff speaker, Smith had prepared some eloquent remarks for the black-tie ESPYs ceremony in New York. But the video-taped testimonial, which included moving words from old friends Reverend Bob Seymour and UNC professor Chuck Stone, as well as Michael Jordan, left Smith choked up as he watched from the audience. Then the surprise appearance of former players Brad Daugherty, Billy Cunningham, Walter Davis, Doug Moe, Charlie Scott, and James Worthy, who presented him with the Ashe Award, caused Smith to lose his train of thought about halfway through his speech. The players had been sequestered backstage by ESPN, and Smith seemed genuinely stunned to see them walk out.

With his old team having lost one game through Valentine's Day and ranked No. 1 in the country, Smith continued mostly casual conversation with Guthridge about game plans and strategies. He did, however, watch extra tape of archrival Duke, the Tar Heels' top challenger in the ACC during the 1998 season. He increased his time in the film room after Carolina's poor performance in a six-point home loss to seventh-place N.C. State, helping Guthridge prepare for the last week of the regular season and rematches with Wake Forest and Duke, followed by the annual ACC Tournament. The irony was not lost on those who knew what was happening. While most programs had volunteer coaches barely out of school, the Tar Heels' "candy striper" just happened to have the most wins in major-college history. One way or another, Smith had his hand in Carolina's 13-3 ACC record, two wins over Duke and the conference tournament title.

By then, of course, he had surprised many people by accepting a six-figure offer to join CBS-TV as a studio analyst for "Championship Week" and all six rounds of "March Madness." A participant in the last twenty-three NCAA Tournaments, Smith spent three straight long weekends in New York as a member of the broadcast media, sitting around the CBS set with Greg Gumbel and Clark Kellogg. Draggan Mihailovich, a CBS producer who grew up in Chapel Hill and was raised on Carolina basketball, saw the man he had idolized for years eating alone in the network cafeteria one afternoon during the first weekend. With a lump in his stomach, Mihailovich immediately instructed his own administrative assistant to make sure she knew where Smith was at all times and that he had anything he wanted or needed – including company. However, Smith quickly bonded with Gumbel and Kellogg, who took their new broadcast partner out to dinner on several occasions after the last nightly show, and the trio grew closer over the course of the month.

Because television is a contrived medium, it proved to be a difficult assignment for Smith. The coach who could speak to his players and fans whenever and for however long he wanted now had to condense his thoughts into short sound bites. Although he improved as the tournament wore on, Smith admittedly was uncomfortable in the role and, in his own words, "not very good" at dropping in ten-second comments while producer Eric Mann talked to him through a small receiver in his ear. Once, while commenting on the Tar Heels, Smith said "we" and grimaced as Mann chirped, "It's they now, Coach; gotta be objective." Smith joked later that his finest moment had been a pre-taped blackboard session on the Princeton backdoor offense that did not air because Michigan State upset the Tigers in the second round of the East Regional. "That was my best, but it never got on," Smith said.

Gumbel, Kellogg, and Mann remembered Smith "really sweating" during Carolina's narrow wins over UNC Charlotte and Connecticut on the way to the Final Four. "It looked like he was still coaching and we were right there on the bench with him," said Mann, referring to Smith's body language. "But when it was time to go on, he pulled it together and did a nice job. He's a national hero, a coaching legend, but he was part of the team and very down to earth." Mann added that Smith was understandably in agony on the broadcast platform in San Antonio during Carolina's fretful first-half performance against Utah. "We've got to shoot better and find a way to stop them," Smith said to no one in particular during UNC's semifinal loss.

✪

Smith's loyalty and dedication to his players was never tested more than after the Final Four, where Makhtar Ndiaye had made an embarrassing (and false) accusation that a Utah player called him a "nigger" during the game. It was the worst in a series of outbursts from Ndiaye, whom Smith had trusted enough to be his first-ever major-college transfer. Upset by his own horrid play and the team's lackluster loss, Ndiaye somehow got into a dialogue with four sportswriters that resulted in his accusing Utah sophomore Britton Johnsen of making the slur during the game. Meanwhile, in the other locker room, Johnsen said that Ndiaye had spit on him during a battle under the basket.

Remaining in San Antonio for the national championship game between Utah and Kentucky, Smith was not involved in the apology Ndiaye and UNC issued to Johnsen and Utah on Monday. Even so, the media severely criticized Carolina for not allowing Ndiaye and Guthridge to appear at a press conference. A shocked university community outside the basketball office was ready to disavow the controversial Senegalese player who had already been involved in several public controversies. Even chancellor Michael Hooker blasted Ndiaye in the *Raleigh News & Observer*, although Hooker later said his strong remarks came after a reporter had caught him by surprise. Just when the incident had died down, Ndiaye was charged with misdemeanor assault in yet another bizarre, off-campus case. At his eventual trial, Ndiaye denied that he had ever apologized for the Johnsen remark and said the university had done it without his approval. That was a lie, as Ndiaye had signed off on the statement before it was released.

When Smith returned from the Final Four, he had several long talks with the disconsolate and troubled player, encouraging him to attend anger-management counseling and then pro tryout camps that spring. While some coaches might have regretted taking Ndiaye in the first place, Smith instead saw it as a valuable lesson for someone whom he long ago understood came from a decidedly different culture. Growing up in Africa, Ndiaye had played mostly soccer, which in the Eastern Hemisphere is a far more violent game than in the youth leagues of America. Smith had spoken with other basketball coaches who had had African players on their teams and learned of sometimes uncontrollable aggression on the court. He stayed in regular contact with Ndiaye during the spring. "Hustle and play smart," Smith told him one day when Ndiaye called in from the Portsmouth, Virginia, tryout camp.

In May, Smith orchestrated the "hardship" decision of Antawn Jamison, National Player of the Year as a junior, to turn pro ("an easy choice for him"), and he went through the motions with Vince Carter, whose mother, Michelle Robinson, had already made the decision that her son was also leaving school. Early in the season, Robinson had been upset with the results of Smith's first query of pro scouts and general managers that revealed Carter was rated no better than the fifteenth pick in the NBA draft. "We want to get a second opinion," Robinson told Smith in January. Meanwhile, Carter finished the season on a tear, hitting double figures in sixteen of his last seventeen games, averaging twenty-one points and six rebounds, and playing more aggressively than he had for most of his career. In Smith's second round of calls to his NBA contacts, Carter had moved up to a top-ten pick. By then, Robinson had gotten similar feedback and decided her son should go pro. When Smith set up his annual "agents day" for the players and their families, Carter and Robinson did not attend because they had already selected Michelle's friend William "Tank" Black to represent them.

However, the most difficult time of Smith's retirement stemmed, ironically, from something he had done before stepping down. Vasco Evtimov, one of thirty-six McDonald's All-Americans Smith had signed over the years, took a sabbatical after a disappointing freshman season. A dual citizen of France and his native Bulgaria, Evtimov had to satisfy a military commitment in either country before he turned twenty-five to preserve his citizenship in both. Smith went to work after the 1997 season arranging a "red-shirt" year for Evtimov, who wound up playing for a club team during his ten months in the French army in order to qualify for France's national team. Smith had read the NCAA rule and thought it was clear that Evtimov could serve his country and follow guidelines for national team tryouts set by the French Basketball Federation, but he did not check it out with the NCAA. Though this was not quite the same, Smith had made numerous foreign arrangements for players over the years.

However, after returning to Chapel Hill in July of 1998 and getting ready to begin his sophomore season under Guthridge, Evtimov was suspended by the NCAA because the club team for which he played had several paid professionals on the roster. Smith got involved in the appeals process and was despondent on December 17 after participating in a conference call that afternoon with the NCAA and the French Basketball Federation. Evtimov's suspension had not only been upheld, but also extended to eighteen games – through January 13 – or more than half the season.

"Blame me, punish me," Smith told the NCAA, "I'm the one who told him (Evtimov) he could do this." For the first time since he retired, Smith felt stung by the criticism of fans who believed he hadn't done his homework and should have called the NCAA to get specific clearance for Evtimov. But it seemed like more than that, beyond the NCAA's explanation that it was carefully monitoring the college eligibility of all foreign athletes.

No longer as visible, Smith's power base in college basketball was slipping. Had he still been coaching, the NCAA might have embraced his arguments more warmly. Carolina was also seeing the difference on the recruiting front, as competition now came from new and different places. Kentucky, which had rarely tried to recruit players from North Carolina when Smith ran the program, was suddenly scouting prospects all over the state. The Wildcats apparently no longer assumed the Tar Heels were going to get any kid they wanted within their own borders. During his first season off the bench, Smith also caught some second-hand blame for the team's over-enthusiastic, often cocky behavior. The trash-talking, body-banging, and occasional crowd-taunting had begun in Smith's last few years, and speculation arose that Guthridge did not crack down more on the 1998 team because his old boss was still in the background.

Much to his embarrassment, Smith continued receiving honors and accolades outside and inside UNC. "I get so much credit it gets to be ridiculous," he said, adding without his usual modesty, "I think we can coach, I will say that." Smith received the prestigious University Award for "illustrious service to higher education" at a black-tie banquet on November 12 attended by his family, closest friends, and dozens of his former players, including the world's most famous athlete. "When I came to the University of North Carolina, you saw two people in me, my mother and my father," Michael Jordan said sweetly from the podium. "Now you don't just see my mother and my father; you also see Dean Smith." (Exactly two months later, Smith would hold a press conference for his reaction to Jordan's own retirement from basketball). While also renewing old acquaintances within the UNC faculty, Smith smoothed out any residue from his clash with the chancellor over the new athletic director. "Dean and I get along better than ever, now that he's a full-time philosopher," Hooker said in late autumn. The following January, Smith was among the first to call when Hooker was diagnosed with lymphoma and began chemotherapy treatments.

Meanwhile, Guthridge's second season proved far more difficult on the court, with two freshman starters and a lack of outside shooting that left the Tar Heels vulnerable to zone defenses. Smith resisted what had to be strong temptation to tell his former staffers what to do, even though they certainly could have used all the wisdom available to work around the team's obvious shortcomings. Occasionally, when in town, Smith wandered into the video room where assistant coaches were reviewing tapes and debating strategy. Asked for his opinion, Smith's brilliance at the game often settled the issue in a matter of minutes. But on the way out, he would inevitably say, "Who knows? Maybe I was wrong all those years."

Among Carolina alumni and fans, at least, the specter of Dean Smith remained large – and never very far from the question of who would be the next Tar Heel coach. How long would Guthridge stay? And was it really a done deal that Roy Williams would succeed him? Members of the Rams Club fueled rumors that Williams was ready to leave Kansas at a moment's notice and take over the Carolina program. There were unsubstantiated reports that Williams had bought property at the exclusive Governors Club golf community outside of Chapel Hill and planned to build a new home there. "I do know this," said one prominent member of the booster club. "Roy will accept the job here if it is offered. He has told people that."

Whenever it happened, such an offer would come from the university chancellor, but merely as the messenger. By his own engineering, Smith had changed roles more than he had entered true retirement – that serene realm where the accomplishments of a Hall of Fame and record-breaking coach could be properly scrutinized and fully appreciated by friend and foe alike. It was not quite time for that. Although he would be the last to say so, Dean still very much presided over his Domain.

INDEX